Digital Imaging

Digital Imaging

Ron Graham
Ph.D., C.Phys., M.Inst.P, ASIS., FRPS

Whittles Publishing

Typeset by
Whittles Publishing Services

Published by
Whittles Publishing,
Roseleigh House,
Latheronwheel,
Caithness, KW5 6DW,
Scotland, UK

ISBN 1-870325-12-5

Printed by Interprint Ltd., Malta

To my wife, Joan,
who provided the necessary encouragement and support
that made this book possible

Contents

Introduction   1

Part One Theoretical Background

1   Radiometry   **7**
1.1   Electromagnetic Radiation   7
1.2   Coherent Sources of Light   10
1.3   Geometrical Optics   11
1.4   Wave Theory of Light   12
1.5   Quantum Theory of Radiation   14

2   Photometry and Visual Science   **19**
2.1   Basic Photometry   19
2.2   Camera Image Photometry   23
2.3   The Visual System   25
2.4   Colour   30

3   Fundamentals of Imaging systems   **37**
3.1   Types of Imaging Systems   37
3.2   Information Capacity   39
3.3   Spatial Resolution and Modulation Transfer Functions   45

Part Two Charge Coupled Devices and Imaging Systems

4   The Electrical Properties of Semiconductors   **55**
4.1   Electrical Conductors and Insulators   55
4.2   Semiconductors   56
4.3   Metal-oxide-semiconductor (MOS) Technology   58
4.4   Charge Coupled Devices (CCDs)   60
4.5   Video Technology and the Digital Revolution   65
4.6   CCD Imagers   67

5   Digital Cameras   **77**
5.1   Introduction   77
5.2   Basic Types of Digital Camera   78

viii 5.3   Single Exposure, Single Area-array (Spatial Multiplex)
             Cameras (Type 1)   81
      5.4   Single Exposure, Three Area-array (Parallel Acquisition)
             Cameras (Type 2)   98
      5.5   Three Exposure, Single Area-array (Temporal Multiplex)
             Systems (Type 3)   99
      5.6   Scanned Linear Array Systems (Type 4)   101
      5.7   Scanning CCD Backs for Studio Cameras (Type 5)   102
      5.8   Single Exposure, Single Area-array Camera Backs (Type 6)   103
      5.9   Future Developments   104

      6   Scanning Methods   105
      6.1   The original and its Reproduction   106
      6.2   Scanner Principles   108
      6.3   Hand-held Scanners   111
      6.4   Flat-bed Scanners   113
      6.5   Film Scanners   116
      6.6   Drum Scanners   118

      7   Image processing   119
      7.1   Practical Applications of Image Processing   119
      7.2   Image Analysis with Photoshop 3.0   126
      7.3   Spatial Filtering   128
      7.4   Image File Formats   133
      7.5   Image Compression   134

      8   Digital printers   137
      8.1   Dot Matrix Printers   137
      8.2   Inkjet Printers   137
      8.3   Laser Printers   140
      8.4   Dye-sublimation Printers   141
      8.5   Thermal Wax Transfer Printers   142
      8.6   Thermo-autochrome Printers   142
      8.7   Pictrographic Printers   142

      9   CD-ROM and Photo CD   144
      9.1   CD-ROM Drives   144
      9.2   CD-ROM Writers   145
      9.3   CD-Rewritable Drives   146
      9.4   Kodak Photo CD   146
      9.5   CD-ROM Advantages and Applications   147

Part Three Applications   ix

10   Digital Imaging Applications   **151**
10.1   Press Photography and Photo-journalism   152
10.2   Commercial and Industrial Photography   153
10.3   Holographic Interferometry   153
10.4   Medical Photography   156
10.5   Forensic Science and Police Work   159
10.6   Military Applications   160
10.7   Aerial Surveys and Remote Sensing   161
10.8   Applications in Astronomy   172
10.9   Scientific Laboratory Applications of CCD Imagers   177
10.10 Freelance Photography   180
10.11 Conclusions   180

Appendix A   Binary and ASCII Codes   **183**
Appendix B   Fundamental Constants and Conversion of Units **185**
Appendix C   Manufacturers and Agents, Institutions
                         and Publications   **187**

        Glossary   189
        References   195
        Index   199

Preface

When I first started this book in the summer of 1996, I could find reference to only 40 different digital cameras on the market. One year later there were close to 200 digital cameras available, including scientific types. The expansion of this technology has been so rapid that it has been almost impossible to keep up with developments. This applies to cameras and also the associated items such as printers, scanners, software, CD-ROMs and memory cards, not to mention the ever-increasing computer market. As a consequence of these developments, I make no excuse for detailing products that are no longer state-of-the-art in a particular field. For example, it was 1996 when I purchased a Kodak DCS-40 digital camera, an excellent device and one that I use regularly, but after only a couple of years on the market it was replaced with new models and is no longer manufactured. Nevertheless, Kodak did me the favour of releasing more technical information concerning this camera than for any other of their products. Accordingly, the DCS-40 has proven to be an extremely useful example for the purpose of this book.

Digital Imaging comprises three parts and aims to form a general text that will include something for everyone. It is written for students, lecturers, professionals and amateurs, in fact all who wish to engage with this new technology. Although I say *new*, I was actually teaching CCD imaging in 1980, anticipating the introduction of the Sony Mavica digital camera, but it has taken a full decade for this early promise to be realised.

Part One is an introduction to imaging and is intended mainly for those who have little background in optics, electronics or photography. Part Two deals with MOS, CMOS and CCD technology and from this base goes on to discuss digital cameras, scanners, image processing, printers and CD-ROM. Part Three covers various applications with an emphasis on technical and scientific work.

If the reader wonders why so many of the images shown in this book have been taken from the air, it is because this particular environment is one of the most difficult to control and digital imagery has an economic importance in the field of small format aerial mapping. Aerial photography (air-to-ground) faces a number of difficulties, not least being the atmosphere and the moving platform. Getting the colour, contrast, brightness, resolution and geometric conditions correct is a constant challenge. It therefore seemed appropriate to use these examples as a yardstick for measuring the professional value of digital systems since they can readily be compared to conventional (film) methods. In making these comparisons it is important to keep a rational outlook, no matter what the application. In aerial (mapping) work, for example, we cannot compare the tiny digital camera format to the 23 cm square format of a conventional air camera. But we *can* compare these cameras when we look at a small area of cover where there are requirements for remote sensing and geographic informations systems (GIS).

Above all, digital imagery offers much more than conventional photography! Access to an image without the inconvenience of a darkroom, water or chemicals is certainly foremost, but there is also the speed of access via the computer and also the possibility of sending an image around the world via the Internet.

Ron Graham
Ph.D., C.Phys., M.Inst.P., ASIS., FRPS

Acknowledgements

I should like to express my appreciation to Dr Jon Mills, University of Newcastle-upon-Tyne, for his unstinting help with many parts of this work and for his critical preview of the first draft of the book. My thanks also go to the many people in Kodak Ltd. who helped with information and the use of some of their digital cameras. To Drs Rick Curr, Fiona Strawbridge and Alex Koh of the RSGIS Unit, Bath Spa University College, I extend my grateful thanks for their cooperation with our joint mapping and remote sensing research projects in Yorkshire and for the images included in this book.

Finally, my gratitude goes to two people who made this book possible. To my wife Joan, for her practical assistance with information and records and last, but not least, to my publisher Dr Keith Whittles, for his constant encouragement and valuable advice.

Introduction

The human eye-brain mechanism must represent the ultimate imaging system where, for a given scene, the visual mechanism provides spatial information in three dimensions and full colour.

The visual appreciation of a scene comprises both objective (measurable) and subjective (perceptual) components involving many disciplines including: physics, psychophysics, chemistry, anatomy, physiology and aesthetics.

Early humans strove to record their world by carving crude drawings on stone; and this developed through the ages, by way of materials and skill, with an ever-growing appreciation for perspective, scale and artistic impression. By the mid-nineteenth century photography was well established in monochrome, and by the turn of the twentieth century stereoscopy and colour had also been exploited within the medium. Indeed, stereoscopy was more popular in the nineteenth century than it ever was in the twentieth!

As the quality of photographic materials advanced, in terms of speed (sensitivity to light), spectral sensitivity (embracing radiation from X-rays to the near infrared), spatial resolution (sub-micrometer) and accuracy of representation, so did camera technology.

Until the mid-twentieth century most practical photography was restricted to monochrome and it is interesting to reflect that few people really cared about colour – what they never had they never missed! Monochrome images served very well, and the average person was perfectly content to accept achromatic representations of what they actually saw in full colour. Similarly, the same acceptance was given to two-dimensional representations of a scene, the viewer being content to assume the third dimension from limited visual cues, such as perspective, scale, obscuration, atmosphere, etc. These visual assumptions continue to be accepted today as much as they ever were! And we need look no further than the monochrome images seen in newspapers and journals to appreciate this fact. Even so, only the dedicated amateur photographer will be happy with monochrome these days – colour is the expected norm and its quality is good. Stereoscopy is still available of course (but not a popular option) and although its 'cardboard cut-out' appearance is little more than a historic oddity to most people, it still remains highly important for technical purposes, such as scientific recording, photogrammetry and mapping. Indeed, large format aerial (mapping) photographs are now digitised and viewed on computer monitors via spectacles (softcopy

2   photogrammetry) in much the same way as the old anaglyph and vectograph processes, with all the advantages of computer software to assist in the manufacture of accurate maps.

Since the advent of the laser we have had holography – a system where a truly 'solid' form of imagery can be realised. As one of the earliest practitioners of this technology I employed this medium as a scientific tool where, with its ability to form a three-dimensional image that can be inspected (with full parallax along its entire depth) at leisure, even fast transient events could be recorded for subsequent analysis. Holography remains an important scientific aid and although the detail resolved by a hologram is extremely fine, and requires photographic materials capable of the highest spatial resolution, it is interesting to note that in one significant industrial application, holographic interferometry, digital cameras are now employed to record the low resolution interferometric fringes created on various materials under mechanical, thermal or electrical stress loads.

So, as we approach the twenty-first century, we can justly applaud the many new developments that have occurred in photography and, because of the vast scope of its scientific importance, have made the process invaluable as a diagnostic tool, as well as a graphic form of communication and an exciting medium for artistic expression. Nevertheless, apart from the innate acceptance of a two-dimensional representation of a scene, or object, equally important features, such as parallax (the apparent change in position of an object, or image, due to change in position of the eye of the observer) and viewpoint remain as unchallenged today as they have ever been. And now, in the final decade of the twentieth century, we have another significant development in photography, but this time it is the medium itself!

The title adopted for this book is 'Digital Imaging', but it could equally be 'Digital Photography', or 'Electronic Imagery', and no doubt the reader will have his or her own views regarding the semantics at issue. It could be argued that 'photography' is not an appropriate term for a recording system that employs a CCD (charge coupled device) array rather than chemically produced silver-halide grains. But since (roughly speaking) photography means 'drawing with light', the term surely denies any need to specify the medium employed! As to the use of the word 'electronic' this is equally lacking in any specific discrimination between AgH (silver halide) and the silicon-based MOS (metal oxide semiconductor) used in CCDs, since both sensors activate free electrons under exposure to appropriate radiation!

Purists might argue that, since a CCD camera employs an array that directly stores an electronic charge in proportion to image radiation, then the appropriate term should be 'electronic imagery'. But this tends to ignore the most significant aspect of CCD imaging, which is its system compatability with computers! After exposure each cell in the array is 'clocked-out' by the system's electronics so that each CCD (thousands or millions of them) is given a digital code according to its signal strength (image intensity) and x, y position within the array. At this point in the imaging process, the system becomes 'digital' and as such can be stored in the camera – and subsequently downloaded into a computer.

Digital systems have many advantages, and as the manufacturers improve their products it is safe to say that digital cameras will get better, less expensive and more popular, just as their host – the computer has done before them.

Although this book is devoted to digital imagery it cannot satisfactorily address the subject in isolation, that is to say, without reference to the fundamental physics and perceptual phenomena that relate the image to its subject, and to the four basic types of two-dimensional imaging systems. As a consequence, the first part of the book is devoted to basic theory in order to emphasise underlying concepts and to provide a foundation for those without a traditional background in optics or photography.

Part One

Theoretical Background

1 Radiometry

Whereas we usually refer to 'light' when dealing with photography, this can be misleading when we discuss radiation below or above the visible spectrum. This is particularly true when dealing with the ultra-violet or infrared. As can be seen from Fig. 1.1, the radiometric spectrum projected by the sun is a continuum extending from high-energy (high-frequency) cosmic and gamma rays, through X-rays and the ultra-violet to the relatively narrow band of visible rays, before extending through the infrared to radio waves.

1.1 Electromagnetic Radiation

In Fig. 1.1 we see the entire spectrum of electromagnetic energy which, as the name suggests, exists in the simultaneous form of electricity and magnetism. These two forms of the same energy are transmitted together as electromagnetic radiation (EMR). One cannot exist without the other: a flow of electric current always produces magnetism, and magnetism is used to produce electricity.

EMR is propagated outwards from its source at a velocity (c) of 300 000 000 metres per second (3×10^8 ms^{-1}). Both the electric and magnetic fields are propagated as transverse waves. Wave motion and the transfer of energy are best explained by looking at what happens to water when a stone is thrown into a perfectly calm pool. As the stone enters the water it sets up a disturbance to create waves that eventually reach the edges of the pool. But the particles of water do not move towards the edges of the pool – they simply move up and down. Only the disturbance (energy) moves outwards from the stone – as a series of wavefronts. A wave in which the particles move at right angles to the direction of travel of the wave is called a transverse wave.

Electromagnetic waves have an electrical field (E) associated with a magnetic one (H) at right angles to it, and both are at right angles to the direction of propagation as shown in Fig. 1.2. The electric field is known as the optic disturbance field and is the one we are interested in when dealing with light.

Although our natural source of EMR is the sun, there are also a number of man-made sources which, among many others, include tungsten filament lamps, gas discharge lamps, and lasers. Light is that narrow band of EMR mediated by the human eye, and is limited to a spectrum extending from 380 nm to 760 nm. Other animals also see light of course, but to different extents. As we shall see

8

later, light and colour *can* be quantified – but the human observer must always be taken into account when studying the visual sciences and photometry.

When considering the passage of light it is important to stress the medium of propagation, because in media other than space (vacuum) light will slow down – as in glass or water, for example. And if the velocity of light in a vacuum (V_0) is 300×10^6 ms^{-1}, then its velocity in a medium of refractive index (n) is (V_n) and can be found from:

$$V_n = V_0/n \qquad (1.1)$$

So, for glass of $n = 1.5$, the velocity of light travelling through that glass will be 200×10^6 ms^{-1}.

Inspection of Fig. 1.3 shows that the distance between one wave crest and the

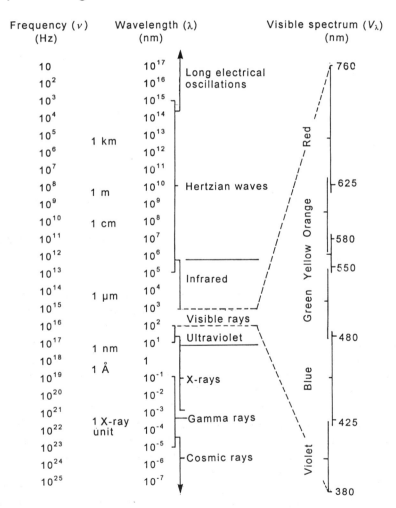

Fig. 1.1 The spectrum of electromagnetic radiation (EMR). Units are in nanometers (10^{-9}m).

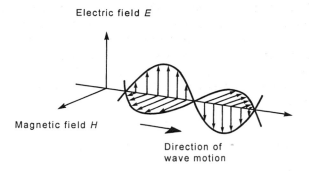

Electric field *E*

Magnetic field *H*

Direction of
wave motion

Fig. 1.2 The electromagnetic wave.

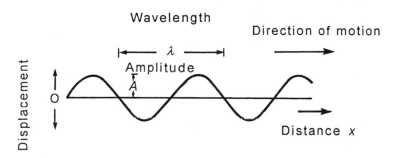

Wavelength

Direction of motion

λ

Amplitude

Displacement

O

Distance *x*

Fig. 1.3 A transverse electromagnetic wave of wavelength (λ) and amplitude (A).

next is the wavelength (λ), which has an associated frequency (*v*) directly related to c by the equation:

$$\lambda \ = \ c \, / \, v \tag{1.2}$$

Commonly known as the speed of light, c is a universal constant, and although it is convenient to discuss optics mainly in terms of wavelengths, it is the associated frequency that is fundamentally more important since, regardless of whether light is radiated in vacuo (V_o) or media (V_n) the frequency remains invariant and only the wavelength changes (Eq: 1.2). But, apart from this, it is more convenient to discuss optical matters in terms of λ since frequencies have such high values. An example will make this clear.

In visual optics we often refer to green light since this is the region of maximum human eye sensitivity, and if we consider green light at a wavelength of, say, 500 nanometres (500×10^{-9} metres) it is easy to fit this value into various calculations. But if we look at the associated frequency we find (from Eq: 1.2) that $v = c \, / \, \lambda = 300 \times 10^{6} \, / \, 500 \times 10^{-9}$, which is 6×10^{14} Hz or, to be more emphatic, 600 000 000 000 000 cycles per second! Obviously, it is more convenient to discuss EMR in terms of wavelengths (nm) rather than frequencies (Hertz)!

The amplitude of the wave (A) shown in Fig. 1.3 indicates the amount of light (EMR) associated with that wave, but since the human eye and sensors such as photographic film and solid-state devices are what are known as *square law detectors* all measurements of EMR are taken from the intensity of radiation *I* where

$$I = A^2 \tag{1.3}$$

(Only in holography do we manage to record information by amplitude of the waves, and that is due to the phenomenon of optical interference.)

The travelling wave equation

As shown in Fig. 1.3, the travelling wave repeats itself every wavelength unit (λ) along the *x*-axis of propagation, and its sine wave can be described by the function

$$\psi(x, t) = A\sin(kx - \omega t) \tag{1.4}$$

where
   k (the circular wave number) $= 2\pi/\lambda$
   ω (the circular frequency) $= 2\pi\nu$
   t is the situation at time t

1.2 Coherent Sources of Light

Before we can explain *coherence* it is necessary to understand the rather chaotic nature of radiation and examine the atomic process that gives rise to the emission of light. And although we shall deal with the quantum theory of EMR at a later stage (albeit very superficially), it is worth mentioning the role of the atom at this point.

   Inside the atom electrons exist in discrete energy levels, and if an electron falls from one energy level to another with lower energy, the excess energy is given off as EMR with a corresponding frequency. Under appropriate conditions therefore, the atom can be regarded as an oscillator, and when it stops vibrating those frequencies of radiation cease to be emitted. Each atom of the material emits waves of radiation during a period of about 10^{-8} seconds, this process being repeated again and again in a random fashion. Even if waves from different atoms all had the same frequency (as with a laser) they would always have a different phase. As a consequence a wave-train of light will only have constant phase during a period of roughly 10^{-8} seconds.

Optical coherence

According to Fig. 1.3 and Eq: 1.4, the travelling wave looks rather simple, but in reality the frequency of the sinusoidal disturbance will vary (very slowly) and the amplitude will fluctuate too.

   As we have seen, if a light source is totally coherent then each point on the source will give rise to the same type of wave, at the same instant of time, and all in phase with each other. Unfortunately this is not the case (apart from some lasers) and although it is of no great concern in photography it does provide some theoretical and practical problems with interferometric apparatus and in holography.

Optical coherence can be divided into two parts, *temporal coherence* and
spatial coherence.

Temporal Coherence

The average wave-train will exist for a time period (Δt_c) which is known as the
coherence time and is the inverse of the *frequency bandwidth* (Δv). Coherence
time is also known as temporal coherence and is given as:

$$\Delta t_c = 1/\Delta v \qquad (1.5)$$

Coherent waves need not be exactly in phase (where each wave emits a crest or
trough simultaneously) but the phase relationship should remain fixed during the
period of observation.

In holography temporal coherence is very important since it controls the *coherence length* of the wave-train (Δx) where:

$$\Delta x = c\Delta t_c \qquad (1.6)$$

or, in terms of wavelength bandwidth $(\Delta \lambda)$, an easier equation is:

$$\Delta x \approx \lambda^2/\Delta \lambda \qquad (1.7)$$

For a typical HeNe laser emitting at $\lambda = 632.8$ nm, we can expect a bandwidth
$(\Delta \lambda)$ in the region of 0.002 nm (the related frequency bandwidth follows the proportional relationship: $(\Delta v/v) \propto (\Delta \lambda/\lambda)$, giving an associated frequency bandwidth
$\Delta v \approx 1.5 \times 10^9$ Hz). Both Eq: 1.6 and Eq: 1.7 show that the HeNe laser can be
expected to provide a coherence length (Δx) of about 20 cm, within which distance we can assume reasonable phase relationships to exist. Under these circumstances it is possible to arrange for a small object to be placed within the coherence length of a holographic optical set-up.

Spatial coherence

A light source that is spatially coherent offers a planar wavefront at the object. To
do this, it is necessary that each point of the source acts in phase with every other
point. The classical way of approaching this condition is to restrict the size of the
source to point dimensions – but this can only be done at the expense of restricting the intensity of the source. However, with the advent of the laser the problem
became much easier since this type of source can produce beams with very high
spatial coherence, and which (in the TEM_{oo} mode – an almost perfect state of
laser radiation) generally have a divergence of only one minute of arc or less.

1.3 Geometrical Optics

Inspection of Fig. 1.3 indicates that we can think of light radiating in straight lines
– in every possible direction! This is the classical theory for the propagation of
light, and it is just as useful today as it was in Isaac Newton's time. Known as the
rectilinear propagation of light, it is the basis of geometrical optics and is generally employed to demonstrate ray-paths for all optical instruments, including cameras, and for calculating optical relationships such as image formation and scale.

Typical examples of geometric optics are those used to show image formation

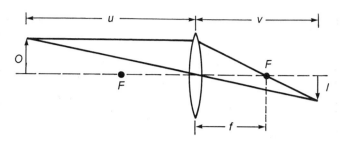

Fig. 1.4 Image formation with a single lens. Object and image conjugates (*u* and *v*) are related to focal length (*f*) by: $1/f = 1/u + 1/v$ where the focal length is the distance from the node of emergence of that lens to point *F*.

by a lens, as shown in Fig. 1.4, where ray-paths for image formation with a positive lens are illustrated. The well-known 'lens equation' relates object and image conjugates (*u*) and (*v*) respectively, to the focal length of the lens (*f*) according to:

$$1/f = 1/u + 1/v \qquad (1.8)$$

and since the size of the image (*I*) to that of the object (*O*) is the magnification of the system, we have:

$$M = I/O \qquad (1.9)$$

Combining Eq: 1.4 with Eq: 1.5 allows us to employ two further equations of great use to photography:

$$v = f(M + 1) \qquad (1.10)$$

$$u = f(1/M + 1) \qquad (1.11)$$

1.4 Wave Theory of Light

The wave theory, as illustrated by Fig. 1.3, allows us to explain optical phenomena such as *diffraction* (the bending of light around an edge), *interference* (the interaction of divided wave-fronts such that they form *interference fringes*) and *polarisation* (where light rays are polarised into one particular plane, rather than every direction). The diagram shown in Fig. 1.2 is an illustration of a single *plane-polarised* wave of light.

Diffraction

Diffraction theory is very important when considering the optical resolution of a lens system where, in the limit, the highest possible resolution is a function of the wavelength of light employed and the relative aperture of the lens (*N*), (see Box 1). Commonly known as the *f/No* of a camera lens, the relative aperture will provide an image resolution (for a theoretically perfect lens) known as the *diffraction limited resolution* (*r*) given as:

$$r = 1.22\lambda N \qquad (1.12)$$

Thus, for a lens operating at *f/4* (*N* = 4) and with a filter limiting the bandwidth to

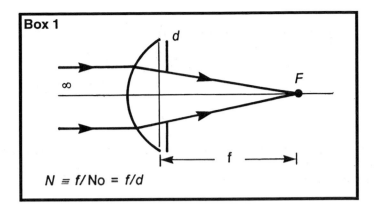

Box 1

d

∞

F

$|\!\!\leftarrow\!\!-\!-\!-\! f \!-\!-\!-\!\!\rightarrow\!\!|$

$N \equiv f/No = f/d$

a peak radiation of, say, 410 nm, the theoretical resolution limit (r) is 2000 nm, or 2 μm. This suggests that the image would resolve two points separated by 0.002 mm. It is common practice to refer to the reciprocal of r in terms of spatial frequency where:

$$R = 1/r \text{ (line-pairs/mm)} \qquad (1.13)$$

In the above example this would mean: 1/0.002 mm = 500 LP/ mm. (Note: With small apertures, such as f/22, resolution is degraded by the effects of diffraction, i.e., where light is bent from its normal path at the edges of small apertures.)

Interference

As mentioned above, when two common wavefronts interfere they can create bright intensity fringes where the crests or troughs of individual amplitudes come together and, conversely, dark fringes where troughs meet crests. It is possible to employ an optical set-up that will exploit such conditions: holography is based upon interference phenomena, and many scientific instruments rely on either wavefront-splitting or amplitude-splitting techniques to provide for the interferometric analysis of matter.

Polarisation

Natural polarisation of light can take place either by scattering or by specular reflection. With the former condition we find that blue sky is a result of preferential scattering of blue wavelengths according to Wein's law where scatter is given by:

$$\text{light scatter} \approx 1/\lambda^n \qquad (1.14)$$

where the exponent can be anything from 1 to 4 (for perfect blue skies).

But since this phenomenon is accompanied by partial polarisation, we can use a polarising filter (which reduces the transmitted light to a single plane of polarisation – and to reduced intensity of course) to exclude the scattered short wavelength light and thus darken the blue sky in colour photography. It must be noted, however, that the entire sky will not be polarised to the same degree. Scattered

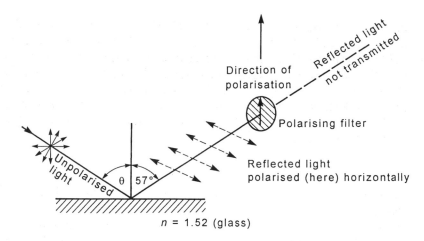

Fig. 1.5 Specular reflections are polarised at the Brewster Angle θ, where $\theta = \text{Tan}^{-1}n$.

skylight is mainly polarised in directions at right angles to the line-of-sight of the sun.

Another use of a polarising filter is to reduce unwanted specular reflections coming from glass or water surfaces. According to 'Brewster's law' specular reflections are polarised at an angle given by:

$$\tan \theta = n \tag{1.15}$$

(where $n = 1.333$ for water and 1.52 for crown glass).

Thus, for glass ($n = 1.52$) the angle whose tangent is 1.52 is close to 57°, as shown in Fig. 1.5.

1.5 Quantum Theory of Radiation

Although we usually think of light as a wave, when it is absorbed by matter it behaves as if it were a stream of tiny particles of energy called *photons* and which can be represented by finite wave-trains, or wave-packets. In general we talk of *photons* when discussing all forms of EMR.

In this book we make use of all three concepts of light, but the quantum theory is perhaps most useful when considering the interactive nature of EMR on sensitive materials such as the crystal structure of silver halides (AgH), and silicon sensors such as MOS (metal oxide semiconductors) or CMOS (complementary metal oxide semiconductors) as used in CCDs. In all of these materials the imaging theory is the same – a packet of EMR energy is incident upon a sensitive material, and an electron is released from the valency band of the crystal into the conduction band (see below).

The energy band model of an atom

The usual model of an atom is that of a dense nucleus of positively charged *protons* surrounded by an equal number of negatively charged planetary *elec-*

trons. This model can be used to explain the behaviour of electrons in a solid, where they are arranged within a series of concentric shells (bands) with a maximum of eight electrons per shell – in the stable state. The bands farthest from the nucleus have the greatest energy level. The outer shell is known as the *valence band*, and the number of valency electrons determines the chemical properties of the atom and also its functional relation in semiconductors. An even higher energy level is the outermost *conduction band* in which electrons can move freely in conducting an electric current.

The electron and electron volt

An electron (e) has a mass of 9.109×10^{-31} kg and a charge of 1.602×10^{-19} coulomb (amp seconds). (One ampere $= 6.24 \times 10^{18}$ electrons/second.)

The electron volt (eV) is the amount of work done when one electron is accelerated by a potential difference of one volt. One eV $= 1.602 \times 10^{19}$ joules (watt seconds).

Generally speaking, a normal atom is most stable when it has its lowest energy E_0, that is to say, when it is in its *ground state*, and at room temperature most of the atoms in a gas or solid occupy the ground state. In Fig.1.6, we suppose that most of the atoms are at the ground state energy level (E_0) and that a single atom is in the first excited state at E_1. As the temperature rises more atoms will occupy a number of discrete excited states (the energy of an atom may occupy any one of the allowed higher energy levels – but not an intermediate energy value) but the population of atoms in the excited state(s) will still be much less than those at E_0. This is known as a *normal population* of atoms.

If the atom absorbs energy (which could be EMR in the form of a photon) and is excited to one of its allowed energy levels, say E_1 (from A to B in Fig. 1.6) it will emit EMR (of frequency v) when it falls to its ground state. The quantum of energy

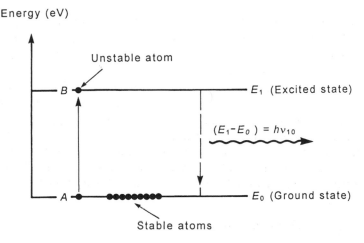

Fig. 1.6 Simple energy level diagram. An atom excited to an allowed level E_1 will emit EMR of frequency v when it falls to its ground state E_0.

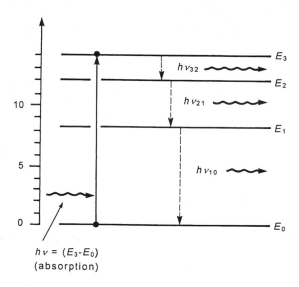

Energy (eV)

$hv = (E_3-E_0)$
(absorption)

Fig. 1.7 Incoherent emission of radiation. An atom with three discrete energy levels above the stable ground state (E_0).

(Q) emitted is given by:

$$Q = E_1 - E_0 = hv \qquad (1.16)$$

where h = Planck's constant = 6.6262×10^{-34} Js

This is known as *spontaneous emission* of radiation, where energy is absorbed from the radiation field and re-emitted as radiation.

Fig. 1.7 represents an atom with three discrete energy levels above its stable ground state E_0. The first excited state is shown at E_1 (8 eV), the second at E_2 (12 eV) and the third at E_3 (14 eV). The atom cannot absorb incident energy that is less than the E_1 level, and if the atom were struck by a photon of, say, 5 eV, it would not be absorbed by the atom. However, if the incident quantum is greater than 8 eV then it can be absorbed and will put the atom into its first excited state, where it will stay for a little while then fall back to the ground state, emitting its 8 eV as a packet of EMR with energy equal to $E_1 - E_0 = hv$.

If now a photon of energy $hv = (E_3 - E_0)$ is incident on a normal population of atoms (as shown in Fig. 1.7) the probability of excitation from level E_0 to level E_3 is high since there are many more atoms in the ground state than there are in the E_3 level (shown here at 14 eV). As mentioned above, excited atoms eventually fall to the ground state – either directly or via intermediate states. In Fig. 1.7, an atom is shown in the E_3 level, first falling back to E_2 (where it emits energy $hv_{32} = E_3 - E_2$), then makes further transitions from E_2 to E_1, and E_1 to E_{0}, with emissions hv_{21} and hv_{10} respectively.

Under these circumstances, the three spontaneous emissions depicted in Fig. 1.7 will not only have different amplitudes and frequencies but, since they occur at slightly different times, will result in totally incoherent wave-trains. If an atom in its ground state absorbs sufficient energy just to remove an electron completely from the atom, then the absorbed energy is known as the *ionisation energy*.

Photon energy

From Eq: 1.16 we saw that a photon of light will have the energy $Q = hv$. As an example we can take an incident photon of $\lambda = 500$ nm, and from Eq: 1.2 find a value for the frequency, where $v = c/\lambda$, or $300 \times 10^6 \,\text{m s}^{-1}/5 \times 10^{-7} = 6 \times 10^{14}$ Hz

The energy $Q = (6.6262 \times 10^{-34} \,\text{J s}) (6 \times 10^{14} \,\text{Hz}) = 39.76 \times 10^{-20} \,\text{J}$, and since 1 eV is equal to 1.602×10^{-19} J, the energy (Q) is 2.48 eV.

Spectral power distribution

The spectral power distribution of a source is quoted as the number of watts radiated over some wavelength interval, for example over a specific spectral band-width ($\Delta\lambda$). If, for example, we look at a bandwidth of 400 nm to 410 nm, the radiated power within this 10 nm bandwidth can be specified. But the amount of radiation falling at exactly 400 nm is meaningless. It is possible to choose any size of bandwidth – but the interval must be specified!

The solar spectral power distribution is shown in Fig.1.8, with the ordinate scaled in units of watts per square metre per nanometre, that is to say, the amount of spectral radiant power ($\Phi_{e\lambda}$) that falls on a square metre of the earth. If the total spectral radiant power under the curve shown in Fig. 1.8 is summed then we have the total solar radiant power per unit area as shown by the integral:

$$\Phi_e = \int_0^\infty \Phi_{e\lambda} \, d\lambda \quad \text{watts} \tag{1.17}$$

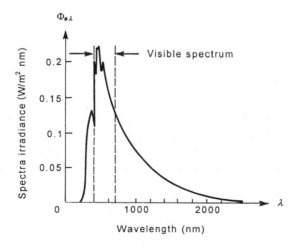

Fig. 1.8 Spectral power distribution of the sun.

18 The total radiant power per unit area falling on the earth's upper atmosphere is known to be 1400 watts per square metre, with the amount falling on the earth's surface reduced to about 1 kW m^{-2} on a clear day. The associated energy is given by:

$$Q = \Phi_e t \quad \text{joules} \tag{1.18}$$

where t = time of exposure in seconds.

2 Photometry and Visual Science

2.1 Basic Photometry

As the name suggests, photometry is the science of measuring light, that is to say, measuring EMR within the visual limits of 380 nm to 760 nm as shown in Fig. 1.1. Whereas radiometry is pure physics, photometry is concerned with psychophysics – where the eye mediates between EMR and the brain. As a consequence we find that our observations, being totally subjective, are less accurate than those in radiometry – simply because we must take the average human observer into the equation!

Photometry accepts only a small band of the EMR ($\Delta\lambda = 380$ nm) and in many ways seems to be at odds with the more accurate system – radiometry! But photometry was already well developed before much was known about EMR and to this day we still have photometric units that reflect its historical past, that is, the unit for luminous intensity (the candela) was originally a 'standard candle' burning a specific amount of wax per hour! Nevertheless, for those dealing with visual optics alone (ophthalmics, lenses, instruments and most of photography) photometry still serves a useful purpose. But for technical and scientific purposes photography is a highly useful tool and can 'see' further than the visual limits. Film is capable of recording high-frequency radiation such as X-rays and gamma rays, as well as the near ultra-violet (including a narrow band around 320 nm using quartz optics); and is capable of recording in the near infrared up to about 1200 nm with special plates. Similarly, CCD imagery can be used outside the visible spectrum, MOS sensors being sensitive up to about 1100 nm.

The photometric radiation equivalent

The unit of luminous intensity (I) is the candela (cd) which, by definition, is 1/60th of a square centimetre of the surface of a black-body radiator at the absolute temperature of 2045 K. (Note: A black-body radiator is one that absorbs all the radiation incident upon it and has no reflecting power. The radiation from a heated black-body source is called black-body radiation, and is always quoted in Kelvin – the SI unit of thermodynamic temperature. Zero degrees Kelvin is equal to –273.16°C, i.e. *absolute zero*.)

From this specification and a knowledge of the sensitivity of the human eye ($V\lambda$) it is possible to quantify the physical radiant unit into photometric terms. The

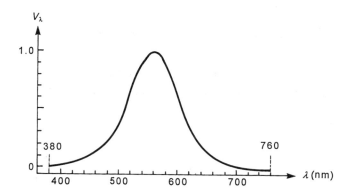

Fig. 2.1 The V_λ curve. Human eye sensitivity to daylight (photopic vision) shown against wavelength (λ).

human eye sensitivity for daylight (*photopic* sensitivity) is shown against wavelength in Fig. 2.1, and is known as the V_λ curve.

The photometric radiation equivalent (PRE) for monochromatic radiation is given by:

$$K_\lambda = \Phi_{\nu\lambda}/\Phi_{e\lambda} \tag{2.1}$$

The maximum value for K_λ is:

$$K_{\lambda(max)} = 673 \text{ lumen/watt} \tag{2.2}$$

and this parameter allows us to find the PRE from:

$$K_\lambda = V_\lambda K_{\lambda(max)} \tag{2.3}$$

From inspection of the V_λ curve we can see that at a wavelength of 510 nm the value is 0.503, and from Eq: 2.3 we can calculate:

$$K_\lambda = 0.503 \times 673 = 338 \text{ lumen/watt}$$

The reciprocal value of $K_{\lambda(max)}$ is known as the *mechanical equivalent of light* (M):

$$M = 1/K_{\lambda(max)} = 1/(673 \text{ lmW}^{-1}) = 1.47 \text{ mW/lm}$$

Luminous flux

The amount of light energy flowing from a source is known as the *luminous flux*, and is defined as:

$$\Phi_\nu = K_{\lambda(max)} \int_{380\,nm}^{760\,nm} \Phi_{e\lambda} V_\lambda d\lambda \quad \text{(lumens)} \tag{2.4}$$

and in a given period of time (*t*) the *luminous energy* (exposure) is given by:

$$Q_\nu = \Phi_\nu t = 673t \int_{380\,nm}^{760\,nm} \Phi_{e\lambda} V_\lambda d\lambda \quad \text{(lm / s)} \tag{2.5}$$

Luminous intensity

By definition, the luminous intensity (I) of a source is given by:

$$I = d\Phi_v / d\omega \qquad (2.6)$$

where $d\omega$ is the elementary solid angle into which the source emits a flux of $d\Phi_v$.

For a luminous flux radiating into a perfect sphere of 4π steradian, a source of 1 candela provides a flux of 4π lumens:

$$\Phi_v = I \int_0^{4\pi} d\omega = 4\pi I \qquad (2.7)$$

So, for 1 candela of luminous intensity we get a theoretical total of 12.56 lumens.

Illuminance

If a flux (Φ_v) is incident upon a surface of area S (usually S is given in square metres) it is said to be *illuminated,* and the illuminance (E) at any point on that surface is given by:

$$E = \Phi_v / S \qquad (2.8)$$

If S is quoted in square metres (m²) then E is given in lumen/m², or lux.

$$E = 673 \int_{380\,nm}^{760\,nm} \Phi_{e\lambda} V_\lambda d\lambda \quad \text{lm}/\text{m}^2 \quad \text{(lux)} \qquad (2.9)$$

The inverse square law

The law of inverse squares is well known in photography and is the basis of the f/no sequence found on all camera lenses, and by which we can allow twice as much, or half as much, light to reach the film or CCD – simply by adjusting the f/nos, up or down, as they run in the geometric progression of √2 (i.e. f/2, f/2.8, f/4, f/5.6, f/8...).

The law is illustrated in Fig. 2.2, which shows a source of 20 Cd illuminating a

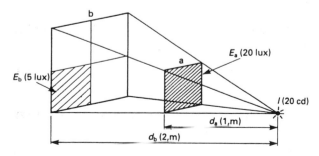

Fig. 2.2 The law of inverse squares: The illumination of a surface falls off inversely as square of the distance from the source.

1 metre square card (*a*) at a distance of 1metre from the source.

The illuminance of a surface is given by:

$$E = I/d^2 \quad \text{(lux)} \qquad (2.10)$$

and for surface (*a*) in Fig. 2.2, we have $E_a = 20 \text{ Cd}/1^2 = 20$ lux.

If we now want to calculate the illuminance on a second surface, such as (*b*), when we only know the value of E_a, then we may use:

$$E_b/E_a = (d_a/d_b)^2 \qquad (2.11)$$

Substituting, we now have

$$E_b = E_a(d_a/d_b)^2 = 20 \, (1/2)^2 = 5 \text{ lux.}$$

Reflectance

Reflectance (ρ) may take the form of *specular reflectance*, as shown in Fig. 2.3a or as *diffuse reflectance* shown in Fig. 2.3b. Specular reflectance is that exhibited by a mirror and follows a regular law where the angle of incidence (*i*) is equal to the angle of reflectance (*t*). But in photography we are more concerned with the light that is reflected from objects – and although some of the light will undoubtedly be specular (from shiny surfaces) most of it will be diffuse, and follow an irregular distribution known as an *indicatrix* of reflection with a unique form like

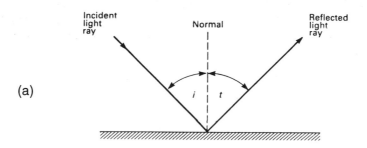

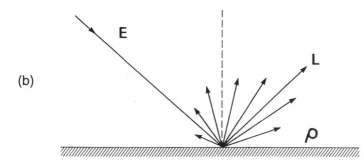

Fig. 2.3 (a) Specular reflection. (b) Diffuse reflection.

that shown in Fig. 2.3b. The indicatrix not only illustrates the different directions of reflected light, but (by their vectors) their strengths also, and serves to describe the nature of the reflecting surface.

Luminance

Although we see *by* light, we cannot actually *see* light itself! What we *do* see are the various luminances coming from an object and it is these that we interpret through eye and brain. Each luminance (L) can be calculated (in units of Cd/m^2) as:

$$L = E\rho/\pi \quad (Cdm^{-2}) \tag{2.12}$$

For an object (O) with an even and diffusely reflecting surface (ρ), the luminance from that surface will follow Eq: 2.12, which in terms of incident flux is given by:

$$L = \frac{673}{S} \int_{380\,nm}^{760\,nm} \Phi_{e\lambda} V_\lambda \rho_\lambda d\lambda \tag{2.13}$$

2.2 Camera Image Photometry

For a camera, the image photometry is illustrated in Fig. 2.4, where a camera lens of relative aperture (N) = f/d, is exposed via a spectral filter (F) of bandwidth F_λ. Under these circumstances we can say that the spectrally defined luminance of the object is now:

$$L_{o\lambda} = \frac{673}{m^2} \int_{380\,nm}^{760\,nm} \Phi_{e\lambda} F_\lambda V_\lambda \rho_\lambda d\lambda \quad (Cdm^{-2}) \tag{2.14}$$

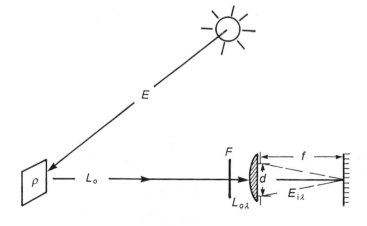

Fig. 2.4 From an illuminance (E), an object with reflectance (ρ) presents a luminance (L_o) incident on the filter (F). The camera lens receives a spectral luminance ($L_{o\lambda}$) through the relative aperture ($N = f/d$), to provide an image illuminance $E_{i\lambda}$.

24 *Image illuminance*

In simple terms image illuminance (E_i) is only a function of object luminance and camera aperture, as shown:

$$E_i = L_o/N^2 \quad \text{(lux)} \qquad (2.15)$$

and if a filter is employed then the spectrally limited (monochrome) image illuminance is given by:

$$E_{i\lambda} = L_{o\lambda}/N^2 \quad \text{(lux)} \qquad (2.16)$$

Note: The lens aperture (N) is squared because of the law of inverse squares which is responsible for the *f*/no progression and the common acceptance that camera exposure is controlled by factors of 2, that is, it is the area of the lens aperture that doubles when the diameter goes up by $\sqrt{2}$ (one stop): area $\propto$ diameter^2.

Unfortunately camera image illuminance is complicated by three additional factors:

- lens transmission (T_g),
- off-axis image illumination,
- non-image light (lens flare).

Lens transmission

Lens transmission is never 100%, but suffers from internal reflections at each air/glass interface. The degree of attenuation can be normalised for most compound lenses, with m air/glass surfaces, and is given by:

$$T_g = (0.98)^m \qquad (2.17)$$

Typically, for an uncoated compound lens with six air/glass surfaces, $T_g = 0.88$.

Off-axis image illuminance

The angle (θ) made between the optical axis and extreme off-axis image points gives rise to less image illuminance $(E_{i\theta})$ at those points, and should be accounted for when considering an average level of image illuminance. If we look at a mid-field image point that lies at an off-axis angle (θ), we can allow for this problem by calculating the off-axis illuminance as a fraction of the axial illuminance E_i.

$$E_{i\theta} = E_i \cos \theta^4 \qquad (2.18)$$

Thus, for off-axis points lying 25° from the axis, the image illuminance at these points will be reduced to $0.67E_i$. Taking the above values for T_g and $E_{i\theta}$ into account, we can modify Eq: 2.15 and 2.16 by including the factor (k), where k is the product of the two values, that is $0.67 \times 0.88 = 0.59$. The general equation for monochromatic spectral image illuminance is therefore:

$$E_{i\lambda} = k \, L_{o\lambda}/N^2 \quad \text{(lux)} \qquad (2.19)$$

and specifically, for the parameters calculated for k (above), we can put:

$$E_{il} = 0.59 \, L_{o\lambda}/N^2 \quad \text{(lux)} \qquad (2.20)$$

Lens flare

In all optical instruments there is an amount of non-image light present, usually known as lens flare (E_{if}). Most of this 'flare-light' is caused by the internal reflections mentioned above, but in addition there are possible reflections from the inner walls of the lens barrel and, in the case of CCD images, the influence of the MOS sensors themselves – including cell filters, chip thickness and also the direction of the image illuminance (front or back lit illuminance).

As a consequence the total image illuminance (E_{iT}) is given by:

$$E_{iT} = E_i + E_{if} \text{ (lux)} \tag{2.21}$$

Generally speaking the value of E_{if} is rarely known with any degree of accuracy, nevertheless it is always present. But with cameras that are of good quality and in fresh condition flare-light can usually be ignored.

Camera exposure

For the general case it only requires the exposure time (t) to be included and we have the equation for camera exposure:

$$H_i = (0.59 \, L_o/N^2) \, t \quad \text{(lux seconds)} \tag{2.22}$$

If a filter is included in the system, as shown in Fig. 2.4, then the luminance should be that indicated in Eq: 2.20.

2.3 The Visual System

Brightness

Brightness (B) is the subjective correlate of luminance and its relationship to luminance is a highly complex function depending upon the adaptive state of the eye, inhibitory factors (such as the influence of adjacent image areas) and lightness and colour constancies. [1] Brightness is a function of both achromatic (black and white) and colour scenes and its values can only be determined approximately by means of psychological scaling procedures. It is perhaps strange that the most obvious feature of imagery – the varying degrees of brightness we perceive when viewing the image of a scene – is the least understood part of the entire reproduction cycle. Regardless of the medium, silver or silicon, the final result still has to be interpreted through the vagaries of the human visual system.

For simple fields (such as a single luminance prominent within a uniform background) Stevens and Stevens[2] have shown that the magnitude of the brightness sensation can be determined by direct estimation and by judging brightness ratios. The variability of each observer and the variations due to personal interpretation all contribute to brightness being a statistical quantity with a basic uncertainty. Nevertheless, according to a number of authorities [3, 4, 5] the power law which satisfies the basic relationship for simple fields is:

$$B = kL_o{}^n \tag{2.23}$$

26   where

B is the psychological magnitude of brightness,

L_0 is the luminance of a scene element observed within a simple field,

n is the exponent for brightness, generally agreed to be of the order of 0.33 for simple fields,

k is a constant which depends upon the conditions of the test.

In complex (everyday) scenes, certain modifications are needed to basic brightness scales, because of adaptation, induction and lightness constancy. As an example of the complexity involved in this subject the reader is invited to inspect Fig. 2.5, where an everyday example of lightness constancy has been recorded in a photograph. The panel fixed to the wall above the table is evenly illuminated to match the luminance of the panel fixed below the table. The upper panel has a reflectance (ρ) of 0.18, whereas the panel below the table has a reflectance of 0.84. Although the illuminance (E) has been adjusted to provide conditions of equal luminance (L) between the two panels there is no doubt that the lower panel looks 'lighter' than the one above. A 1 : 1 relationship exists between the print and the scene, with respect to the panels, and it can be shown that they both have

Fig. 2.5 An example of lightness constancy. Although the luminance is the same for both grey patches, the upper patch ($\rho = 0.18$) still *looks* darker than the one below ($\rho = 0.84$).

Box 2

If I is the light incident upon a surface of reflectance (ρ), then the opacity of the surface (O) is given by $O = I/\rho$. Since I can be considered as unity, we have $O = 1/\rho$. For example, for $\rho = 0.5$ the opacity is 2. Similarly, for a semi-transparent medium we can put $O = 1/T$ (a photographic negative has numerous transparencies (T) in its image). Density (D) is given as $D = \log_{10} 1/T$ or $1/\rho$.

---

identical reflection densities[1] (see Box 2). But if a mask is placed over the photograph, obscuring all but the two panels, then it will be seen that they exhibit identical brightness – thus illustrating the well-known fact that at least two different surfaces must be in view at the same time in order to gain *lightness constancy*.

From this single example of the problems associated with brightness in the visual scene, it is evident that brightness in complex fields cannot be estimated with an expression as simple as that shown in Eq: 2.23.

Through research investigating complex field brightnesses in interior scenes Graham[6] has shown that an empirical expression, in the form of a polynominal, gave good results over three levels of illuminance. The second term in Eq: 2.24 may be considered as the departure from the simple power law that is to be expected for an expression concerned with a complex field.

$$B_o = aL_o^b + \text{antilog } c(\log_{10} L_o)^n \qquad (2.24)$$

where:

n is the logarithm of the scene luminance range (for E_o – 640 lux, $n = 1.862$), and the constants

a, b and c are found by iteration to be 1.025, 1.53 and –0.32 respectively. Fitting the above values into Eq: 2.24 gives the empirical equation:

$$B_o = 1.025L_o^{1.53} / \text{antilog } 0.32(\log_{10}L_o)^{1.862} \qquad (2.25)$$

The plot of Eq: 2.25, showing log of brightness (B) against log of scene luminance (L_o) is shown in Fig. 2.6. It can be seen that Eq: 2.25 provides a good fit for the three adaptation levels of 40, 174 and 640 lux.

Monochrome tone reproduction with photographic film

In an attempt to reproduce an exact monochrome likeness to original scene interiors Graham[1, 6] selected materials and processes with specific controls to gain optimal results. With the aid of an eight block cascade of tone reproduction diagrams (Fig. 2.7) it was possible to show an almost perfect result for restricted conditions. Although such monochrome reproductions were proven possible, the system was difficult and time consuming.

Inspection of Fig. 2.7 shows the reproduction cycle as it reads from Block 1, going clockwise to the final Block 8. It is instructive to note the laborious cycle of

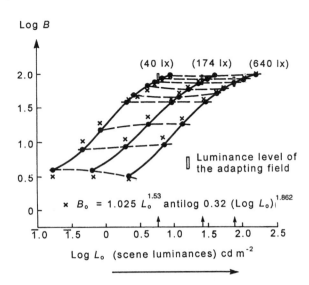

$$B_o = 1.025\, L_o^{1.53} \quad \text{antilog } 0.32\, (\text{Log } L_o)^{1.862}$$

Fig. 2.6 Logarithm of relative scene brightness (*B*) plotted against scene luminance (*L*$_o$) at three adaptation levels.

reproduction, as set out in Table. 2.1.

Table 2.1 *(see also Fig. 2.7)*

Block 1.	Log scene luminance (*L*$_o$) v log scene brightness (*B*$_o$).
Block 2.	Camera lens flare (non-linear in shadow areas of image reproduction).
Block 3.	Kodak Plus-X film: density v log exposure (typically non-linear, as are all films).
Block 4.	Enlarger flare (almost linear in this instance).
Block 5.	Bromide paper density v log exposure scale (typically sigmoid in shape).
Block 6.	Print viewing: log print luminance v log print density (linear).
Block 7.	Log print luminance (*L*$_p$) v log print brightness (*B*$_p$).
Block 8.	Overall tone reproduction (almost linear).

Table 2.1 serves to illustrate the extended process of photography, from camera through film, enlarging and printing. Although a very reasonable monochrome facsimile *can* be gained, it is obvious that the process is far from straight forward – mainly due to the non-linearity of photographic films and papers. Leaving aside the purely subjective issues involved, the simple relationship between scene luminance (*L*$_o$) and print density (*D*$_p$) indicates a non-linear objective tone reproduction, as shown in Fig. 2.8.

Monochrome tone reproduction with digital cameras

It has long been recognised that CCD imagers provide a linear response to scene

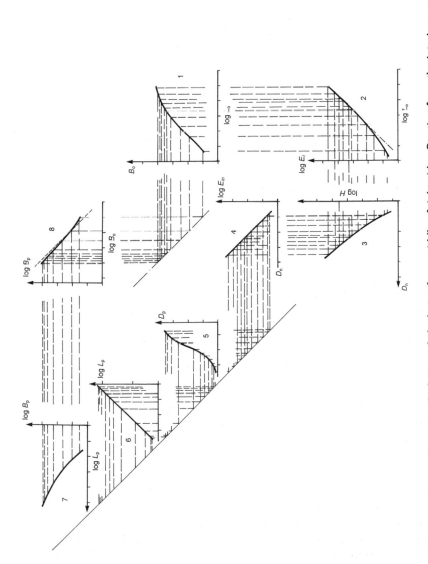

Fig. 2.7 Overall tone reproduction diagram which is read clockwise from middle of right side. Starting from the interior scene brightness function (1), camera lens curve (2), Plus-X film (3), enlarger curve (4), printing paper curve (5), print-viewing conditions (6), print brightness function (7) and final tone-reproduction curve (8).

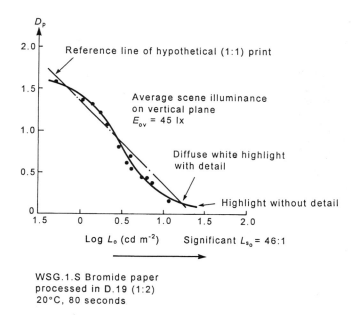

WSG.1.S Bromide paper
processed in D.19 (1:2)
20°C, 80 seconds

Fig. 2.8 Experimental plot of log print density D_p against log scene luminance L_o. Recorded on Kodak Plus-X film type 4147 via Wratten 8 filter. Processed in Kodak Microdol-X, 12 minutes at 20 °C.

luminances, and there can be little doubt that this also extends to colour reproduction. Naturally a 1 : 1 response between scene and image must also depend upon the camera optics (digital sensor arrays are not always free from flare) and the computer printout, but from a simple experiment carried out by me it appears that a 1 : 1 response can be assumed for even modest digital cameras.

Using the Kodak DC-40 digital camera with a 3 diopter close-up lens attachment, a monochrome grey scale was recorded and its image downloaded into Kodak PhotoEnhancer software. The resulting computer image was then printed out on an inkjet printer to yield a facsimile grey scale. The original and facsimile grey-scale densities are shown in Table. 2.2, and plotted to show the linear 1 : 1 response shown in Fig. 2.9.

Obviously the linear response of CCDs will prove to be a significant advantage in the development of digital camera applications.

2.4 Colour

The physical nature of colour was first understood by Isaac Newton (1642–1727), who used a glass prism to display a colour spectrum from incident white light, as shown in Fig. 2.10 (see colour section). Newton also realised that colour is a *perception*: it needs someone to receive the rays of light in order to interpret them as colour. He made this quite clear in a passage from his major work *OPTIKS*: 'For the rays, to speak properly, are not coloured. In them there is nothing else

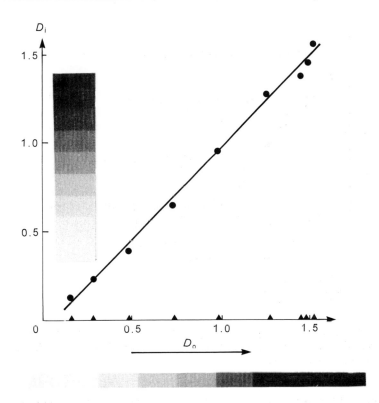

Fig. 2.9 Typical CCD linear response between original and facsimile grey-scale densities: Kodak DC-40 camera.

Table 2.2

Original grey-scale densities	Printed grey-scale densities from Kodak DC-40 camera
D_o	D_i
0.16	0.12
0.29	0.24
0.49	0.38
0.73	0.65
0.99	0.95
1.27	1.26
1.44	1.37
1.48	1.45
1.52	1.55

than a certain power and disposition to stir up a sensation of this or that colour.'

If a material should absorb white light evenly throughout the spectrum, then it will appear neutral; as a shade of grey, or (if absorption is almost complete) as black. But most materials absorb only parts of the visible spectrum and reflect the rest. This selective absorption gives rise to the sensation of colour – we see the light that is not absorbed.

Colour is an entirely subjective phenomenon and relies on special nerve cells, called cones, in the retina of the eye. Three different types of cone exist, each being responsible for the detection of a different part of the visible spectrum: one to red light, one to green and one to blue light. The three types of cone are arranged in a random mosaic in the fovea of the retina. If red light falls on the retina, essentially only the red sensitive cones send signals to the brain, and we perceive this radiation as the colour red.

It was Thomas Young (1773–1829) who first discovered that the eye perceives colours as a mixture of only three different *primary colours*. His famous demonstration is illustrated in Fig. 2.11a (see colour section). Three projectors are arranged so that overlapping circles of red, green and blue light are projected onto a screen. At each overlap the coloured lights add to produce different colours. In the centre, all three colours add to give white light. This is called the *additive synthesis of colour*. These three primary colours (red, green, blue) are fundamental to our understanding of colour vision, but more important they are, with their complementary colours (cyan, magenta and yellow – formed by overlapping primary colours of light), basic to colour imagery, both photographic and digital.

Just as the *additive* (spectral) *primaries* add to form white, so we can use their complementaries, cyan, magenta and yellow, to subtract colour. If, instead of using beams of coloured light, we start with a white screen and add coloured filters to it, a different effect is obtained. This is because the white screen already reflects white light containing all three additive primary colours. Adding coloured filters *subtracts* portions of the spectrum. If we take, say, a yellow filter and hold it in front of a white screen, then the yellow absorbs the blue light and reflects a mixture of red and green light, which appears yellow to the eye, so we see a yellow screen. If we now put a cyan filter over the yellow, then we see green. Finally, if we put cyan, magenta and yellow filters together all three additive primary colours have been absorbed (subtracted from white) so we get black. For this reason the complementary colours are known as *subtractive primaries*. This type of colour synthesis is shown in Fig. 2.11b.

Summing up we can put:

Additive primary colours
Red + Green + Blue = White

Additive primaries	**Complementary colours**
Red + Green	Yellow
Red + Blue	Magenta
Green + Blue	Cyan

Subtractive primaries
Cyan + Magenta + Yellow = Black

A convenient way of remembering these relationships is to use the simple matrix
given below:

R   G   B

C   M   Y

Each complementary colour is made up of the two additive primaries not directly
above, for example: C = G + B. And each of the additive primaries can be seen
by combining the two complementary colours not directly below. Obviously there
are more than just six colours – in fact if we take differences in brightness and
purity (restricted bandwidth) into account then we can distinguish millions of discrete colours, but only a few hundreds at any one time!

   To be correct we should discuss 'colour' in terms of *hue*, *saturation* and *lightness*, where 'lightness' is the term used instead of 'brightness'. Two major systems
for depicting colour are the Munsell system and the CIE system.

Munsell colour system

The Munsell system is shown schematically in Fig. 2.12. It is a practical system
and as such is built as a three-dimensional model known as a Munsell tree (or
colour solid), or can be purchased as a book. Essentially the Munsell system of
colour notation identifies colour in terms of three attributes: hue, value (lightness)
and chroma (saturation).

Hue
This is simply the name we give to a colour (red, yellow, etc.), and in the Munsell
system these are represented around a three-dimensional colour tree, with forty
leaves of constant hue.

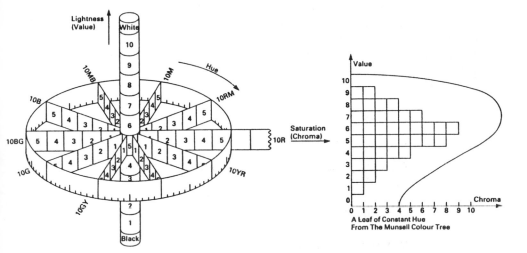

Fig. 2.12 The Munsell colour system.

34 Saturation (chroma)

Saturation is the purity of a colour. Most colours have some grey in them (they are not pure) but if a colour has no grey in it is said to be fully saturated. The 'leaf' of constant hue shows increasing saturation as the colour squares shift to the edge of the leaf.

Lightness (value)

Lightness is simply a scale going from black (1) at the bottom of the tree, to white (10) at the top. The complete Munsell notation for a colour is written as: HV/C. Thus, for a 'rose' colour its notation might be 5R 6/4.

The CIE colour system

The CIE (Commission Internationale de l'Éclairage) system takes the form of strongly modified colour triangle and also takes into account the source of illumination when specifying the colour under investigation. It is a scientific system which allows the user to plot the colour characteristics of a filter or paint or whatever, at some point within the locus of the CIE diagram. The locus of the diagram

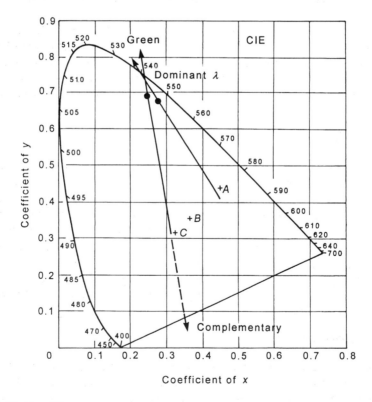

Fig. 2.13 The CIE colour diagram. Construction of dominant wavelengths is shown for the Wratten 58 green filter (coordinates within the locus of the diagram), and light sources A and C.

starts at 700 nm at the bottom right-hand edge of the figure and extends through green at 520 nm down to 400 nm (blue) at the lower left. The straight line connecting the blue and red ends represents the non-spectral colours of magenta (i.e. complementary to green opposite).

As shown in Fig. 2.13, the CIE diagram also places the light source within the figure. In the example shown, three well-known illuminants A, B and C are provided. However, if the x, y coordinates of any other light source are known then it too can be positioned within the locus. In Fig. 2.13 the x, y coordinates for a Kodak Wratten 58 filter are plotted for light sources A and C. Kodak provide full information on their filters and for the illuminant A (high wattage tungsten lamp at 2854 K) the standard green 58 filter has coordinates $x_A = 0.269$, $y_A = 0.683$ and a total visual transmission of 16.9%. For the C type illuminant (sunlight plus skylight at 6500 K) the x, y coordinates are 0.242 and 0.692, with visual transmission at 12.5%.

The location of these two coordinates are shown in Fig. 2.13, and if a line is extended from the light source through the appropriate coordinate point then it will cut the locus at the dominant wavelength transmitted by the green filter when used under that illuminant. In this instance the dominant wavelengths are 539.5 nm for the A source and 541.2 nm for the C source.

The saturated colours lie along the locus and become less saturated as the coordinates move towards the centre of the figure. Lightness is not available directly since this is only a two-dimensional representation of a colour. To find the complementary colour of the dominant wavelength the line that cuts the locus need only be extended backwards. For the greens this backward extension reaches the non-spectral magenta line.

Photographic colour films and papers

All modern colour films (except Polarcolor) and papers are based on the subtractive principles of colour reproduction and consist of multi-layered emulsions with complementary dyes coupled to the oxidation products of silver halide development. The greater the amount of silver image, the greater the amount of dye. Thus, for negative colour film, a scene colour of say, yellow, will affect the red and green sensitive layers of the tri-pack and these, in turn, will produce cyan and magenta dyes. The resulting negative colour will be a combination of the cyan and magenta dyes – giving blue! When printed, a similar type of tri-pack emulsion will receive blue light in its blue sensitive layer – which then couples to the original scene colour of yellow.

Digital colour images

For digital colour both additive and subtractive principles are involved. The pixel array camera has an array of many thousands of small picture elements (pixels), each of the order of about 10 μm as a rule. These pixels are covered with individual filters, such that red, green and blue sensors are always adjacent. When this additive colour array is downloaded to the computer (via an analogue to digital converter) the information is compiled as an additive colour system and what we see on the monitor is an image made up from RGB phosphors. But when the image is transported to the colour printer the data are then converted to CMYK for either inkjet, laser or dye-sublimation printing with cyan, magenta, yellow and black inks. The black (K) is added to give printing strength to the image, for although in theory cyan, magenta and yellow inks combine to give black, in practice they rarely do so because of ink imperfections.

Whereas in theory a colour photograph could have an infinite number of colours, in digital imagery colour is restricted to what is known as *colour depth*. Colour depth is expressed in terms of the amount of computer memory allocated to defining the colours for each pixel. An 8 bit colour, for example, gives a palette of 2^8 or 256 colours per pixel, a 16 bit gives 65 536, and a 24 bit gives 16.7 million.

Although we have mentioned the pixel array camera, this is not the only way of producing colour in digital cameras and, as we shall see later, there are special cameras that take three simultaneous or consecutive exposures through separate red, green and blue filters. The advantage of these systems is that the original pixel resolution is not reduced to account for the filters. But these cameras are really only suitable for stationary subjects and limited to studio use.

3 Fundamentals of Imaging Systems

3.1 Types of Imaging Systems

According to Klein[7] and Metz, Ruchti and Seidel,[8] imaging systems can be classified into four basic types according to the character (stochastic or multilevel), and to the spatial arrangement (regular or random) of the constituent image elements.

Regular/stochastic

The regular arrangement of newsprint images (such as letterpress) employs only black dots on a white ground to enable the appearance of whites, greys and blacks. When viewed under normal observation the eye confuses these dots (image elements) to yield a picture that appears as one of continuous tone. But under moderate magnification the dot structure is revealed and it can be seen that, although regular in spatial distribution, dot size governs image density. In such a system the stochastic (statistical) nature of the image is one of binary elements (on-off detectors) that can only assume extremes of a given density range, for example, black (1) or white (0). Any grey tone between black and white being achieved only within an area considerably larger than a single element, and with a suitable statistical mix of black and white elements.

Random/stochastic

If we make an image with a very high-contrast high-resolution film, we can expect the image structure to be a random collection of black image points, each with a point spread function (PSF) of about 1.0 μm diameter at the 10% intensity level. When scanned by an aperture much larger than the PSF (such as the human eye, or a microdensitometer) we would interpret a large number of such dots as a continuous black area. But if only half this number occupied the same area, then the impression would be a grey, and so on down to white – where perhaps only a single dot (PSF) occupies the scanned area. A typical PSF for Kodak Plus-X film is shown in Fig. 3.1, where the 10% level is 26 μm diameter. It can be seen that with either regular or random arrangements, both of the stochastic systems rely on statistical distributions of black and white image elements (dots or PSFs).

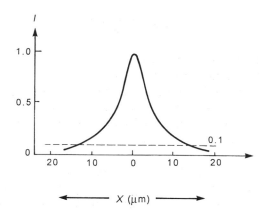

Fig. 3.1 Point spread function (PSF).

Random/multilevel

Whereas high-contrast films have a random distribution of small, almost equally sized grains of AgH, conventional panchromatic films also have a size distribution which allows for a wide range of density levels. As a result, there is a greater latitude for accepting various scene luminances in a single exposure. We can therefore say that conventional photography is of the random/multilevel type of imaging system. A typical sample of grains taken from a fast panchromatic film is shown in Fig. 3.2, where the grain-size distribution ranges from about 0.5 μm to 3 μm diameter. The 'printed-out' specks shown within individual grains in Fig. 3.2, are microdensities due to microscope illumination and not to any development.

From such a system the developed image can be expected to have multilevels of density (*M*) given by:

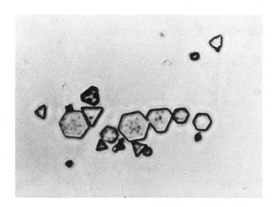

Fig. 3.2 Typical silver halide grains taken from a fast panchromatic film. Grain size distribution ranges from 0.5 mm to 3 mm.

$$M = (\Delta D/2kG_S)A^{0.5} + 1 \qquad\qquad (3.1)$$

where

ΔD is the density range in the image,

G_s is the Selwyn granularity averaged over ΔD,

k is the number of standard deviations (σ) by which adjacent density levels are separated; for a normal distribution of densities k is $\pm 5\sigma_D$, but intervals of $10\sigma_D$ are recommended to avoid abnormal distributions of density readings,

A is the area of scanning aperture (cell size).

Film granularity (system noise) is usually given in terms of G_S (quoted above) and is the statistical variation of microdensities (usually found for an image density of 1.0) that can be expected for a given film material. Selwyn granularity is calculated as:

$$G_S = \sigma_n A^{0.5} \quad \text{(density microns)} \qquad\qquad (3.2)$$

where σ_D is the root mean square (RMS) granularity value (statistically the standard deviation σ) taken from multiple microdensitometer readings and calculated according to Eq: 3.3.

$$\sigma_D = ((\Sigma(\Delta D)^2)/(n-1))^{0.5} \qquad\qquad (3.3)$$

Kodak Ltd use an aperture of 48 µm diameter for their quoted RMS granularity values,[9] which are simplified to the form of:

$$G_{RMS} = 10^3 \sigma_D \qquad\qquad (3.4)$$

As an example, we could calculate the density levels (M) for Kodak Plus-X film with the following parameters: $G_S = 0.8$, $\Delta D = 1.4$, $k = 10$, and $A = 530$ square microns (an area provided by the diameter of a typical Plus-X, PSF at the 10% level). From Eq: 3.1, we have:

$$M = ((1.4/20 \times 0.8) \times (530)^{0.5}) + 1 = ((0.0875) \times (23)) + 1 \approx 3$$

So we can say that, for Plus-X film under the above conditions, we can expect three separate density levels in a single PSF. We shall see later that M is important when calculating the information capacity of an imaging system.

Regular/multilevel

Regular/multilevel imaging systems include CCD imagers, where we have a regular array of pixels each with a multilevel capacity (M) of grey tones or colour. When CCD type imagers were first put on the market they were very coarse with arrays of the order of only 400×400 pixels. Nevertheless, by the mid-1970s CCD cameras were being used in astronomy; in the 1990s we have cameras with multi-million pixel arrays available for conventional camera work. For CCD imaging systems with their multilevel character and regular arrangement of elements (pixels) the information capacity (I_c) can be determined very easily.

3.2 Information Capacity

According to Shannon[10] information capacity (I_c) is defined as the maximum amount of information a system is capable of storing under optimum conditions of encoding. For a multilevel system comprising n elements, with M levels each, the capacity (in binary digits, or bits) is given by:

$$I_c = n\log_2 M \quad \text{(bits)} \qquad\qquad (3.5)$$

(Note: The bit is the smallest piece of information that can be stored on a computer and is a binary value of either 1 or 0. The byte is a unit used to measure the size of computer files, memory and storage capacity. One byte is made up from eight contiguous bits and stores the equivalent of one character. See Appendix A.)

As stochastic systems have only black and white levels, they have the same information capacity as a multilevel system with the minimum possible number of levels, that is, two. Using Eq: 3.1 and Eq: 3.5 it would seem possible to compare imagery between different systems, be they conventional photographs, or solid-state images (such as those made by a CCD imager comprising of n MOS elements). And as this section of the book is intended to introduce and explain the complex nature of images (particularly digital systems) it is useful to see if information capacity correlates with perceived image quality.

For example, a 35 mm negative on Plus-X film might have something like 2×10^5 cells/cm^2, when calculated from a PSF at the 10% intensity level, which means a total of something like 1.7 million cells within the whole 24 × 36 mm format. And if we accept that Plus-X has three density levels (10σ), then the information capacity of this frame would be:

$$I_c = (1.7 \times 10^6) \log_2 3 = (1.7 \times 10^6)1.585 = 2.7 \text{ million bits}$$

But if we make k equal to 4 rather than 10 standard deviations in Eq: 3.1, then our density levels are increased by a factor of 2.5 to yield $M = 7.5$, and the corresponding information capacity becomes 4.93 million bits.

By comparison, the Kodak DCS-420i digital camera (monochrome version) has 1524 × 1012 pixels framed in a chip of 14 mm × 9 mm, and 256 levels (although 12 bits are quoted, only the best 8 of these are employed). The information capacity of this system is given by:

$$I_c = 1\,542\,288 \times \log_2 256 = 1\,542\,288 \times 8 = 12\,338\,304 \text{ bits}$$

We can see that the digital camera is far superior in its information capacity! So much so, that the high data capture of these cameras can be a problem, and one that is usually solved by compressing the image to a much lower capacity before downloading it to a computer. But can we say that the image quality is better than that provided by Plus-X film? Perhaps as good (depending on enlargement) but, even when printed on a high-quality dye-sublimation printer and on the best glossy paper, the digital image will be hard pressed to better film – in terms of quality. However, this argument must also consider other factors, such as subject, lighting, presentation, etc. and, above all, the rapid improvements now being made to digital systems.

I think digital imagery is capable of reaching film quality – at a price! And when the capital outlay for high-quality digital cameras and supporting computer hardware becomes less, then the many advantages of digital systems will soon outpace those of traditional methods.

It is obvious that high values of I_c are not enough on their own. From the above examples we can see that the Plus-X image will be improved as M increases, but this cannot be extended without limit! Indeed, would the average observer really need 256 grey levels, or colours, in a photograph? Could he or she see more than, say, a 100, or appreciate more than 20 or 30? Would it not be better to adopt a stochastic system?

For monochromatic images stochastic systems work reasonably well:
since at least two alternative states are required for the recording of information, maximum packing occurs when the cell is reduced to the size at which only two density levels are permitted by the granularity. Put in another way, maximum information packing on the photographic emulsion occurs for the case of binary (stochastic) recording. Brown, Hall and Kosar[11]

Reciprocity between tone levels and resolution

In an experiment to determine the best compromise between regular/stochastic and regular/multilevel images, Metz et al.[8] illustrated a number of variants under each system. From their work they make it clear that 'information capacity and image quality are two very different quantities with no fundamental correlation between them.'

In their experiments they scanned a portrait photograph and reproduced facsimiles with varying amounts of n and M. As might be expected, the quality of these reproductions improved with increasing the number of picture elements (n) and with increasing the number of grey levels (M). However, they found but limited reciprocity between values of n and M. The best correlation (in terms of acceptable quality) was found to be between a stochastic image with 1408×1216 elements (n), and a multilevel image made up of 704×608 elements and 16 levels. As the reader can calculate from Eq: 3.5, both systems have equal capacity (1 712 128 bits) and although the stochastic image appeared rather 'grainy' it came close to the good-quality image provided by the 16 level system – even though the latter had less resolution.

Regular/multilevel imagery

In Fig. 3.3 we have an interior photograph of a modern cathedral, and in Fig. 3.4, its scanned reproduction (Canon IX-4015). Held at some distance, or with the eyes screwed tightly enough to reduce edge definition of the pixels, the scanned image is almost passable with a resolution (n) of 64 pixels wide by 48 pixels high, and eight grey levels (M). From Eq: 3.5 the information capacity is 9216 bits. Obviously the scanned image has faults! Apart from its pixellated appearance the shadows are empty of detail and there is room for grey-tone improvement, but at a distance it will pass!

In Fig. 3.5(a) and (b), the same scanned image has been reproduced at one third the information capacity of Fig. 3.4, with noticeable effects. When viewed at sufficient distance to remove the obvious pixellation Fig. 3.5(b) approaches the

Fig. 3.3 Photograph of an interior scene (a modern cathedral with daylight illumination).

Fig. 3.4 Scanned image of Fig. 3.3 has a pixel resolution (n) 64 pixels wide × 48 pixels high, with eight grey levels (M). Information capacity I_c = 9216 bits (binary digits).

quality of Fig. 3.4, but Fig. 3.5(a) is far too contrasty. The important feature of the two images in Fig. 3.5 is their reciprocity, for both have equal capacity at 3072 bits. In (a) the resolution is 37 pixels by 28 pixels with eight levels, giving $1024 \times 3 = 3072$ bits. Whereas in (b) we have a lower resolution of 32 pixels by 24 pixels with sixteen levels, giving $768 \times 4 = 3072$ bits.

(a)

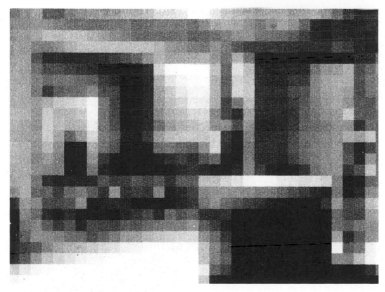

(b)

Fig. 3.5 Images (a) and (b) have identical information capacity ($I_c = 3072$ bits). In (a) pixel resolution is 1024 pixels with eight grey levels, whereas in (b) resolution is only 768 pixels, but with twice the number of grey levels. Despite their reciprocity the images have a different appearance.

The trade-off between resolution and grey levels is not a simple matter that can lead to global conclusions, particularly since other criteria are involved, such as viewing conditions, image contrast, 'graininess', pixellation, etc. But it remains obvious that given the largest possible number of n and M the image will always be at its best. As mentioned before, digital imaging systems involve a considerable amount of data storage and inevitably this puts a strain on tranmission systems and computer storage. In an attempt to determine the minimum practical number of data required to store and reproduce a recognisable image, I used a monochrome passport photograph of a college lecturer in an experiment to find the smallest value of I_c that could be employed to reproduce a pixel picture with a 50% chance of the face being recognised among fifty of his students.

To begin with, the passport photograph was enlarged and the image analysed with a densitometer to divide the overall density range of the face into a number of nearly equal sub-ranges. Eventually, after a number of trials, four significant grey-tone levels were selected, and from four sheets of different grey paper a suitable pixel picture was mosaiced as shown in Fig. 3.6. With a crude resolution of only 15×14 pixels ($n = 210$) and four grey-tone levels, the information capacity came to 420 bits. Allowing each individual viewer an opportunity to observe the mosaic image at any given distance, it was found that 53% of the observers could recognise the face. A smaller sample was taken a year later with the stochastic version shown in Fig. 3.7, but on this occasion only 44% could recognise the subject.

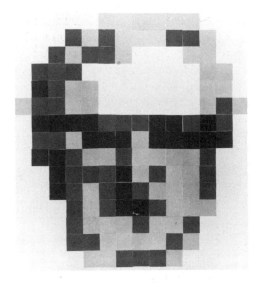

Fig. 3.6 Image of a face at minimum resolution ($15 \times 14 = 210$ pixels) and four grey levels provide an information capacity of 420 bits. held at some distance with eyes screwed tightly the face becomes marginally recognisable.

Fig. 3.7 A stochastic version of the face shown in Fig. 3.6.

These experiments were carried out many years ago and without the advan- **45**
tage of today's technology. It is now a simple matter to use a colour scanner, as
shown in Fig. 3.8 (see colour section), where the original has been reproduced
with $n = 374$ pixels and $M = 32$ colours, giving an information capacity of 1870
bits.

3.3 Spatial Resolution and Modulation Transfer Functions

It now seems common practice to discuss the resolution of digital imagery in
terms of the sensor's packing density, that is, pixels per unit area or the number of
pixels on the chip. This is certainly a useful form of discussing *pixel resolution*
provided one can size the pixel-to-pixel distance. The Kodak M5 chip, as used in
the DCS-420 camera, is a suitable example. This chip has an array of 1524 × 1012
pixels in an active area of 14 mm by 9.3 mm. Dividing 1524 pixels into 14 mm
tells us that the M5 pixel resolution is of the order of 9.2 μm between pixel centres.
We can also state this as the *sampling spatial frequency* (k_s).

$$k_s = 1000 / \Delta p \quad \text{(pixels/mm)} \tag{3.6}$$

where Δp is the inter-pixel distance expressed in mm, and k_s the sampling frequency.

The point spread function (PSF) and Airy discs

The PSF shown in Fig. 3.1 illustrates the nature of an image point created on film,
and in many ways is representative of most image points that are less than theoretically perfect. The PSF shown in Fig. 3.9 shows the symmetrical figure of an
image point that can be found on the central axis of a good-quality lens – but it is
not the theoretically perfect image point defined by what is known as the diffraction limited lens.

For a theoretically perfect image point, the PSF shown in Fig. 3.9 would be
surrounded by an ever decreasing series of annular rings, known as an Airy disc
(after the great astronomer of that name), and two such image points separated
as shown in Fig. 3.10 would provide the limit for spatial resolution.

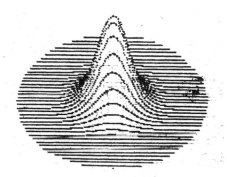

Fig. 3.9 Point spread function (PSF) of a good image point.

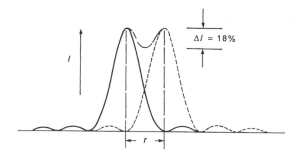

Fig. 3.10 Image resolution (*r*) for a perfect (diffraction limited) lens. In practical terms $r = \lambda N$, where *N* is the *f*/no of the lens.

Rayleigh limited resolution

The criteria for image resolution for a perfect (diffraction limited) lens is shown in Fig. 3.10, which shows that two Airy discs can be just resolved if the central maximum of one coincides with the first minimum of the other, the resulting dip in intensity between the two points being of the order of 18%.

The distance *r* (the Rayleigh limit) is given in Eq: 1.12, but in practical terms can be approximated by:

$$r = \lambda N \qquad (3.7)$$

where λ is the wavelength of light employed, and *N* is the relative aperture (*f* number) of the lens.

Although Eq: 3.7 suggests simplicity, we must remember that λ represents a dominant wavelength out of a given bandwidth. For example, we might employ a filter which transmits between 480 and 540 nm, but its dominant wavelength could be 500 nm (0.5 mm). In this case, with a lens operating at *f*/4 (*N* = 4), the image resolution would be about 2 μm.

For the practical testing of spatial resolution it is usual to employ a simple square-wave type test target as shown in Fig. 3.11. The distance between the centre of one black line to the next being the same as *r* in Eq: 3.7.

Fig. 3.11 A square-wave test target. Black and white bars are of equal width.

The reciprocal relationship between resolving power (r) and image spatial frequency (k_i) is given by:

$$k_i = 1/r \quad \text{(line-pairs/mm)} \tag{3.8}$$

and if we combine the spatial frequencies of lens and sensor then, to a first approximation, we can put:

$$(1/k) = ((1/k_i)^2 + (1/k_s)^2)^{0.5} \quad \text{(line-pairs/mm)} \tag{3.9}$$

If we take a good-quality lens capable of providing an average resolution of, say 250 LP/mm, and if the sensor is Plus-X film with a known spatial resolution of 125 LP/mm then, from Eq: 3.9, we can calculate:

$$1/k = ((0.004)^2 + (0.008)^2)^{0.5} = \sqrt{((16 \times 10^{-6}) + (64 \times 10^{-6}))}$$
$$= \sqrt{(80 \times 10^{-6})} \approx 9 \times 10^{-3}$$

from which $k \approx 111$ LP/mm.

Although Eq: 3.9 works reasonably well when the sensor is film there can be problems when the sensor is a regular array such as that found in CCD cameras.

The Nyquist sampling theorem

With sensors that have regular cell arrangements (such as CCD imagers – with spatial frequency f_s), unambiguous resolution of image detail with a spatial frequency $k_i > 0.5 \, k_s$ is not possible since this would contravene the Nyquist sampling theorem.[12] The theorem states that the sampling of any signal that has a spatial frequency (k_i) close to the sampling frequency (or multiples thereof) gives rise to intensity modulations in the displayed image in the form of 'beats' between the two frequencies (i.e. $k_i \pm nk_s$), commonly called an 'alias' or 'moire' pattern. These are most noticeable about and above the Nyquist limit and arise because the intensity maxima and minima in the image do not always fully coincide with a sensor element. This is a fundamental limitation of all solid-state image sensors that have discrete sensor elements (such as CCDs) but as the spatial frequency of the sampling systems improves to higher values, so the problem becomes less important. The Nyquist limit is given by:

$$k_i \leq 0.5 \, k_s \tag{3.10}$$

Contrast and modulation

Contrast is simply the ratio of high intensity to low intensity, in either object or image. It can be expressed as:

$$C = L_h / L_l \tag{3.11}$$

and can have any value. The contrast in the test target shown in Fig. 3.11 is very high, of the order of 100 : 1 or more.

Modulation, on the other hand, is a more useful parameter since it quantifies contrast with a scale that corresponds closely with that of visual perception. For example, there is little visual difference between a contrast of 100 : 1 and 1000 : 1, and this is shown by the small differences in modulation for these two contrasts. Modulation (M) is given by:

$$M = (I_{max} - I_{min}) / (I_{max} + I_{min}) < 1.0 \tag{3.12}$$

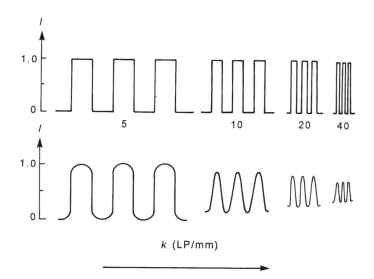

Fig. 3.12 Top: an ideal square-wave target at spatial frequencies (k): 5, 10, 20 and 40 line-pairs/mm. Bottom: their expected reproduction.

For a contrast of 100 : 1, the corresponding modulation is 0.98, and for 1000 : 1 the modulation is 0.998, whereas for an average sunlit scene M could be anything from 0.33 to 0.96.

Analysis of a square-wave test target

Fig. 3.11 shows a simple square-wave target. But the image of such a target becomes less simple as we inspect its reproduction at higher frequencies (smaller scale). In Fig. 3.12, the upper diagram shows the ideal image of a square-wave target at spatial frequencies, 5, 10, 20 and 40 LP/mm. But the lower diagram illustrates the kind of reproduction we can expect!

It is obvious from Fig. 3.12 that whereas the lower frequencies only suffer degradation to the edges, the higher frequencies also suffer a loss of modulation.

Fourier analysis

The square-wave form shown in Fig. 3.11 may be represented mathematically by a Fourier series composed of a fundamental sine wave (with the same spatial frequency k as the square-wave target), plus a series of odd harmonics with spatial frequencies, $3k$, $5k$, $7k$, ..., nk. Indeed, a very close approximation to the square wave would result if the Fourier series were to be taken to enough terms. The square-wave function f_x is given by:

$$f_x = 2\left(\sin x + \frac{1}{3}\sin 3x + \frac{1}{5}\sin 5x + \ldots \frac{1}{n}\sin nx\right)$$

(3.13)

In most types of photography (film), a microdensitometer trace across the image

Amplitude

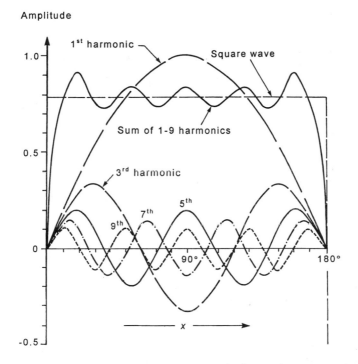

Fig. 3.13 Fourier analysis of a square-wave target. The sum of odd harmonics (1 to 9) produces a rough approximation to the square wave at a mean height of $\pi/4$ of the first harmonic.

of a square-wave target seldom includes terms above the ninth harmonic, as shown in Fig. 3.13, where it may be seen that the sum of the first, third, fifth, seventh and ninth harmonics produces a rough approximation to the square wave (which has a mean height of $\pi/4$ of the first harmonic). Higher harmonics than the ninth are, generally speaking, removed by atmosphere, lens aberrations and the photographic emulsion until, at frequencies of about 5 LP/mm and higher, only the fundamental frequency is left in the signal.

Once the signal has been reduced to the fundamental frequency, we may consider square-wave targets to be effectively sinusoidal in character; and the only change left possible is for their images to be reduced in modulation, as shown by Fig. 3.12. If the original target could be made with a sinusoidal distribution of luminance, then the problem of harmonic stripping would not arise, and the difference between object modulation (M_o) and that of the image (M_i) would be the only variable involved. Although difficult to manufacture, sine-wave targets can be produced by photographing a square-wave target with the aid of a cylindrical lens. An example is shown in Fig. 3.14 accompanied by its associated wave-form. Once again it is important to remember that the amplitude of light cannot be seen, and that intensity (which can) is proportional to the square of amplitude

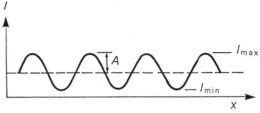

Fig. 3.14 Sine-wave target.

(Eq: 1.3). For a more comprehensive treatment of the Fourier approach to image formation the reader is recommended to read Saxby.[13]

The modulation transfer function (MTF)

It is obvious from Fig. 3.12 that modulation in the object (M_o) suffers on transfer to the image (M_i), and for a given spatial frequency (k) the modulation transfer function (MTF) is given by the transfer factor T_k, where:

$$T_k = M_{i(k)}/M_{o(k)} \tag{3.14}$$

For a perfect (diffraction limited) lens the MTF is given by:

$$T_k = (2/\pi)(\pi/180) \cos^{-1}(k/k') - (k/k')(1 - (k/k')^2)^{0.5} \tag{3.15}$$

where k is the spatial frequency for which T_k has to be calculated, and k' is the cut-off spatial frequency, given by $k' = 10^3/\lambda N$ (λ in nm).

A family of diffraction limited MTF curves are plotted in Fig. 3.15 for a range of apertures (with λ at 0.55 nm) along with the MTF for a Zeiss Pleogon air-camera lens.

A particular advantage of the MTF system is that it allows an entire system, that is, lens, sensor, atmosphere, image motion etc. to be cascaded (by algebraic multiplication of the individual values for each spatial frequency) to provide a total answer concerning the final image.[14]

CCD arrays: resolution and MTF

Since we traditionally express optical resolution in terms of line-pairs/mm (Eq:

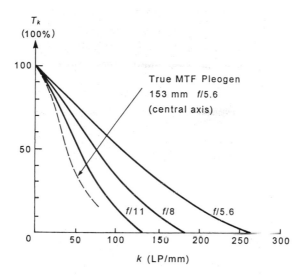

Fig. 3.15 MTF curves for an ideal (diffraction limited) lens at three apertures, compared with the MTF of an actual air-camera lens.

3.8) then we also need to equate the frequency of CCD pixels in much the same fashion (Eq: 3.6). A straightforward relationship would suggest that two pixels are equal to one line-pair, but in practice two pixels can often fail to resolve one black line and an adjacent white line (a line-pair). For this reason it has been suggested by Konecny, Schuhe and Wu[15] that a more reasonable solution is 2.8 pixels = one line-pair, and Makarovic and Tempfli[16] concluded (from MTF data) that 3.3 pixels would be needed to equal one line-pair. From these figures a compromise is recommended where:

$$3 \text{ pixels} = \text{one line-pair}$$

Although the structural topography of CCD arrays will be discussed at length in Part Two, it can be said here that the active part of each CCD element (in which charges are located) is called the *channel* and this region is bounded by electrically inactive p-type *channel-stop* regions. The horizontal element spacing (Δp) is determined by the spacing of the charge transfer columns (as defined by the channel-stop regions) and the vertical pitch by the centre-to-centre spacing of the CCD elements. These limits provide the optical aperture of the elements (w), usually expressed in micrometres.

If we employ a sinusoidal intensity target, such as that shown in Fig. 3.14, then the theoretical MTF of the sensor is given by:

$$\text{MTF} = \sin (\pi s(w/\Delta p))/(\pi s (w/\Delta p)) \qquad (3.16)$$

where s is the 'normalised spatial frequency' ($s = k_i/k_s$).

In general there is little difference in the size of w and the inter-element spacing Δp; consequently for all practical purposes we can put $w \approx \Delta p$ and the term ($w/\Delta p$) becomes unity.

A plot of MTF (Eq: 3.16) against the normalised spatial frequency (s) will approach 100% for relatively coarse image detail, that is, where $k_i << k_s$, and decreases as k_i increases. At the Nyquist limit the MTF is reduced to 64%.

The MTF of a CCD image can also be degraded by inefficient charge transfer. It is a fundamental limitation of CCDs that, although charge is not lost, a small proportion of the charge signal is left behind at each transfer.[17] This residual charge adds to the next charge signal following through the array, which itself leaves a similar charge behind, and so on. As a consequence there is a loss of MTF which can be expressed as MTF' and accounted for as:

$$MTF' = MTF \exp^{\left(-n\varepsilon\left(1-\cos\left(2\pi k_i / k_s\right)\right)\right)} \qquad (3.17)$$

where

n is the number of transfers from point of charge generation to the output.

ε is the fixed fraction of charge left behind at each transfer.

However, in modern buried channel CCDs (BCCD) the above effect is very small since ε is only of the order of about 10^{-5}.

Part Two

Charge Coupled Devices and Imaging Systems

4 The Electrical Properties of Semiconductors

4.1 Electrical Conductors and Insulators

The resistance of conductors (as well as insulators and semiconductors) is partly determined by the number of electrons in the outermost energy level known as the *valence band* of the substance's constituent atoms (see Chapter 1). Under suitable conditions, such as the application of energy from an external source, electrons can be forced from the valence band into the even higher energy level of the conduction band. This transport of electrons is called an electric current.

In the case of a solid crystal the atomic nuclei are so close that the electrons of any given atom are influenced by those of its neighbours such that the energy levels (see Fig. 1.7) are broadened into bands of allowed values, grouped so closely together as to appear as a continuous band. Energy bands which electrons cannot occupy are called *forbidden bands*.

The maximum possible number of electrons in a valence band is eight, and an atom with eight valence electrons is normally an excellent insulator. This is because the valence band is filled, and may be considered to be in a state of equilibrium with a reluctance either to contribute or to receive an electron from the unfilled valence band of a neighbouring atom. All the inert gases (helium, neon, argon, krypton, xenon and radon) have eight valence electrons and are electrical insulators. But elements with six or seven valence electrons are also found to be good insulators, mainly because the gap between the valence and conduction bands is too great.

Atoms having only one, two, or three electrons in their valence band are usually very ready to accept electrons from, or contribute electrons to, neighbouring atoms and are therefore good electrical conductors. Metals like silver and copper have a single valence electron and make excellent conductors since they have a very small forbidden band – or none at all. When a battery is connected to a metal conductor some of the valence electrons gain a small amount of energy and move to the adjacent (unoccupied) higher energy level of the *conduction band* where they can move freely from atom to atom along the conductor. But with an insulator the valence electrons cannot gain sufficient energy from a battery to bridge the extremely wide gap to the conduction band. As a consequence there are no carriers available for conduction. Fig. 4.1(a) broadly illustrates these conditions for an insulator.

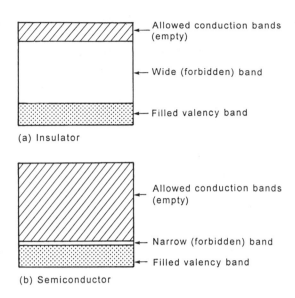

Fig. 4.1 Typical energy bands for (a) an insulator, and (b) a semiconductor.

A basic electrical property of a material is its *resistivity* (ρ), which is a function of a material's *resistance* (R) given in ohms (Ω), and the dimensions of that material. From the well-known Ohms Law, which relates voltage (V) and current (I), we have:

$$R = V/I \quad \text{(Ohms)} \tag{4.1}$$

We can then obtain ρ from:

$$\rho = R\,(A/L) \quad (\Omega\,\text{cm}) \tag{4.2}$$

where A is the cross-sectional area in square centimetres, and L is the length in centimetres.

Materials with values of $\rho < 10^{-2}\ \Omega$ cm are known as *conductors*; aluminium is an excellent conductor for example, and has a resistivity of $10^{-6}\,\Omega$ cm at room temperature. At the other end of the scale we have *insulators*, with values of $\rho > 10^5\,\Omega$ cm, Silicon dioxide, for example, has a resistivity of $10^{16}\,\Omega$ cm. In between these two types of material we have the *semiconductors*.

4.2 Semiconductors

Those elements with four electrons in the valence bands of their atoms, and compounds made up of one element with three valence electrons and another with five valence electrons, may be semiconductors.

Semiconductors are used to make solid-state electronic components, and some of these are light-sensitive devices that employ the *photoelectric effect*. One such photo-cell is the cadmium sulphide (CdS) photoresistor, which has a resistance that can vary from millions of ohms in total darkness to a few tens of ohms when illuminated. Another device is the metal oxide semiconductor (MOS) employed in CCDs.

Semiconductors have an energy band diagram similar to that of an insulator, but the gap between the valence and conduction bands is very narrow, as shown in Fig. 4.1(b). At absolute zero (zero degrees Kelvin) a pure semiconductor is an insulator, but at room temperature (about 20°C, or 290 K) the mean thermal energy of an electron follows the expression:

$$E_t = 3kT/2 \qquad (4.3)$$

where:

E_t is the mean energy of translation of a molecule,
k is Boltzmann's constant, 1.38×10^{-23} JK^{-1} (joules per Kelvin),
T is the absolute temperature of the molecule (in degrees Kelvin).

If we take a value for T as 290 K, and since 1 eV = 1.6×10^{-19} joules we can calculate the mean thermal energy of an electron at room temperature to be in the region of 0.04 eV. However, some of the valence electrons will have much more thermal energy than this, and can easily overcome the 0.75 eV forbidden energy gap of a germanium semiconductor, or the 1.1 eV forbidden gap of a silicon semiconductor.

Semiconductors are often 'doped' with controlled amounts of impurities so that the dopant lowers the resistance of the semiconductor to allow more current to flow through the device. If we introduce a pentavalent element (i.e. with five valence electrons), such as phosphorus, arsenic or antimony, into a pure silicon crystal (the host material, with four valence electrons) then each substitute atom has one more electron than necessary to make a covalent bond. These pentavalent atoms are called 'donors' since they donate an extra electron. And since they are not in a valence band, these excess electrons are free to carry a negative charge and leave behind a fixed positive charge (positive hole) in the substitute atoms. In this way the charge-neutrality condition is preserved. An absolutely perfect semi-conductor is known as an *intrinsic* semiconductor where the concentration of electrons (n) and holes (p) are equal. Under these conditions an *intrinsic* semi-conductor is not particularly useful, which is why dopants are employed.

Silicon doped with phosphorus is known as an *extrinsic* semiconductor of the negative type (n-type) because the concentration of free electrons is much larger than that of holes. If, on the other hand, a trivalent element such as boron, alu-minium or gallium, is used as the substitutional impurity, a single electron is now missing from the bonding arrangement of elements, and a positive hole is pro-duced with a fixed negative charge remaining in the impurity atom. Materials with an excess of holes are called p-type semiconductors. It is the movement of elec-tron-hole pairs that carry the charge in solid-state junction devices.

The junction diode formed by an interface of p-type and n-type semiconduc-tor materials is characterised by its ability to block the flow of electrons in one direction (reverse bias) while permitting electron flow in the opposite direction (forward bias). If electrons are directed into the p-type side of the diode they will not cross the interface of the pn junction, because the electrons already present in the n-type region repel them. But if electrons with sufficient energy are directed into the n-type side of the junction, they can easily cross over the junction to combine with the positive holes and create an electrical current.

It should be noted that all microelectronic devices make use of the pn junction in some form or other. And while the operation of the diode described above is discussed in terms of electrons as carriers of electrical charge, it is also possible to consider the holes on the p-type side of the junction as being charge carriers, because holes continually migrate toward the pn junction to combine with arriving electrons.

The transistor is an important semiconductor component incorporating multiple pn junctions, and although there are numerous types of transistor they all allow a relatively large electric current flowing through the device to be controlled by a very small current or voltage at a third electrode, or gate.

4.3 Metal-oxide-semiconductor (MOS) Technology

Since the mid 1980s MOS technology has superseded the bipolar junction transistor both in sales and in applications, mainly through its simple structure and low fabrication costs. In this book it is important to discuss MOS structures since the MOS capacitor is basic to the charge coupled device (CCD), and although a silicon-silicon dioxide system is mentioned here, MOS technology is ever improving, and insulating materials other than pure SiO_2 are currently under consideration.[18]

The MOS capacitor

The basics of a MOS capacitor are shown in Fig. 4.2, where it can be seen that the structure comprises an aluminium gate (Al) over a dielectric material (SiO_2) deposited on a p-type silicon substrate. The band gap of the silicon dioxide insulator is 8 eV, and that of the p-type silicon semiconductor 1.1 eV.

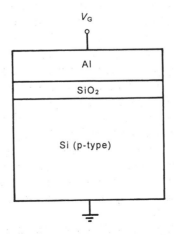

Fig. 4.2 Basic MOS capacitor structure.

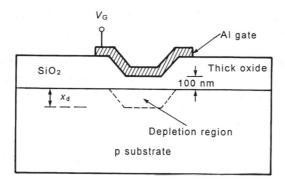

Fig. 4.3 Details of MOS capacitor with aluminium gate.

As there is only a negligible voltage drop in the metal gate, the applied voltage V_G is shared by the voltage across the oxide (V_o) and the *surface potential* (ψ_s), as:

$$V_G = V_o + \psi_s \tag{4.4}$$

The surface potential is the voltage across the semiconductor, and by using the bulk Si as reference, ψ_s can be considered as the potential at the Si–SiO$_2$ inter-face. For this reason it is known as the surface potential.

It should be noted that the SiO$_2$ layer is a good insulator and does not allow the conduction of current between the metal and semiconductor – even under bias, that is, as a dielectric the oxide will, under an applied electric field, cause a displacement of charge – but not a flow of charge.

Depending on the polarity and magnitude of the applied voltage, three differ-ent surface conditions are possible: (i) carrier accumulation, (ii) carrier inversion, and (iii) carrier depletion. Although all three conditions are important to the theory of the MOS capacitor,[19] it is the third condition that we shall consider here, since this allows us to explain the function of MOS elements in the CCD.

Fig. 4.3 shows a typical cross-section of a MOS capacitor. In this diagram the gate is shown as an aluminium type, but it could equally be a semi-transparent polycrystalline (polysilicon) gate as suited to a CCD imaging sensor. Other gate variants employed in CCD structures include polysilicon-aluminium, or two or three levels of polysilicon. Typically the SiO$_2$ layer will vary from a thin deposit of about 100 nm to a thick one in the region of 1 µm (10^{-3} mm).

When a positive step voltage (up to about 10 volts) is applied to the gate of a MOS, the majority of carrier holes are repelled – resulting in a depletion region of negatively charged acceptor states under the gate, near to the surface of the silicon. In time, electron-hole pairs are generated in the depletion region, and electrons accumulate at the Si–SiO$_2$ interface to create an inversion layer, while the holes are driven to the substrate.

The surface potential (ψ_s) of a MOS capacitor, as a function of the applied voltage at the gate electrode (V_G), is given by:

$$\psi_s = V_G + Q_s/C_o \tag{4.5}$$

where

Q_s is the total charge per unit area in the semiconductor surface region (C/cm^2),

C_o is the SiO$_2$ capacitance (F/cm^2).

The oxide capacitance (C_o) is given by:

$$C_o = K_o \, \varepsilon_o / x_o \tag{4.6}$$

where

K_o is the oxide dielectric constant (3.9 for silicon dioxide),

ε_o is the free space permittivity (F/m),

x_o is the oxide thickness.

Surface potential is also controlled by the substrate doping concentration, as well as the silicon oxide thickness.

4.4 Charge Coupled Devices (CCDs)

Essentially a charge coupled device is a silicon integrated circuit of the MOS type with a basic structure such as that shown in Fig. 4.4. A CCD comprises an oxide (SiO$_2$) covered silicon substrate upon which is formed an array of closely spaced electrodes. Signal information is carried in the form of an electric charge, usually electrons (although opposite polarity CCDs are also possible). The charge is lo-

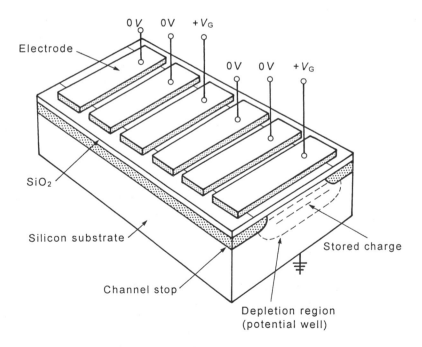

Fig. 4.4 Typical CCD structure.

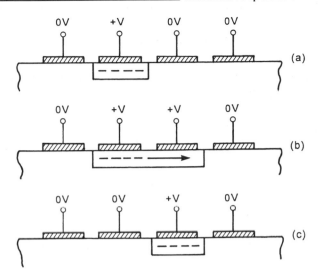

Fig. 4.5 Signal transfer by charge coupling.

calised under the electrodes with the highest applied potentials because the posi-tive potential of an electrode (V_G) causes the underlying silicon to be in depletion (Fig. 4.3) and so assume a positive potential, which attracts the signal electrons. We can then say that the electrons are being stored in a 'potential well'. The active part of the CCD (where the charges are stored) Is known as the channel, and this region is bounded by electrically inactive p-type 'channel stops' as shown in Fig. 4.4.

The term 'charge coupling' refers to the method by which signal charges (which can be photoelectrons created from an image falling on the CCD array) can be transferred from under one electrode to the next. This is accomplished by taking the voltage on the second electrode also to a high level, and reducing the voltage on the first electrode, as shown in Fig. 4.5. By sequentially pulsing electrode voltages between high and low levels, charge signals can be transported down an array of very many electrodes with hardly any loss and with very little noise. This CCD transport system is often compared to the action of a 'bucket brigade' used to convey buckets of water to fight a fire. This simile is made good by the fact that each 'bucket' is a potential well of electrons – carried along a 'shift register' to a final output.

Three-Phase CCDs

By connecting up three closely spaced MOS capacitors into storage elements, and applying a set of three-phase drive pulses ϕ_1, ϕ_2 and ϕ_3 (typically from +5 to +15 volts), charge signals can be stored under every third electrode in each line of the array, as shown in Fig. 4.6. Under this system each storage element (or pixel if the input signal is optically generated) has every third electrode connected

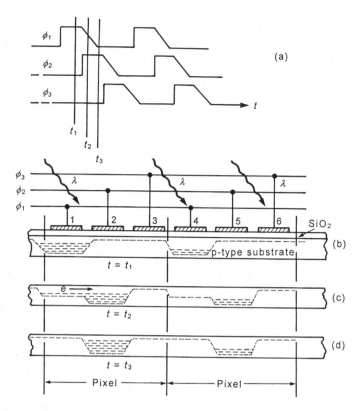

Fig. 4.6 Three-phase CCD, showing storage elements (pixels) and drive pulses.

to the same clock voltage and consequently three separate clock generators are required, as shown in Fig. 4.6(a). If the positive voltage applied to ϕ_1 is higher than that applied to ϕ_2 and ϕ_3, surface potential wells are formed under the ϕ_1 electrodes, as explained for Fig. 4.5. Charge packets, introduced either optically or electrically, are accumulated in these depletion wells at $t = t_1$. These charge packets may be of different signal strengths. For example, those illustrated in Fig.4.6(b) show the charge under gate 4 to be less than that under gate 1. It should be noted that the MOS capacitors must be close enough to allow their depletion layers to overlap; this is necessary so that the surface potential has a smooth transition at the boundaries of the neighbouring electrodes.

In order to move the charges to the right, a positive step voltage is applied to ϕ_2 to ensure that the potential wells under the ϕ_1 and ϕ_2 electrodes are the same in depth. In this way the charge packets are allowed to spread out to the right, as seen at $t = t_2$, Fig. 4.6(c). Immediately after the pulse to ϕ_2, the the voltage at ϕ_1 decays so that the potential wells under the ϕ_1 electrodes slowly rise. The charge packets now spill over to the potential wells under gates 2 and 5 at $t = t_3$; see Fig. 4.6(d).

By repeating the same procedure the signals can then be moved from ϕ_2 to ϕ_3, and then from ϕ_3 to ϕ_1, and so on. At each full cycle of clock voltages the charge packets advance one storage element (pixel) to the right.

Developments in CCD technology

It is perhaps appropriate at this stage to mention that the principle of the charge coupled device dates back to 1934[20] and since that time the CCD has developed from being a shift register memory store in computers to solid-state imaging systems. Bell Systems USA first announced the use of CCDs for a solid-state camera in 1972, and from there we had the well-known Sony Mavica in 1980. But it wasn't until the start of the 1990s that CCD technology had improved sufficiently to provide electronic imagery of good enough quality to interest people in its future as an alternative to film. Improvements are constantly being made of course, and it must be said that the technology mentioned in these pages can only provide a guide to the reader – in terms of future CCD developments. Indeed, some of the detail written here is likely to remain valid for only a few years at the current rate of technical progress! Nevertheless, it may be assumed that the basic theory will not alter too much, even as the fabrication of CCD imagers changes and improves at a steady pace.

Significant improvements already put into production include smaller storage elements, and a much higher pixel resolution of CCD imagers due to better fabrication techniques. There is also a continuous improvement in charge-transfer efficiencies and noise reduction through the use of *buried-channel CCDs*, and more advanced methods in clocking the electrodes using *two-phase* systems and *triple-polysilicon gates*.

Further improvements include semiconductor doping techniques, and the use of optical filters over storage elements to provide micro-colour pixels in the architecture of CCD imagers.

Two-phase CCDs

Whereas in a three-phase CCD the potential wells are symmetrical, and charges can flow to either right or left, we have a much simplified system with two-phase clocking since the flow can only go in a single direction, as shown in Fig. 4.7.

To provide charge transfer with a two-phase shift register, potentials on adjacent electrodes are clocked between high and low levels (Fig. 4.7a) to direct charges to the right. A deep potential well (PW) which attracts electrons is formed under a 'high' electrode clock voltage and disappears under a 'low' voltage pulse. At $t = 0$ (Fig. 4.7b), ϕ_1 voltage is high and the finite charge packet lies in the potential well under gate electrode 2 of storage element A. At a half-cycle time later (Fig. 4.7c), the potential well at gate 2 has collapsed due to ϕ_1 going low, and the charge packet is now attracted to the new potential well under gate electrode 3, as ϕ_2 goes high. At $t = 1$, the potential well under gate 3 has now collapsed with ϕ_2 going low, and the electron packet moves to a new potential well under gate 4, which has gone high with ϕ_1.

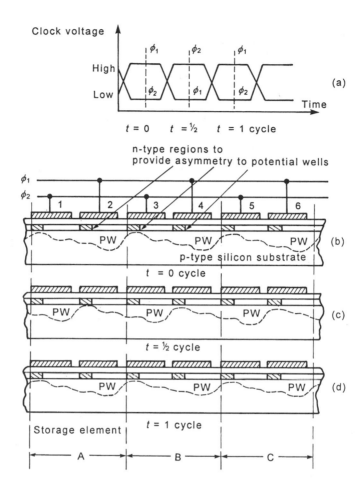

Fig. 4.7 Two-phase CCD. (a) Two-phase clock voltages. Stages of charge transfer are shown at (b), (c) and (d). PW – potential well.

Usually we find that both two-phase and three-phase CCDs, employ optically transparent polysilicon-aluminium gates with an overlapping structure of the kind shown in Fig. 4.8.

Buried channel CCDs

As we have seen from the previous diagrams, the CCDs described so far store and transfer their charges in potential wells situated at the silicon surface directly beneath the SiO_2 layer. For this reason they are known as *surface-channel CCDs* (SCCDs). But these surface states can adversely influence such things as transfer efficiency and noise levels – particularly if the signal strength is low.

A suitable arrangement for overcoming the worst of these problems is to fabricate what is known as a *buried-channel CCD* (BCCD). The buried channel is

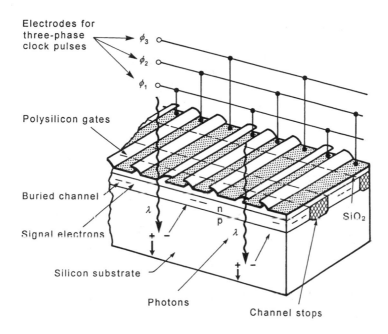

Fig. 4.8 Three-phase buried channel CCD (BCCD).

created by forming a diffused n-type layer on a p-type substrate, as shown in Fig. 4.8. And if a large positive voltage is applied to the channel (via the input and output diodes) a depletion layer is formed under the MOS capacitors. The potential well formed in the n-type buried channel will then store the signal electrons, which can then be transferred by the same clock pulses as used with SCCDs.

With BCCDs a transfer efficiency better than 99.99% can be achieved as well as higher clocking frequencies, up to 100 MHz.

4.5 Video Technology and the Digital Revolution

The term video was originally used in television to separate the picture from sound signals, but today it broadly refers to all systems that involve electronic imaging, including television, video cassette recorders (VCRs), camcorders and still video cameras. It is the last of these products that concerns us in this book, and although the term 'still video camera' is currently simplified to 'digital camera', we often find the former expression is still being used to differentiate digital cameras from camcorders.

As the technology moves forward, we find that many of the terms are either misunderstood or misplaced, and this is as much to do with a lack of standard terminology as it is careless advertising. Certainly we can class the digital camera to be part of video technology, but it has now grown out of its early origins, where a video (movie) camera was used to provide a 'still' image via an external device known as a *frame grabber*.

All video images are essentially in analogue form, that is to say, as electrical signals conveying luminance and colour with a continuously variable voltage. And up to the early 1970s TV signals were almost all analogue. But as CCD and digital technology developed, much of the analogue video processing circuitry was replaced by high-speed sampling methods that convert continuously changing signal gradients into binary digits, each representing a discrete signal level.

The CCD camcorder was introduced in the latter part of the 1970s, and as a home-videotape camera it rapidly overtook the amateur cine camera, since it offered immediate access to the TV screen. It also took on a professional role with outside television crews, electronic newsgathering, documentary filming and scientific recording. In the latter role there was a need for analysing certain frames and so the frame grabber was introduced to convert analogue signals into digital ones (A/D conversion), in order to grab a still picture (see Box 3).

Box 3 The analogue-to-digital converter

The analogue-to-digital converter converts analogue signals into a numerically equivalent form suitable for input to a digital computer. Analogue signals are of a continuously varying nature, but computers can only handle discrete bits of information. The A/D converter allows analogue data to be stored and handled by the computer with conversion rates as high as 1 GHz possible.

The required input voltages are the upper and lower reference voltages, the voltage to be measured and a clock pulse. The A/D converter comprises a series of binary voltage comparators supplied with the input signal and a reference voltage which is scaled between the low and high values. At each clock pulse the comparators are simultaneously read and a binary code is then generated, a process often referred to as *image quantisation*.

In short, an A/D converter is a register that can hold a digital value, an operational amplifier, and a series of binary voltage comparators. The register outputs are electrically summed to produce an electric current proportional to the digital value of the register. This current causes a proportional voltage gain at the amplifier output, and the amplified voltage is compared with the unknown input analogue signal. Provided there is a discernible difference, the voltage comparators allow the register value to change one step at a time until there is no difference. The register then holds the digital value equivalent to the analogue input.

A/D converters are common computer input/output devices used for control applications, and have resolutions that can vary from 8 to 14 bits. Frame grabbers usually have an A/D resolution of 8 to 12 bits (256 to 4096 grey levels). Conversely, computer produced control signals may require the complementary device, a digital-to-analogue (D/A) converter, for example for monitor display.

Usually a frame grabber is a printed circuit board fitted to a host computer, with its analogue entrance port matching the impedance of the incoming video signal which is then split into the synchronisation and analogue pre-processing modules. The A/D converter then translates the video signal into digital values by sampling the 0 to 0.7 V analogue voltage range and a digital image is constructed from each pixel, sampled at a rate based on the pixel clock and other synchronisation signals.

4.6 CCD Imagers

Often referred to as charge coupled imagers, digital cameras can take many forms, as we shall see in Chapter 5, but the main differences, apart from pixel specifications, centre on the type of sensor array employed.

So far we have concentrated on the basic mechanism of CCDs, but we must now look at the CCD imaging sensor in terms of its pixels (storage elements) which, as we have seen, can be formed by either two or three electrodes. Common to all CCD imaging sensors is the *photogate* (the optical window of the photosite) which is qualified by its *fill factor* or the percentage of the pixel that can be filled with light. These days manufacturers quote fill factors as high as 100% for some of their products.

At exposure to image light, each pixel will receive electrons in proportion to the incoming radiation and, as we have seen, each charge packet of electrons is then passed down the line of pixels by the process of charge coupling. Once a charge packet reaches the end of its line it is transferred to the output register and measured. It is important to remember that the signal received at the output register is in analogue form and remains so until put to the analogue-to-digital (A/D) converter. After A/D conversion each individual pixel receives a digital number (DN) according to its strength and corresponding to its sensor location within the array. (Note: The CCD's elements are only equivalent to pixels if the sampling rate at the A/D conversion is the same.) Naturally we can expect some of the charge to be lost at each potential well as the signal is passed down the line, but this is only a small amount with modern CCDs since they generally exhibit charge-transfer efficiencies as high as 99.99%, or one electron in 10^5, a negligible amount when one considers that it takes over 10^5 electrons to fill each potential well.[21]

CCD linear imaging arrays

The linear (one-dimensional) array represents the simplest form of CCD imager and has been employed since the early 1970s in applications varying from space-borne military intelligence gathering to flat-bed scanners. A single line of CCD pixels are clocked out into the parallel output register as shown in Fig. 4.9.

However, in order to produce a two-dimensional image, a line array CCD imager has to be used as a scanning device either by moving the array over the object, or vice versa. In aerospace imaging the former method is employed by a process known as *push-broom*, where the space vehicle or aircraft moves over the terrain and, akin to sweeping a floor with a broom, the linear array sweeps forward to

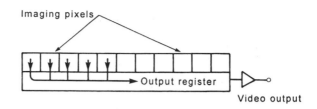

Fig. 4.9 A single-line CCD linear array.

scan the terrain in a regular pattern that is read out strip-by-strip via the output register into storage or direct transmission.

This technique has been instrumental in producing one of the earliest and most important forms of CCD digital imagery, not only for military reconnaissance but also for SPOT (Système Probatoire d'Observation de la Terre) the French earth resources satellite cover, and airborne multispectral line-scan imagers such as the Canadian MEIS II. SPOT, for example, employs linear arrays of 6000 elements in its panchromatic mode and 3000 in its multispectral mode (see Chapter 10). Similar methods are employed for flat-bed scanners, using either moving or static arrays (see Chapter 7).

CCD area imaging arrays

Two-dimensional area imaging arrays come in three basic architectures: (a) interline transfer, (b) field-frame transfer and (c) full-frame transfer. All of these array types continue to be manufactured and are subject to constant change and variation as the technology improves. The basic outlines considered here lack finite detail, but perhaps this is just as well, since there is little to be gained by detailing systems that are constantly in a state of change. Nevertheless, the three array types mentioned above are likely to remain as standard architectures for many years yet, with the full-frame transfer arrangement the most likely CCD architecture for current and future digital cameras.

Interline transfer arrays

Interline transfer CCDs require twice as many pixels as a full-frame type, because columns of image sensors (pixels) are interspaced by columns of opaque transfer elements as shown in Fig. 4.10. Charge packets are accumulated in the sensor elements during image exposure, then shifted into the transfer columns and finally transferred, row by row, into the horizontal output (shift) register. The image is detected as two vertically interlaced modes and can be operated in either high resolution or standard TV interlace mode. Interline transfer arrays are generally employed in the broadcast and home markets for video imaging systems, where they are favoured for their improved vertical resolution.

Field-frame transfer arrays

The basic architecture of a three-phase, field-frame CCD imager, is shown schematically in Fig. 4.11. As a three-phase system, there are three MOS capaci-

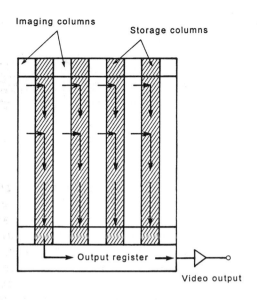

Fig. 4.10 CCD interline transfer.

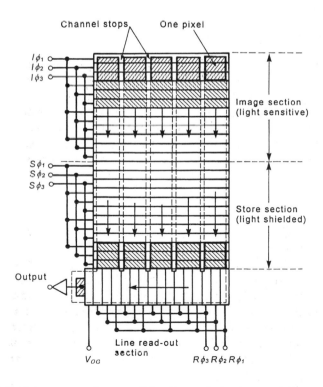

Fig. 4.11 CCD field-frame transfer array (After Hoare & Matthews. 1988). OG – output gate.

tors to each (vertical) storage element, and so a square-shaped pixel is formed by appropriately spaced channel stops.

The device must be considered as an array of horizontal pixels above a number of vertical charge-transfer channels (or columns) defined by *channel-stop* regions. The horizontal electrodes (pixels) are grouped into two sections; the upper one is the 'image reception' section, and the lower one a 'storage' section. In Fig. 4.11 there are twelve horizontal electrodes broken up into four layers of pixels in both sections. At the bottom is the 'line read-out' of the horizontal shift register, which transfers the charges in each pixel line to the video output amplifier. This amplifier is electrically shielded from the line read-out section by an output gate (OG) which is held at a fixed direct current (DC) bias voltage (V_{OG}).

The clock pulses applied to *image, store* and *shift register* sections are designated $I\phi$, $S\phi$ and $R\phi$ respectively. Naturally the store and read-out sections are shielded from image illumination by opaque masking.

When the image section is illuminated, photons can pass through the semi-transparent polysilicon electrodes to generate electron-hole pairs within the silicon substrate. The electrons then diffuse to the nearest biased electrode where they are collected as a signal packet (Fig. 4.5) and the holes diffuse down to the substrate where they are effectively lost (Fig. 4.8). A single pixel is therefore an area bounded by the channel stops and the three (or two) electrodes centred on the biased electrode.

In the example shown in Fig. 4.11, there is a matrix of five pixels in each of four rows, and the quantity of charge collected is proportional to the local radiation intensity and time allowed for collection, that is, the exposure time. At the end of the exposure time, the entire array of charges collected in the image section is transferred to store by applying drive pulses to electrodes in both sections. In the example shown here, this would amount to four pulses in each phase. Radiation is still incident on the image section of course, and so the fastest possible transfer is desirable to avoid spurious signals being picked up as the charges are moved from one section to the other.

By applying appropriate pulses to the electrodes of store and shift register sections, all the image-generated charges are moved as a block, one element at a time, down the store section. The lowest row of pixel charges is transferred in parallel into the line read-out section (shift register). This last transfer is achieved through one cycle of the $S\phi$ drive pulses with one of the phases of the shift register held high, for example, $R\phi_2$ in Fig. 4.11. As the potential on the last electrode of the store ($S\phi_3$) goes low, the transfer takes place across the upper edge of the $R\phi_2$ electrodes. Then, by application of $R\phi$ pulses, the line of charges is sequentially transferred to the on-chip charge detection amplifier which converts the charge signals into a voltage modulated video output. The next line of signals is then passed down from store to shift register and read out in the same way. As the first pattern of image charge is being read out to video a second pattern can be recorded in the image section. Once the first image has been completely read out, a second image will be transferred to the store section, and so on.

Normally the integrated charge detection amplifier is configured to provide a voltage output, where the output corresponding to each pixel (V_p) is proportional to the charge collected (Q_p). This can be achieved through a change of potential on the capacitance (C) of the charge detection node, that is,

$$V_p = Q_p/C \qquad (4.7)$$

Whereas most of the earlier types of CCD cameras employed field-frame transfer systems, current models adopt a simpler configuration that does away with the store section, and is known as the full-frame transfer system.

Full-frame transfer arrays

It would seem that current developments favour a full-frame transfer array as the state-of-the-art architecture for modern digital cameras.

As may be seen from inspection of Fig. 4.12, a full-frame transfer arrangement is much the same as that shown in Fig. 4.11, except for the store section and its associated clock phases. In operation it follows the same basic pattern of events as the field-frame transfer system, but here the image section occupies the entire array, and its pixels are then transferred directly to the shift register.

This increased efficiency is made possible by improved clocking frequencies, and the use of a mechanical shutter to prevent *smear*. Smear is a problem common to all types of frame transfer systems and can be defined as the ratio be-

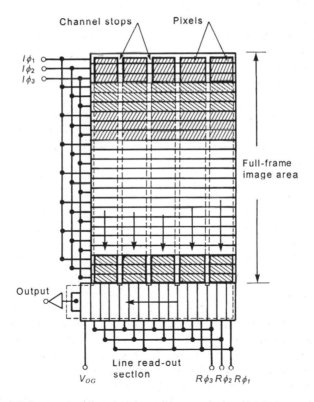

Fig. 4.12 CCD full-frame transfer array (containing only incident light receptors).

tween the change in image illuminance above or below a bright area covering 10% of the sensor extent in the column direction.[22] Smear is proportional to the ratio between illumination and transfer periods, typically in the region of 40 : 1. So, for a 10% extent on the sensor, the smear will be about 0.25% for a saturated image and would not be noticed normally. But if the image is over-saturated at any point, then the smear becomes apparent as 'image trails'.

All frame transfer imagers can be illuminated either from the top through the semi-transparent polysilicon gates, or through the back of the substrate – provided it is suitably thin. Unfortunately, thin wafer substrates are very fragile, so their use is generally reserved for CCD cameras that are attached to instruments, such as astronomical telescopes and microscopes.

CCD transfer efficiency

The fraction of charge transferred at each gate is called the *transfer efficiency* (ε). The fraction left behind, or loss-per-transfer, is designated with the symbol α. So the sum of these two components is given by:

$$\varepsilon + \alpha = 1.0 \tag{4.8}$$

Since ε determines how many transfers can be made before the signal output is seriously distorted and delayed, it is a highly important figure of merit for a CCD imager. If a single charge-pulse of amplitude P_0 is transferred down a CCD register with n transfers, the output will be:

$$P_n = P_0\, \varepsilon^n \approx P_0(1 - n\alpha) \tag{4.9}$$

When the product $n\alpha = 1.0$, then the original pulse is completely lost and distributed among several trailing pulses.[23] Obviously α must be very small where a large number of transfers are required, as the following example makes clear.

If we consider a 1000 stage shift register and allow an overall loss greater than 10%, then the product $n\alpha \leq 10^{-4}$, and a transfer efficiency (ε) of 0.9999 is required.

For imaging applications the entire field of CCD stages are biased into deep depletion (Fig. 4.3), and then exposed to a focused image for a short period of time as the generation of carriers under a CCD gate is enhanced according to the image illuminance at that point. But there is a lower limit for the speed of operation of a CCD, where the signal has to be transferred into and out of a stage at a rate that is fast compared with the *dark current* generation rate at a depleted silicon surface. No stage in a CCD array can be held for a long time in conditions of deep depletion, and noise (such as that caused by dark current) will be continuously added because of thermal generation. Most CCD signal charges usually range from about 10 to 10^7 electrons. By comparison, a thermally generated dark current density of 1 nA cm^{-2} corresponds to about 60 electrons per second under a 1 µm^2 gate.[24]

Dark current in CCDs

Rather akin to the non-image light known as 'fog' in photographic films, *dark* current (I_D) arises from the thermal generation of electrons that accumulate in CCD elements and add to the photo-generated signals. A typical value is about 1% of the peak signal level (I_p). At 25 °C, typical values are in the region: $I_p \approx 250$ nA, and $I_D \approx 3$ nA.

Ideally I_D would be uniform – adding equally to the output of all pixels – but there will be some spatial variations due to inhomogenities in device manufacture, giving a 'pattern noise' that sets a minimum signal level below which imaging is not practical. It is also important to note that the dark signal and its non-uniformity are very temperature dependent and will generally follow the well-known diode law:

$$I_D = Ae^{-V_{bg}/(2kT/q)} \tag{4.10}$$

where

V_{bg} is the band gap for silicon (≈ 1.1 eV),
A is a constant,
k is the Boltzmann constant (1.38054×10^{-23} J K^{-1}),
T is the black body operating temperature of the device (degrees Kelvin),
q is the charge of electron (1.6021×10^{-19} C) (Note: The coulomb $\equiv$ amp-second).

At normal room temperatures (20–25 °C) we can expect values of I_D to follow Eq: 4.10 quite well over the range –60 to 60 °C. Using Eq: 4.10, with a known dark-current value of 3.5 nA for a device operating at 25 °C (298 K), the constant (A) is found to be 6.88, and when this value is inserted back into the equation values of dark current can be found for any other temperatures. Values of dark current relative to that found for 25 °C (3.5 nA) are shown plotted in Fig. 4.13,

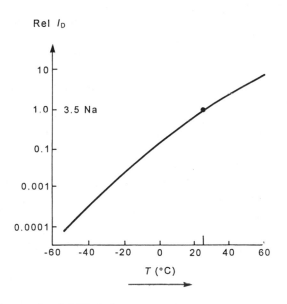

Fig. 4.13 Typical example of CCD dark current (relative to that found for 25 °C, 3.5 nA) plotted against temperature.

Table 4.1 A sample of Kodak full-frame CCD imaging sensors

Sensor: KAF-0400 (colour and monochrome) 0.39 million pixels

Imager size = 6.9 mm (H) × 4.6 mm (V) Chip size = 8.4 mm (H) × 5.5 mm (V)
Pixel count = 768(H) × 512(V) Pixel size = 9 µm × 9 µm
Optical fill-factor = 70% Saturation signal = 85 000 electrons
Output sensitivity = 10 µV / electron Read-out noise (1 MHz) = 15
  electrons RMS

Dark current < 10 pA /cm^2 Dark current doubling rate = 5–6 °C
Dynamic range (signal/noise) = 72 dB Maximum data rate = 20 MHz
Quantum efficiency = 10% (λ = 450 nm), 30% (λ = 550 nm), 35% (λ = 650 nm)

Applications: digital cameras, machine vision, astronomy and microscopy

---

Sensor: KAF-1600 (colour or monochrome) 1.6 million pixels

Imager size = 13.97 mm (H) × 9.29 mm (V) Chip size = 15.5mm (H) × 10mm (V)
Pixel count = 1536 (H) × 1024 (V) Pixel size = 9 µm × 9 µm
Optical fill-factor = 100% or 70% (colour) Saturation signal = 85 000 electrons
  or 40 000 (colour)
Output sensitivity = 10 µV / electron Read-out noise (1 MHz) = 15
  electrons RMS
Dark current < 10 pA / cm^2 Dark current doubling rate = 5–6 °C
Dynamic range (signal/noise) = 72 dB Maximum data rate = 20 MHz
Quantum efficiency = 10% (λ = 450-nm), 38% (λ = 550 nm), 32% (λ = 650 nm)

Applications: digital cameras, machine vision, astronomy and microscopy, aerial survey

---

Sensor: KAF-6301 (monochrome or colour) 6.3 million pixels

Imager size = 27.65 mm (H) × 18.48 mm (V) Chip size = 29 mm (H) × 19.1mm (V)
Pixel count = 3088 (H) × 2056 (V) Pixel size = 9 µm × 9 µm
Optical fill-factor = 100% Saturation signal = 85 000 electrons
Output sensitivity = 10 µV/electron Read-out noise (10 MHz) =
  15 electrons RMS
Dark current < 10 pA /cm^2 Dark current doubling rate = 5–6 °C
Dynamic range (signal/noise) =72 dB Maximum data rate = 10 MHz
Quantum efficiency = 10% (λ = 450 nm), 30% (λ = 550 nm), 40% (λ = 650 nm)

Applications: digital cameras, inspection, film-scanning, astronomy

---

(Kodak product specifications by courtesy of Kodak, Rochester, USA)

from which it can be seen that the *dark-current doubling rate* parameter is a ± temperature shift of 9–10 °C.

Most of the current range of Kodak CCD image sensors have dark-current density values that are smaller than 10 pA/cm^2. But, as can be seen from Table 4.1, the *dark-current doubling rate* is now more sensitive at 5–6 °C and, for special applications, such as the long exposure periods required for astronomy or microscopy, special cooling down to –30 °C is required.

CCD noise

There are three main sources of noise in CCD systems, and in their order of importance we can list them as: (i) photon shot noise (N_s); (ii) dark-current noise (N_d) and (iii) circuit noise (N_c).

Photon shot noise
Owing to the random arrival and absorption of photons, charge generation is a statistical process, and the *signal-to-noise ratio* (SNR) for the sensed image is at a maximum when the pixels are close to their full capacity (around 10^6 electrons). Photon shot noise is given as the square root of the signal level (S), given in electrons:

$$N_s = \sqrt{S} \qquad\qquad (4.11)$$

Dark-current noise
As we have seen, dark current is produced continuously at a rate proportional to the absolute temperature (K) of the sensor material, and is generated at both exposure and read-out phases. Similarly, we find that If we measure the dark current (I_D) in electrons we have:

$$N_d = \sqrt{I_D} \qquad\qquad (4.12)$$

Circuit noise
For a CCD sensor the largest source of circuit noise (N_c) is the on-chip amplifier, which is responsible for amplifying each individual pixel charge to a useful level. After each pixel is read out, the amplifier must be reset to zero, and the uncertainty of the recovered zero level is known as *reset noise*. Reset noise can be kept low, but this depends on keeping the read-out speed very low. According to Janesick et al.[25] a specially constructed CCD imager (with 4096 × 4096 pixels) achieved sub-electron circuit noise levels, but requires 64 samples of each pixel and takes eleven minutes to read out an entire image.

The sum of all the noise contributions is N, where:

$$N = (N_s + N_d + N_c) \qquad\qquad (4.13)$$

Signal-to-noise ratio (SNR)

The signal-to-noise ratio (SNR) for an imaging sensor is defined as the ratio between the signal and its noise, or S/N, where N is the sum of the noise contributions listed above, that is,

$$SNR = S/N \qquad (4.14)$$

Usually expressed in decibels, Eq: 4.14 then becomes:

$$SNR = 10 \log(S/N) \quad \text{decibels} \qquad (4.15)$$

Obviously noise becomes a problem mainly at low image-intensity levels, where the signal (S) is close to the overall noise level (*noise floor*). But as the charge capacity of the pixels increases so does the SNR and the dynamic range of the image.

All CCD image sensors have a maximum output signal (or saturation level) and a root mean square noise threshold, with voltages: V_{sat} and $V_{N(rms)}$ respectively. The characteristic linear response region of the imager lies between these two levels, and when CCD analogue signals are quantised into a binary scale, the dynamic range of the image is typically defined as the ratio between the two levels. Expressed in decibels the dynamic range (DR) is given as:

$$DR = 20 \log (V_{sat}/V_{N(rms)}) \quad \text{decibels} \qquad (4.16)$$

Note: Most modern CCD imagers incorporate a lateral overflow drain to prevent *blooming*, a common problem where excess charge is drained off from bright pixels that are over illuminated. Blooming is the major cause of poor highlight resolution.

CCD linearity

As can be seen from Fig. 2.9, the CCD sensor is capable of generating electronic charges in direct proportion to the incident illumination. This is an ideal imaging system, unmatched by any conventional photographic process, and provided the CCD signal does not suffer from non-linear features in the amplifier circuit, the output signal (S) from a pixel can be given by:

$$S = kq^{\gamma} + I_D \qquad (4.17)$$

where
  k is a constant of proportionality,
  q is the generated charge,
  I_D the dark current signal.
The sensor output is linear when γ is equal to unity.

5 Digital Cameras

5.1 Introduction

Although a number of CCD imagers had been produced as a variety of research tools by the late 1970s, the general public only became aware of the electronic camera when the Sony Mavica camera was exhibited at Photokina (Köln, Germany) in the latter part of 1980. It had a phenomenal impact on those who, like me, saw the Mavica demonstrated – but, despite the many claims made for this camera, neither the market, the media nor the public were ready for such an innovation. There were notable exceptions of course, particularly from Geoffrey Crawley, the far-seeing editor of the *British Journal of Photography*, who had been warning the photographic profession of the CCD future for a number of years and who, in 1972,[26] published a first class account of how a CCD imager worked. This article was republished in 1981 with a review of the Mavica[27] and was immediately followed with a further view on the future of solid state imagery a few weeks later.[28]

But although there was some enthusiasm for CCD imagers it was all too premature! Even if the Mavica had gained the necessary financial support, the market was reluctant to press photographers into purchasing an expensive camera that was really no more than a 'freeze-frame video' system with the limited image quality of 570 (horizontal) $\times$ 490 (vertical) pixels. As Crawley rightly pointed out in 1981:

> *'That announcement of a prototype solid-state imaging camera by Sony should cause nervousness and apprehension is very difficult to understand, especially when one considers that electronic imagery will only broaden the whole scope of photography and its associated industry and trade.'*

One can understand the reluctance of both professional and amateur photographers to take on board an unproven system that offered much less than their conventional cameras. But as Crawley put it in 1981:

> *'The Sony Mavica and its like have nothing to offer the professional except early notice that over the next decade new methods and techniques must be learned – the Journal has been warning about this for years, so it should not come as a surprise.'*

How right he was! At that time, I was teaching CCD imagery to students studying for a degree in Photographic Sciences – but again, it was too early, and without the practical support of an available CCD camera there was little or no interest from either colleagues or professionals.

The Mavica looked like an ordinary 35 mm camera, but loaded a flat 50 mm diameter floppy disk instead of film. According to announcements some fifty colour images could be stored on the magnetic disk, which could then be downloaded into a Mavica viewer or TV set. It must be remembered that the Mavica was not a digital camera: the images were strictly analogue! And for all its promise it was never marketed – not too surprising in hindsight, since the personal computer (PC) and essential peripherals were only in their infancy at this time. In the meantime, while the major photographic manufacturers started to research and develop digital cameras in earnest, few people thought there would be any major developments for at least a decade – a prediction that was mainly true!

5.2 Basic Types of Digital Camera

There are several types of 'digital' camera, and all of them are still in production since they offer various advantages according to application and cost. One can also predict that there will be many further types as technology improves, but it is likely these will only be variations of those designs with popular and economic appeal.

The list of digital camera designs given in Table 5.1 is not exhaustive, but simply shows the various methods of achieving a digital image with a camera designed for a particular role. Image quality, in terms of spatial resolution, colour fidelity and dynamic range, always have to be balanced against cost, operating facilities (such as range of available lenses, shutter-speeds, apertures, number of images, frame recycle time, etc.) and compatibility with computer hardware and software.

In Table 5.1 it must be noted that the name used to describe a given type of imager may well be different from that used by a manufacturer; nevertheless it is hoped that the description of the type's technology will suffice to avoid any confusion.

Although some of the types listed in Table 5.1 are rather specialised and often highly expensive, the range of instrumentation is rich enough to support numerous innovations for the future. Already there have been nearly 200 different cameras manufactured and marketed by about 40 different companies, not including the special types made for scientific and industrial work. Indeed, the growth of this young industry is so rapid that it is almost impossible to keep up with the changes now being made.

It is obvious that the high price of a reasonable quality digital camera must fall significantly before it can compete with its film counterpart. This is sure to happen within the space of a few years of course; meanwhile the market is being flooded with what are known as *low end* cameras in the £200 to £1000 range in order to stimulate interest among those who appreciate their potential. The keen amateur photographer has long been able to satisfy his/her hobby from a need to provide

Table 5.1 Basic types of digital camera design

Design type	Description	Major application
(1) Single exposure single area-array	Spatial multiplex system. Low-to-high definition (mono & colour)	Hand-held general and scientific work
(2) Single exposure three area-array chips	Parallel acquisition via three R, G, B filters (mono & colour)	Studio high-quality advertising etc.
(3) Three-exposures single area-array	Temporal multiplex system via spinning three-filter disk (mono & colour)	Studio high quality advertising etc.
(4) Scanned linear-array push-broom or static array	Scanned CCD (1 or 3 CCD linear-arrays) (mono & colour)	Studio CCD cameras, aerospace sytems, flat-bed scanners
(5) Scanning CCD back for studio cameras	Scanned linear-array, 'slip-in' type camera back (70 mm or 5" × 4") (mono & colour)	Studio high quality digital option
(6) Single exposure single area-array camera-back	Single exposure 'slip-in' type camera back (70 mm or 5" x 4") (mono & colour)	Studio/general work high definition for best quality work

photographic records at the workplace. Professionals in every walk of life (scientists, medics, engineers, teachers, surveyors, estate agents, police officers, technical authors,...) have all been used to providing their own photography for many years – thanks to conventional SLR camera technology and a high-street chain of colour processing outlets. But these same users are also among some 60% of UK households who either own or have access to computers (of which only 10% are Macintosh, the majority being IBM compatible PCs), and their ability to use these computers and their peripherals also gives them an opportunity to engage with digital imagery – without the need for darkrooms, chemicals and other inconveniences.

The so-called low end cameras (among those listed as type 1 in Table 5.1) satisfy numerous requirements, where quality need not be as good as that provided by conventional means. They can provide images of a suitable resolution for purposes such as industrial and commercial reports, technical notes,house agent leaflets of property sales, police records and direct communications via fax or Internet. They are not of sufficient quality to satisfy most commercial or advertising requirements, and are not usually suitable for top-quality brochures and journals, but these needs are taken care of by the *high end* digital cameras (usually found in types 2 to 6 in Table 5.1), costing anything from £12 000 to £50 000. As may be expected, these high end cameras are relatively few because of their high cost, and the fact that their exposures are usually counted in minutes rather than fractions of a second. The important system configurations listed as types 1, 2 and 3 (Table 5.1) are shown in Fig. 5.1.

All this leads us to the more interesting *middle range* of professional digital cameras (to be found in the *spatial multiplex* systems under type 1 of Table 5.1) currently priced between £3000 and £15 000. These must surely represent the primary concern of both manufacturers and users alike. The prime market rests with these middle range types, where one-shot, colour imagery of photographic

(a) Spatial multiplex system (R = red, G = green, B = blue)

G	R	G	R	G	R	G	R
B	G	B	G	B	G	B	G
G	R	G	R	G	R	G	R
B	G	B	G	B	G	B	G
G	R	G	R	G	R	G	R

(Single CCD sensor)

(b) Parallel acquisition system

Full colour input

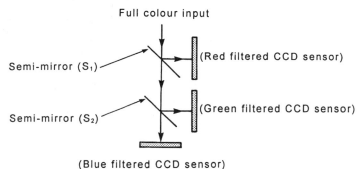

Semi-mirror (S₁)

(Red filtered CCD sensor)

Semi-mirror (S₂)

(Green filtered CCD sensor)

(Blue filtered CCD sensor)

(c) Temporal multiplex system

Full colour input

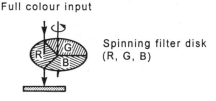

Spinning filter disk
(R, G, B)

Single CCD sensor

Fig. 5.1 Three types of CCD imaging systems.

quality can be attained with SLR type cameras. Such cameras already exist – but the price is high (in the region of £8500 for the Kodak DCS-420 range); nevertheless, at £5000 the Kodak DCS-410 (with slightly less to offer than the DCS-420) shows that prices are already falling as demand steadily increases!

5.3 Single Exposure, Single Area-array (Spatial Multiplex) Cameras (Type 1)

These cameras are the most well-known and popular type of digital imager today, mainly because they operate in much the same fashion as conventional cameras, except that a two-dimensional area-array CCD imager replaces the film.

This type of camera supports much of the full-frame area-array technology mentioned in Chapter 4 and provides a sound basis for future developments. Indeed, hardly a month passes without a new model coming on the market, many of these being modified conventional 35 mm cameras such as the SLRs manufactured by Nikon, Fuji and Canon, with the CCD chip and imaging algorithms provided by another company, such as Kodak.

As we have seen in Chapter 4, monochrome area-array imagers have a spatial resolution accorded by the x, y pixel density. In general the pixels are square shaped with sides of 9 mm. Eastman Kodak are a major provider of CCD imaging chips, such as the KAF-0400 full-frame CCD, as fitted to the Kodak DC-40 and DC-50 cameras, and the KAF-1600 full-frame CCD (usually referred to as the M-5 chip) incorporated in the DCS-200 and its successor, the DCS-420 camera. Full details of these chips can be found in Table 4.1.

Although there are numerous variations with each type of digital camera, many currently follow an almost basic pattern for image capture. Typical of Type 1 cameras is the Kodak DCS-420, which can be supplied in one of three available models: (i) monochrome, (ii) colour, and (iii) infrared false-colour. The DCS-420 is a popular instrument and, although expensive (about £7500 basic to £14 000 CIR), it has a good reputation with many users operating over a wide range of environments. In this respect it represents the middle range of Type 1 digital cameras very well.

Although practical specifications of digital cameras are published, technical data, such as that freely available for conventional cameras, is almost impossible to find. There are good reasons for this of course. Whereas conventional cameras have little to offer that is radically new, every fresh digital camera usually incorporates something unique by way of innovation or advanced technology. As a consequence all manufacturers are reluctant to disclose their secrets – even if in reality they are not secret at all! Naturally much more will be revealed – but slowly – during the years ahead. At this time, however, what *is* known (or thought to be known) about a given digital camera is usually a mixture of truth, conjecture and advertising.

A typical area-array digital camera system

We have seen (Figs. 4.11, and 4.12) how the CCD area-array image is captured, and have discussed how analogue image information is sent to an A/D converter via the output register on the CCD chip. From this point onward the rest of the story takes place inside the camera, within the computer and in the software.

As mentioned, each digital camera has its own system, and although many follow a typical structure and circuitry, the necessary mathematical algorithms that control such things as image compression and colour interpolation are usually unique to a specific camera and associated software.

If we define the archetypical digital camera as one which employs a high-quality SLR camera with an area-array CCD sensor that can provide near photographic quality (in colour), to a diverse population of professional users, then the Kodak DCS-200 camera should take the honours as being the first major success in its field. Although not the first digital camera to be formed from a well-known SLR, it was at least a 'stand alone' system and in this respect a great advance on its (1991) predecessor, the DCS-100. The Kodak DCS-100 was based on the Nikon F3 body and was suitably compact – but in use the camera had to be interfaced with a large external digital storage unit (DSU) carried as a shoulder pack. The DSU also incorporated a inch monitor to display each of the 156 uncompressed images. The camera was designed for photo-journalists, and could be supplied with built-in image compression (400 to 600 images with JPEG compatible compression) to allow news pictures to be sent down telephone lines to the news desk. (JPEG is a standard compression and stands for Joint Photographic Experts Group: see Chapter 6). Such additional (and relatively heavy) burdens as the DSU do not generally endear themselves to itinerant photographers however, and so it was not surprising to see the self-contained DCS-200 camera introduced in 1992.

The Kodak DCS-200 digital camera

The Kodak Digital Science Camera 200, complete with the new M-5 chip housed within a Nikon 801s (N8008s USA) camera body, was an immediate success. With a 1.5 million pixel resolution, an exposure recycle time of three seconds, and a capacity of 50 compressed images stored in a 80 Mb hard disk, the DCS-200 was a leader in its field. As such, although now replaced by the more advanced DCS-420, the DCS-200 serves as an excellent example for further discussion of its type.

Although larger and heavier than its host camera, the DCS-200 is still a very compact unit as may be seen from Fig. 5.2a. For any necessary servicing the digital back can be removed to reveal the CCD sensor, as shown in Fig. 5.2b. The front view of the digital back can be seen in greater detail in Fig. 5.3a, and its rear view (Fig. 5.3b) shows the various controls and a SCSI (an acronym, pronounced *scuzzy*, which stands for 'small computer system interface') port for connection to Mac or PC.

The DCS-200 was manufactured in a number of versions. The basic model 200 was monochromatic and came without an internal hard disk. Then there was the DCS-200c, the colour version; and the most expensive version (at £8500): the DCS-200ci with colour and hard disk. All models have the same chip, but the

(a)

Fig. 5.2 The Kodak DCS-200, incorporated with the Nikon N801s host-camera: the first of a highly successful series using the M-5 sensor. (From the Kodak DCS-200 manual.)

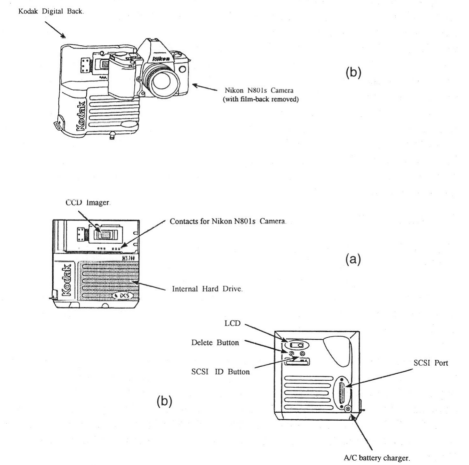

Kodak Digital Back.

(b)

Nikon N801s Camera
(with film-back removed)

CCD Imager.

Contacts for Nikon N801s Camera.

(a)

Internal Hard Drive.

LCD

Delete Button

SCSI ID Button

SCSI Port

(b)

A/C battery charger.

Fig. 5.3 The DCS-200 digital camera back. The M-5 CCD sensor has a matrix of 1524 × 1012 pixels, each 9.2 mm square, within a 14 mm × 9.3 mm format. (From the Kodak DCS-200 manual.)

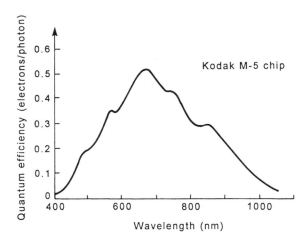

Fig. 5.4 Spectral response curve for the M-5 CCD sensor.

colour version has mosaiced R G B colour filters overlaying the pixels. The M-5 chip with dimensions 14 mm × 9.3 mm contains a matrix of 1524 × 1012 pixels in a full-frame area-array imager. Each of the 1 542 288 pixels are 9.2 μm square and have a spectral response that extends usefully into the near infrared, as shown in Fig. 5.4.

Apart from the four usual batteries that power the Nikon 801s camera, the digital back operates from six AA type rechargeable NiCd batteries. When the camera is awake, the *battery indicator* (shown by the liquid crystal display (LCD) Fig. 5.3b) displays the current battery life, with the bottom indicator blinking to warn when battery life is exhausted. The same LCD provides a *frame counter, disk indicator* (to inform how much hard disk space is left), *frame-delete indicator, SCSI connection indicator* and an *ISO warning indicator*. The ISO warning indicator refers to the four prescribed ISO settings on the camera back, and since the DCS-200 can provide images at only one of the prescribed ISO values, the LCD will display 'ISO' if the camera has not been set either to: ISO 50, 100, 200 or 400 for colour work, or to ISO 100, 200, 400, or 800 for black and white photography.

The digital back also incorporates two control buttons: *Delete* and *SCSI ID* (Fig. 5.3b). The Delete button allows the operator to delete the last image on the hard disk, and the SCSI ID button is used to select the correct ID value on the camera as used by the PC.

The following descriptions (based on the DCS-200, with uncompressed images) provide a notional explanation of the image route taken by both monochrome and colour CCD imagers and will it is hoped give the reader a reasonable grasp of the digital image route from camera to screen.

The monochrome image route

Once a picture has been taken with a monochrome CCD imager, each image point is then clocked-out, pixel-by-pixel, along the *shift register* to the *output amplifier*, and then to an 8 bit A /D converter where each pixel-charge value (along with its x, y location) is registered in the form of a binary code. From here the image data are temporarily stored in an 8 bit *buffer memory* before being sent to a programmable *digital signal processor* (DSP) where the image is stored with other data in the 2 Mb of *dynamic random access memory* (DRAM). Once the data are in the single-frame DRAM, the camera's hard disk is started and image data transferred to it. Hardware in the camera's digital back generates a *thumbnail*, which is a subsample of image data, with data sampled from every eighth pixel. The thumbnail is subsequently stored with the full image on the hard disk. This process takes just over three seconds on the DCS-200 before the camera is ready to expose another picture.

After the image data (up to a maximum of 80 Mb) have been stored on the camera's hard disk, the digital data can then be downloaded to the computer (via the SCSI) where they are received by the manufacturer's image acquisition software. From this stage in the image route the picture may then be saved into any file format supported by the TWAIN (Toolkit Without An Interesting Name – believe it!) compatible host software, such as the highly popular ®Adobe ®Photoshop variants now at large.

Finally, the image-processed data are then sent to the computer monitor's DAC (digital-to-analogue converter) which does the reverse job of the digital camera's ADC (analogue to digital converter). This conversion is necessary since the monitor only accepts analogue signals (as a stream of rapidly varying voltages) that need to be continuously refreshed at the VESA (Video Electronics Standards Association) rates of 72 Hz. Alternatively, the image can be sent to a printer to provide a hard copy.

The colour image route

For colour work the CCD imager must be modified if it is to be of the type shown in Fig. 5.1a, that is, of the *spatial multiplex* type. This is a popular system as it allows for single exposures and virtually makes the camera little different from conventional film types. The technique is to provide an individual red, green or blue filter over each pixel, in much the same way as the additive colour process used by Agfa in the 1930s. The mosaic chip pattern shown in Fig. 5.5 (see colour section) is only one of many CFAs (colour filter arrays) now in current manufacture, and illustrates the typical repeating 2×2 matrix that uses two green cells for every single red and blue cell. Although this arrangement is common for many imagers, from the Kodak DC-40 to the DCS-200, DCS-420 and high end cameras such as the DCS-460, there are other configurations that employ quite different matrixes (some are even reported to be L-shaped in design). The reason for the two-to-one ratio of green cells is to provide for improved green sensitivity so that the image will parallel the response of the human eye, as shown by Fig. 2.1.

Known as the *adjacent pixel colour interpolation technique,* area-array systems ensure that each pixel filter is always adjacent to the other two. And because each pixel has to be able to record all three RGB colours, camera software looks at the strength of the missing colours recorded by adjacent pixels, and makes a qualified evaluation of the two missing colours on a pixel-by-pixel basis. If, for example, the camera was to record a uniform red object, it would not be just the red-filtered pixels that created a charge signal, but *all* of the pixels red, green and blue! Were this not so there would be open gaps in the resolution.

All of the pixel filters are broad-band types, allowing certain amounts of other colours through, that is, red-green and blue-green; consequently the software algorithm has some signal information on each pixel regardless of the image colour at that point. In the example of the uniform red image, the interpolation algorithm finds little response in the green, and even less in the blue-filtered pixels, and since the entire matrix in the immediate area has the same response the algorithm calculates a totally red image at this point.

The method of colour interpolation degrades spatial resolution by a factor of $\sqrt{3}$ and, as outlined in Chapter 3, if three pixels are equal to one line-pair, we can put the spatial resolution of a monochrome CCD imager as:

$$r_{mono} = 3 \text{ px} \quad (\mu m) \tag{5.1}$$

and

$$R_{mono} = 1000/3 \text{ px} \quad (\text{line-pairs/mm}) \tag{5.2}$$

and, for a colour CCD imager,

$$r_{colour} = 3 \text{ px } \sqrt{3} \quad (\mu m) \tag{5.3}$$

and

$$R_{colour} = 1000/(3 \text{ px } \sqrt{3}) \quad (\text{line-pairs/mm}) \tag{5.4}$$

For the M-5 chip, with 9.2 μm square pixels, monochrome resolution is 36 LP/mm, from which we calculate the colour resolution to be 36/1.73, or 21 LP/mm.

It is obvious that colour quality from spatial multiplexing can only be as good as the interpolation algorithm used to gather data from surrounding photosites. Most manufacturers have their own proprietary algorithms which typically take a 3×3, or 5×5 matrix around each pixel (see Chapter 6). Whereas the DN (digital number) value of the colour band sensed by the photosite in question is assigned directly from the received signal, the other two colours required to create the RGB image are derived from the surrounding 8 pixels (3×3 matrix), or 24 pixels (5×5 matrix).

Spatial multiplex systems are not without their disadvantages, however, the main problem being that because of the averaging or re-sampling of pixel intensities, artifacts can occur in the image of an object that has sharp edges or strong lines. Known as *aliasing* such artifacts manifest themselves as stair-stepped jagged edges, particularly when the display or printed resolution is too coarse to hide the effect. However, a suitable anti-aliasing technique known as *dithering* exists for printing. By this process the edges of an image can be softened to remove the worst aliasing effects.

Although it is possible to derive monochrome images from colour simply by averaging the RGB bands, it is not a recommended practice since this leads to double averaging and reduced discrimination in the image.[29] It should be re-membered that a colour interpolation algorithm already does an averaging job,

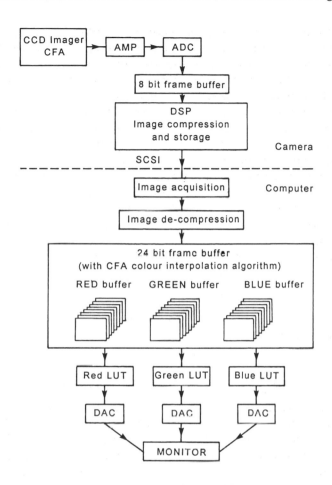

Fig. 5.6 Colour imaging route from CCD imager to the digital signal processor (DSP), image compression and computer (via SCSI interface). After the image has been de-compressed, colour signals are sent to respective buffers and look-up-tables (LUTs) before digital-to-analogue conversion (DAC) and presentation at the monitor.

effectively acting as a smoothing filter across the image.[30] Nevertheless, it is easy to produce a monochrome print from a colour image simply by selecting the grey-scale option in the printing commands, or by selecting a mono-channel from Photoshop's Channel Palette (see Chapter 6).

For the DCS-200, the colour image follows the same style route as its mono-chromatic counterpart, but now there are three channels of data to accommo-date. As shown in Fig. 5.6, each RGB data stream will go to the A/D converter (ADC), and then to the DSP (without compression however) where contrast and detail are adjusted before storage in the hard disk.

In the case of the latest DCS cameras (where image compression takes place) the DSP uses its own special algorithm, known as *run adaptive differential com-*

pression (RADC). Kodak use this proprietary compression instead of JPEG or other standard compression algorithms because RADC allows the camera to store more high-quality images. Compression with JPEG starts with a full resolution colour image, but it's more efficient to start with pixel values coming directly from the CCD chip because they contain only a third of the data of the final colour-image file. Thus for the DCS-420, DCS-410 and the EOS.DCS-5 cameras (which have the same chip as the DCS-200) the 4.5 Mb RGB file is stored in compressed form at around 1.5 Mb on a standard PCMCIA (PC Memory Card International Association) card. In addition, these cameras have frame buffers that hold 12 bits per colour – a total of 36 bits – but from this large capacity only the best 8 bits from each band are selected, leaving the final image capacity at 24 bits of data, as with the earlier DCS-200, but with improved quality.

An important specification for a digital camera is its *pixel depth*, or bit capacity. Pixel depth is set by the number of bit-planes in the frame buffer, and in order to avoid *contouring* (when bands of constant intensity between pixels start to appear) it is essential that at least 24 bit colour is available. A pixel depth of 24 bit planes means a possibility of 2^{24} (16 777 216) colours.

After going through DSP and storage in the camera's hard disk, the images are then downloaded through an SCSI port to the host computer, where proprietary image acquisition software stores the RGB data in a 24 bit frame buffer for CFA (colour filter array) interpolation.

For the Kodak DC-40 camera compressed images are stored on 4 Mb of Flash EPROM (erasable programmable read-only memory) built into the camera (the flash memory retains data even if the batteries run down or are removed). The DSP can compress images at two different levels: medium resolution mode with 256×384 px (32 : 1 compression) and full resolution mode with 504×756 px (16 : 1 compression). The compression mode is selected using Kodak's image acquisition software (PhotoEnhancer) when the camera is connected to the computer.

According to Kodak DC-40 Technical Facts (published via Internet) the three data channels for this camera (and most possibly others as well) are: (i) luminance (based on green wavelengths), (ii) red-green and (iii) blue-green. All of which are compressed and stored on 4 Mb of Flash EPROM which maintains its contents without electrical power, and whose contents can be erased and reprogrammed within the computer.

Each pixel on the CCD is mainly sensitive to only one primary colour of course, either red, green or blue. But the adjacent pixel colour interpolation algorithm is there to make sure that every pixel (despite its designated filter colour) will receive its correct colour identity, according to the image colour at that position in the array.

Kodak CFA interpolation first calculates green values at the red and blue photosites, and then calculates the missing red and blue values at the other photosites. Vertical and horizontal gradients are then calculated to deduce whether the missing green pixel lies along a vertical or horizontal image edge. The missing green value is formed by interpolating the values along the edge. For example, horizontally adjacent green pixel values are used if the missing green pixel is located along a vertically oriented edge. Once the missing green values are interpolated, the missing red and blue values are calculated by linearly interpolating the red-to-green and blue-to-green chrominance ratios. This effectively increases sharpness by adding high frequency luminance details to the red and blue records.

Next, image edges are sharpened with adaptive FIR filters (a computer processing filter used to sharpen edges). Vertical and horizontal high-frequency details are extracted from the green channel and added back to the red, green and blue signals.

Colour correction is then applied to improve colour saturation. This is needed because the filters over the pixels are not perfect, the red photosite having some response to green and blue light, the blue pixel to red and green, and so forth. Fast colour matrixing techniques correct for the unwanted responses to improve colour saturation.

Further image processing can be done by transferring the proprietary camera image file (such as the Kodak KDC file for the DC-40 camera, or other native image files) to any other bit-map file supported by TWAIN compatible software, such as TIFF (tagged image file format) or PCX, or PICT (a native graphics format for Macintosh computers), all standard formats for bit-mapped images (see Box 4).

Box 4 Bit-mapped images and object oriented graphics

Two terms that appear regularly in digital imaging are *bit-mapped images* and *object oriented graphics*. Although we are mainly concerned with bit-mapped images it is important to understand the difference between the two graphic forms.

A *bit-mapped* image is composed of a series of dots (pixels) rather than a set of lines (or vectors), and consists of a grid of discrete pixels, each with its own grey value or colour. The bit-mapped image is located within a high-speed frame buffer, where each pixel (stored as a binary number) has an x, y address that maps to a pixel located in the monitor (CRT) display. Resizing a bit-mapped image without any distortion or aliasing is very difficult, and bit-mapped images consume large amounts of computer memory. Bit-mapped images can be taken from: (a) digital cameras, (b) scanned photographs or (c) digitised (frame-grabbed) video.

Object oriented (vector) graphics allow an image to be defined mathematically, rather than by a set of dots, and are much more economic with storage space. Unlike bit-mapped images, object oriented graphics can reproduce circles or squares without aliasing or distortion, and require much less computer manipulation. For this reason object oriented graphics are mainly used for drawing and CAD (computer aided design) programs.

After being processed and stored in the three (8 bit) frame buffers, the three digital signals are now sent to three *look-up tables* (LUTs) on line between the buffers and the monitor DACs, where real-time colour enhancement takes place. Each LUT is effectively a table of numbers that create an index with pixel values stored in its associated buffer. The number of entries in each LUT is being set by the number of bit planes. For 8 bit planes there are 256 entries in the LUT and it is these that are sent to the display – rather than those in the buffer. By using LUT entries it is possible to preserve the original digital values in each frame buffer, while the computer operator is free to manipulate LUT data for real-time image processing with software such as Photoshop. The advantage of the LUT system is that it allows for iterative experiments to be made with the image. For example, if the blue pixels are too strong (say a DN value of 150) they can be reduced to a DN of say 80, without destroying the original (buffer) values. Colour adjustments can be seen immediately and changed or kept accordingly.

From Fig. 5.6 we see that binary image data (the binary digit can be either 0 or 1) is sent to one of three frame buffers according to the pixel colour in the CCD imager's CFA. For a 24 bit colour system each RGB buffer will have 8 bit planes which means 256 (2^8) brightness levels for each hue.

The bit-mapped image data are now interpolated in the 24 bit frame buffer, pixel by pixel, so that every pixel will have an appropriate brightness in either red, green or blue, up to a theoretical maximum of 256 levels for each colour. After interpolation the binary data are then indexed with their respective LUTs before being sent through their DACs to the three (RGB) electron guns of the monitor.

An indication of CFA interpolation is shown in Fig. 5.7, where a four-bar resolution chart (a) has been recorded with a 24 bit colour imager (Kodak DC-40 camera) via a three diopter close-up lens placed in front of the normal camera lens (one diopter $f = 100$ cm; three diopter $f = 33$ cm). When enlarged 16 times on the monitor screen (Fig. 5.7b; see colour section), the black lines can be seen as an RGB pixel display with only the centre of each line totally black while the white spacings are recorded as pixels of varying colour and intensity. As seen in Fig. 5.7b, digital images have this kind of problem with resolution, as explained by the Nyquist theorem in Chapter 3 (Eq: 3.10).

The colour monitor

Although the bit-mapped image may have a 24 bit capacity, this is not much use if the monitor, or the video graphics card within the computer isn't of similar standard. Monitor resolution is quoted in terms of the number of pixels the screen can display, and also by the VGA (video graphics array) card that supports it. Typically a VGA card will support a monitor that has a resolution of 640 × 480 pixels, with a maximum of 256 colours displayed simultaneously from a palette of 262 144 (2^{18}) colours, and because it is an analogue display the VGA can resolve a continuous range of grey-tones, or colours.

A higher-quality display is provided by the SVGA (super VGA) card, which can support at least an 800 × 600 pixel array (or even twice that resolution), with up to 16.7 million colours displayed simultaneously.

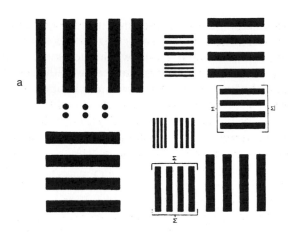

Fig. 5.7a Resolution and CFA interpolation. The 4-bar resolution target.

The interior screen of the monitor's CRT (cathode ray tube) is coated with three RGB phosphors which are held at a strong anode potential. When struck by the electron stream from each gun, the phosphors glow with an appropriate red, green or blue colour, according to the varying strength of the incident beam. However, before the electron beam strikes the phosphor dots, it travels through what is known as a *shadow mask,* which is metal sheet perforated with tiny holes, located just in front of the phosphors. The role of the *shadow mask* is to guide the electrons to the correct phosphor colour and to provide a more precise and rounded point that can reach only one specific phosphor, and not a group.

The electron beam scans the screen (from left to right) in a non-interlaced video mode, each image frame being refreshed at a rate of 72 Hz in order to eliminate screen flicker.

The actual colour displayed on the monitor screen is due to the process of additive colour mixing, as explained in Chapter 2 (see Fig. 2.11a). The eight major colours are: black, white, red, green, blue, cyan, magenta and yellow. All of which, with their variations due to hue, saturation and brightness (HSB), are created from the three primaries RGB. The tiny phosphor dots are then confused by the human eye to appear as a resolved point of a given colour.

Printers, which use inks, work on the subtractive principle of colour synthesis (Fig. 2.11b) and RGB data is changed to CMYK before being sent to a printer for hard copies. An additional black ink is also used, since the theoretical addition of CMY only provides for a rather poor black, consequently we talk of CMYK colour for printing (K is used for black, in order to distinguish it from blue).

As previously mentioned, the above description outlines only one example of an image route for the spatial multiplex type of digital image. It should therefore be treated as no more than a guide since digital technology is constantly on the move, and the division of processing between camera and computer will rarely be disclosed by manufacturers.

92   Although there is little point in listing the entire range of currently available spatial multiple (type 1) cameras, it *is* worth mentioning some of those cameras that currently represent prices and quality within the range. Starting at the low end, we can expect to see cameras with prices below £200 in 1997, and it will be interesting to see if the balance between price and image quality can provide a satisfactory product.

The Kodak DC-20 digital camera

Priced at about £300 (1997) the DC-20 represents a determined effort to introduce digital cameras to the dedicated amateur. Looking like a conventional compact camera (with exclusive software included on CD) and aimed at those with a reasonable computer (PC or Macintosh) plus inkjet printer, the DC-20 employs a 24 bit colour chip, with a 493 × 373 pixel array, and an internal storage capacity of 1 Mb that can store a total of 16 point-and-shoot photos.

The Kodak DC-40 digital camera

The DC-40 is one stage up from the DC-20 and can be considered as a generally useful camera capable of providing reasonable quality for most purposes, particularly photographs of buildings, vehicles and locations required for sales leaflets or low-cost advertising brochures. The cottage shown in Fig. 5.8 is a good example of what can be done by reproducing a DC-40 colour image in monochrome (for economic printing), using the *channel palette* and a little image-processing in Photoshop (see Chapter 6 for details).

Fig. 5.8 A Kodak DC-40 colour image printed in monochrome on a HP-560C colour printer (Photo: Ron Graham).

Where portraits are concerned there is a noticeable, but none too disturbing, granular effect obvious in enlarged areas of skin-tones. The outdoor portrait shown in Fig. 5.9 (see colour section) is a DC-40 image (20 cm × 13.5 cm) printed on Hewlett Packard premium glossy paper with an inkjet printer. But, when viewed at the normal distance of 25 cm, this print is not noticeably different from a conventional colour photograph. Taken on a cold December day under flat lighting, the image required increased contrast and some improvements to the colour balance. Additional image processing included a degree of *gaussian blur* to remove some of the aliasing, some of which can still be seen (in the original at least) in the overhead power cables, and some *unsharp masking* to sharpen up image detail. Specifications for the DC-40 are shown in Table 5.2.

At a current price of around £650 (incl VAT) including PhotoEnhancer software, the DC-40 represents good value for a digital camera that is not going to be asked to produce high-quality images. It is ideal for those who want to engage and experiment with digital imagery and at the same time be able to produce useful images. Basically a point-and-shoot camera, the DC-40 is simple to oper-

Table 5.2 Kodak DC-40 digital camera

CCD image sensor:	Kodak KAF-400
Pixel size:	9 µm square
Fill factor:	100%
Chip size:	6.9 mm × 4.6 mm
Resolution:	756 × 504 pixels
Colour:	24 bit
Storage:	4 Mb Flash EPROM (up to 48 photos)
Image cCompression:	Kodak RADC
	Full resolution 756 × 504px (16 : 1)
	Medium resolution 384 × 256 px (32 : 1)
Colour filter array:	GRGRGRGR
	BGBGBGBG
Camera lens:	8 mm, *f*/2.8 to *f*/16
Exposure:	Auto, with override of ± one stop
Focus:	Auto. Four feet to infinity
Chip speed:	Equivalent to ISO 80
Shutter speeds:	1/30 to 1/175 (Automatic)
Flash:	On camera. Range up to 8 feet
Self-timer:	10 or 20 seconds
Camera controls:	Buttons and LCD
Attachments:	Tele and close-up lenses
Power supply:	Four AA batteries
Weight:	0.5 kg
Hardware recommended:	IBM compatible: 80386 or higher CPU
	AppleMac II or higher 6 Mb available RAM
Operating system	Windows 3.1 or later, MS-DOS 3.3 or later
recommended	Apple-Mac 7.1 or later
Supplied imaging software:	PhotoEnhancer (by Picture Works)

ate, and control settings are neatly displayed on the LCD to the right of the viewfinder. Different flash options are available simply by pressing a button and inspecting the LCD.

The bundled PhotoEnhancer software is capable of producing good prints and is easy to use, but wherever possible PhotoEnhancer files should be transferred from KDC to TIFF, then imported into Photoshop for more comprehensive image processing, as with Figs. 5.8, and 5.9. It is worth noting that both of these images were printed on a humble inkjet printer, but if a higher quality (and much more expensive) dye-sublimation printer had been used, the original prints would exhibit a corresponding increase in image quality.

When operated with a laptop or notebook through the RS-232 serial port (the camera comes with a 9 pin adapter for a 25 pin serial port), the DC-40 only needs a modest portable inkjet printer to provide a complete and convenient field-processing system, as shown in Fig. 5.10.

The Kodak DCS-420 digital camera

Looking very much like its predecessor, and employing the same M-5 chip as the DCS-200, the DCS-420 uses a Nikon N90 SLR as host camera, and provides an image capture with 36 bit colour. It is currently (1997) priced at around £8000. Image storage is accommodated on a removable RAM card (PCMCIA-ATA, type III), and pictures can be exposed at a recycle rate of three seconds. Alternatively, images can be taken at a burst rate of two frames per second for five images, enabling the camera to capture five photographs in just over two seconds.

Fig. 5.10 A complete portable imaging system: Kodak DC-40 camera, notebook computer and printer.

Fig. 5.11 Kodak DCS-420 digital camera, complete with PCMCIA card.

In many ways the DCS-420 can be considered the standard digital camera for general use, particularly since it has sold well in three versions. The most popular version is the DCS-420c, and although it has the same resolution as the DCS-200, its 36 bit colour capability allows for improved rendering of colour in both shadows and highlights. As mentioned previously, only the best 8 bits are used from each band. The 420 also takes advantage of a PCMCIA storage device which allows for extended image capacity. The PCMCIA-ATA type III is a removable 10.5 mm thick hard-disk card, as shown with the DCS-420 in Fig. 5.11. Type III cards offer fast data access times of around 12 ms; they can be obtained with drive capacities from 170 Mb to 510 Mb. The 260 Mb card for example, can store up to 157 raw images.

The advantage of using selected 24 bit colour is the increased dynamic range in the image. It is well known by photographers that reproducing black shadow detail in the same frame as detailed highlights is the ultimate test for any camera medium and, taking an opportunity to test the DCS-420 against this difficult task, I photographed an old bellows camera on top of newsprint carrying a colour photograph. The result, shown in Fig. 5.12 (see colour section), surely justifies the claim that, when printed on a dye-sublimation printer, DCS-420 images can be as good as a conventional colour photograph!

The DCS-420m is a monochromatic version useful for specialist work, as is the DCS-420 CIR, the false-colour infrared variant. Both of these cameras are considered further in Chapter 10. In addition to the imaging functions described above, all of the 420 cameras include 'telephone quality' voice recording via an internal microphone, so that audio annotations can be applied to images as they are recorded.

96 The Kodak DCS-410 digital camera

The DCS-410 deserves special mention if only for the fact that it offers almost the same facilities and all the quality of the 420, but at a much more economic price! Currently priced at around £5000 the 410 offers the same as the 420 with the following exceptions: (i) fixed ISO of 100, (ii) no burst rate of 2 pictures per second, (iii) only 2 Mb DRAM instead of 8 Mb.

The Nikon E2N/E2s digital cameras

Both the E2s and the new E2N are based on the prestigious Nikon F4 camera and employ a 24 bit CCD chip with an area-array of 1280 × 1000 pixels. The E2s sensitivity can be set at 800 or 1600 ISO, and the E2N at 800 (standard) or 3200 ISO. All the usual F4 facilities are available plus special algorithms to provide white balance control and a flash mode designed to match high-powered studio flash equipment at colour temperatures up to 5700 K. An exclusive feature of the E2 cameras is the 'reduction optic' technology that provides approximately the same picture angle coverage for every compatible Nikkor lens. Co-developed with the Fuji Photo Film Company, the Nikon E2 series bears the trade name Fujix as well as Nikon on the camera body.

The E2 pixel architecture is an RGB area-array, but the output from each pixel is said to go directly to the LUT without interpolation. Nevertheless, the observed resolution is of the same standard as that seen in DCS-420 images. Current (1997) prices for the E2N are in the region of £7000 plus VAT.

Image storage is through PCMCIA cards Type I/II, and for a 15 Mb memory card the five different storage modes allow for the following capacities:

HI:	5 (uncompressed)	TIFF images
FINE:	21 (1/4 compressed)	JPEG images
NORMAL:	43 (1/8 compressed)	JPEG images
NORMAL:	84 (1/16 compressed)	JPEG images

Whereas the E2s camera can shoot at a rate of 3 frames/second (up to a maximum of 7 frames), the E2N is restricted to 1 frame/second (according to storage mode). The 1 frame/second framing rate is a valuable facility for some applications, particularly for small format aerial surveys, as described in Chapter 10.

The Fujix DS-505 and DS-515 digital cameras

Yet another Fujix/Nikon F4 combination is found with the DS-505 and DS-515 models. These Fujix cameras lay claim to a 'first' in having a product that captures the entire viewfinder image on CCD by using a special optical system. Like the Nikon E2 series the Fujix models employ an ATA Type I or II flash card, which allows the user to transfer image data to any computer equipped with a suitable card slot. Their similarity to the E2 cameras extends to the same type of chip, JPEG data compression, framing rates and ISO rating (800/1600). Both cameras have a digital output to RS 422 and a video output to NTSC/PAL (NTSC is American 525 lines and PAL British 625 lines with reference to television). These cameras are rather expensive. The 505 costs £9650, including a BP-D5 rechargeable

battery power supply kit, and SD-D5 Photoshop plug-in module, but without lens.
With the same extras the 515 model costs £11 970.

The Kodak EOS.DCS-5 digital camera

What might be considered as the Canon version of the DCS-420, the EOS.DCS-5 uses the Canon EOS-1N as host camera, and since it employs the same M-5 chip can be expected to provide the same quality as the 420. The EOS.DCS-5 has a better burst rate than the Nikon version, providing 10 frames in four seconds, and like the 420 comes in the same three variants; colour, monochrome and false-colour infrared. It is priced higher than the 420, however (£9000 plus VAT), and this is without a PC memory card or lens for the camera! Nevertheless, it is a very worthy example of the upper middle range digital cameras as can be seen from the close-up portrait shown in Fig. 5.13 (see colour section). This off-the-cuff portrait was taken inside a conventionally illuminated (fluorescent tubes) reception room and printed on a dye-sublimation printer. It is worth comparing this portrait with that shown in Fig. 5.9 (DC-40) where it can be seen that a price ratio of 15 : 1 separates the quality of these two digital cameras!

Kodak DCS-460 digital camera

Although the DCS-460 looks just like the DCS-420 (its host camera is the same Nikon N90) the CCD area-array chip has four times as many pixels and yields an 18 Mb file. Currently priced in the region of £24 000 the 460 model represents the high end of the Type 1 area-array cameras which is not too surprising since it incorporates the high-resolution M-6 chip, details of which may be found in Table 4.1 under the Kodak sensor KAF-6301. It has a resolution of over 6 million pixels, in a 2048 × 3072 area array and the sensor size is 18.4 mm × 27.6 mm, which is four times the area of the DCS series 200, 410 and 420 cameras. It is interesting to note that although the nominal spatial resolution of the DCS-460 is the same as that of the earlier models (each pixel is 9 μm square), the image quality is far superior; it easily matches that of any colour film material when output on a suitable printer, such as the dye-sublimation types. The reason for this superior performance is due to the improved CFA (colour filter aray) interpolation algorithm incorporated withn the DCS-460.

Each image (in Kodak proprietary format) is stored in the PCMCIA-ATA card, occupying just over 6 Mb, and during download is extrapolated into a full colour image. The 36 bit colour image (12 bits per RGB colour) is actually used in the form of 24 bits becuse the best 8 bits of each channel are selected for the final image. This can then be saved as a standard image format, say TIFF, to give an image file of 18.6Mb. With a 170 Mb PC card the DCS-460 can hold up to 26 high-quality 18 Mb images but for extra capacity a 510 Mb card will enable 85 high-quality images to be stored.

With an ISO rating of 100, the DCS-460 allows the user to shoot pictures with the same confidence as though using colour film of the same speed rating. The only restriction is an image capture rate of 12 seconds in the standard mode, but this may vary depending on the host computer. Nevertheless, a burst rate of two images in 2 seconds is available, with an 8 second pause to store each image. Above all, for the professional photographer, the DCS-460 offers the high quality required with almost immediate access to the image, and once experienced this is a convenience few can turn their back on. The DCS-460 is available in the usual Kodak range of 460m (monochrome), 460c (natural colour) and 460 CIR (false-colour infrared), the latter being available on special order only.

Perhaps the most critical test for any small format camera is to produce a suitable image in aerial photography, where resoltion and fidelity are of the utmost importance. In this respect the reader is referred to Part 3 of this text where photogrammetric and remote sensing applications of DCS-460 imagery are explained and reproduced in both natural colour and false-colour infrared.

It is obvious that high-end digital cameras such as the DCS-460 are too expensive for popular use, but the cost does not stop there. An 18 Mb image file takes a lot of processing and since most images will require something like three to four times as much free RAM as the file size, the computer's RAM and hard disk capacity become highly important.

Typically, a PC will require 2 Mb of RAM for its DOS and a further 6 Mb or more for Windows. In addition, image processing software such as Adobe Photoshop can eat up at least 5 Mb, so we have used quite a lot of RAM even before an image file is opened! My own system had 32 Mb of RAM and a 500 Mb hard disk which was perfectly adequate to handle images from the Kodak DCS-200 and 420 series, but it came as a shock to realise that this was insufficient for processing DCS-460 images. Once the TWAIN driver had been installed and the first raw colour image brought to the screen it was soon evident that there was not enough RAM to even rotate the image in Photoshop, let alone make a print!

Under these circumstances it is possible to employ Photoshop's *virtual memory* or *Scratch disc* (where Photoshop temporarily borrows some hard disk space) to provide more RAM. A check on the available RAM was made via the Memory Preferences dialogue box (File→Preferences→Memory) which indicated that 75% of the Photoshop RAM field was available; just over 16 Mb out of a total of 22 Mb. By increasing the RAM field to 97%, 21.3 Mb became available, but this was still insufficient to process or print the DCS-460 image.

The answer was obvious. For high end cameras such as the DCS-460, the RAM needs to be at least 48 Mb and in the best interests of speed and ease of operation, the hard disk needs to be at least 1.2 Gb. When these additions had been made, it became possible to process DCS-460 images without difficulty, as shown by Figs 10.13 and 10.14.

5.4 Single Exposure, Three Area-array (Parallel Acquisition) Cameras (Type 2)

The basic architecture of Type 2 digital cameras is shown in Fig. 5.1b and, although only few in number at the present time, they might well take a greater share of the market in future years. The concept of a three-way beam-splitting colour system is not new of course. Indeed the most successful model is Technicolor and, although there are considerable advantages to using parallel acquisition, manufacturers generally seem to prefer Type 1 methods at present.

The obvious advantage of Type 2 systems is freedom from having to use *adjacent pixel colour interpolation* and the reduction of *aliasing* in high-contrast areas of the image. Each chip has its own colour to create an RGB composite file and this means colour quality is improved. The beam-splitting system has to be accommodated however, and if a standard camera is employed the back focal length of its lens has to be increased to take this into account, usually restricting the maximum aperture of the lens.

The Minolta RD-175 digital camera

Based on the Minolta Dynax 500 35 mm SLR camera, the RD-175 provides a full colour image file of 5 Mb onto a PCMCIA card. The three chips are 16.5 × 12.4 mm in size, each holding an area-array of 380 000 pixels. Chip filteration is biased to the green, with two green chips and one red and blue. The two green chips are shifted optically from each other, theoretically doubling the resolution in the all important green channel. According to Tinsley[31] the RD-175 employs both colour and size interpolation so that the RGB output file has an overall reolution of 1528 × 1146 pixels, rather than the 380 000 quoted for each chip. This file is then compressed to 1.1 Mb and stored on a removable 131 Mb PCMCIA card, that allows up to 114 images. The effective speed of the chip assembly is quoted as ISO 800.

From Tinsley's account the resolution of the RD-175 shows some softening (due to size interpolation) but contrast, over-exposure and colour performance are much better. Priced at (1997) just under £10 000 (including VAT) the RD-175 comes complete with a 24-85 mm AF Minolta zoom lens.

The Agfa ActionCam digital camera

Once again using the Minolta Dynax 500 camera, the Agfa ActionCam generates the same 5 Mb 24 bit colour file as the RD-175 which it resembles. This is a one-shot three CCD imager which uses exactly the same chip as the RD-175 with a 28 to 80 mm $f/4$ lens. Recording time is 2.5 seconds per frame and storage is accomplished with a 130 Mb PCMCIA card. White balance is provided for tungsten, flash, fluorescent and daylight conditions.

The minimum system requirements quoted by Agfa are 16 Mb RAM and a 24 bit VGA, and the interface is by SCSI-2. A 1997 price release quotes £4995 (plus VAT), inclusive of lens, PCMCIA memory hard-disk card, battery, battery charger, Adobe Photoshop LE software and Agfa's FotoLook scanner drivers. Truly a good bargain for a parallel acquisition type camera.

5.5 Three Exposure, Single Area-array (Temporal Multiplex) Systems (Type 3)

As shown in Fig. 5.1c, temporal multiplex systems solve their three-colour exposure problem by employing a spinning filter wheel. Such imagers are destined for high-quality studio work not only because of their dynamic nature and lengthy exposure times, but because they are designed to produce high quality colour images of still subjects. Usually these systems are incorporated into special 'camera backs' that replace the conventional film slide used in medium and large (5 × 4 inch) format studio cameras.

The Leaf DCB II digital camera back

Leaf Systems Inc. produce a number of digital camera backs (DCBs) that are rapidly becoming very popular with high-quality advertising studios, and the DCB II is an excellent example of a Type 3 digital system. A measure of the DCB II's imaging potential is mirrored in its Macintosh computer requirements, where at least 64 Mb of RAM are required for efficient operation and this needs to be supported by at least 0.5 Gb of hard disk.

The Leaf has a monochromatic 30 mm square CCD chip with an area-array of 2048 × 2048 pixels, and colour is provided by a rotating RGB filter wheel, as shown in Fig. 5.1c. The filters rotate in front of the chip within a space filled with an inert gas in order to prevent condensation when the sensor is cooled to its operating temperature. As mentioned in Chapter 4, thermal noise is always a problem with CCD imagers, and for high-quality reproduction the Leaf DCB is kept at about 0 Centigrade with the aid of a heat exchanger built into the back.

Each of the single, filtered exposures, can be as short as 1/1000 second with subjects illuminated from any conventional studio source, including studio-flash. The sequence of exposures is red, green then blue with a download time that depends upon the computer. For a correctly configured Power Macintosh this should take about 5 seconds per exposure, or 15 seconds overall.[32] The Leaf DCB has a SCSI interface to the Macintosh, but the latter has to be fitted with a SCSI NuBus board.

A number of studio cameras can be, and have been, fitted with a Leaf DCB including the Hasselblad, Mamiya, Fuji GX680 and Sinar large format monorail. Current (1997) prices are in the region of £20 000.

The Dicomed BigShot 4000

An even more impressive Type 3 system is the Dicomed BigShot 4000. Not only does it have a 4096 × 4096 pixel chip, but employs a novel front-of-lens filter device to expose three sequential RGB images onto a monochrome sensor. Although this is a temporal multiplex system, rather than using a spinning filter disk, the 4000 employs a *liquid crystal tunable filter* that changes filters by rapidly cycling through the RGB sequence during a single flash exposure. In this respect the camera can be considered as a one-shot system, but it still uses three discrete colour images to capture the 48 Mb image file. Exposure speeds range from 1/1000 to 1 second with a cycle time of 10 seconds, and recommended host computer requirements are for a Macintosh with 64 Mb of RAM. Data transfer is by SCSI-3.

The Dicomed BigShot 4000 is currently (1997) priced at £33 000, and is available through Optimum Vision Ltd., UK (Tel: 44-(0)-1730-2640016).

Digital Imaging

Key to Colour Section

Figure 2.10	Page II
Figure 2.11	Page III
Figure 3.8	Page IV
Figure 5.5	Page II
Figure 5.7b	Page V
Figure 5.9	Page VI
Figure 5.12	Page VII
Figure 5.13	Page VIII
Figure 6.7	Page IX
Figure 7.1	Page X
Figure 7.4	Page V
Figure 10.8	Page XI
Figure 10.10	Page XII
Figure 10.11	Page XIII
Figure 10.12	Page XIV
Figure 10.13	Page XV
Figure 10.14	Page XVI
Figure 10.15	Page XIV

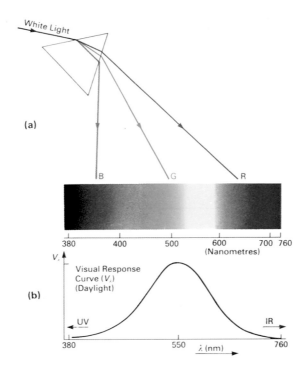

Fig. 2.10 Prismatic spectrum and V_λ curve.

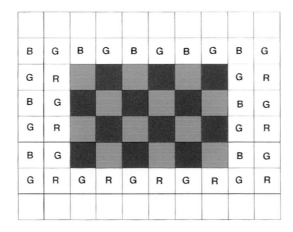

Fig. 5.5 Colour Filter Array (CFA). This Kodak Blue/Green and Green/Red matrix is one of many different CFA geometries used with the ' Adjacent Pixel Colour Interpolation ' algorithms employed for colour CCD imaging.

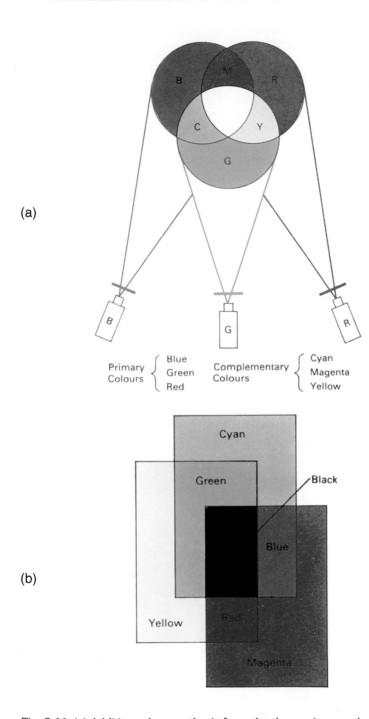

(a)

Primary Colours { Blue Green Red   Complementary Colours { Cyan Magenta Yellow

(b)

Fig. 2.11 (a) Additive colour synthesis from the three primary colours: red, green and blue. (b) Subtractive colour synthesis from the three complementary colours: cyan, magenta and yellow.

Fig. 3.8 Scanned face (Canon IX - 4015) of a colour photograph (inset), reproduced with $n = 374$ and $M = 32$ colours. $I_c = 1870$ bits.

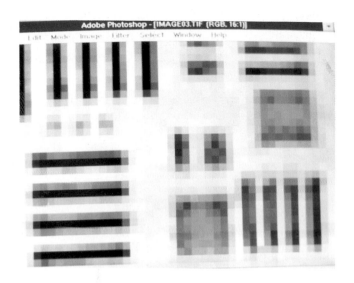

Fig. 5.7 Resolution and CFA interpolation. (b) Reproduction of the target suffers from CFA interpolation (manifest as an RGB pixel display at the outer edges of each black line) plus Nyquist limitations.

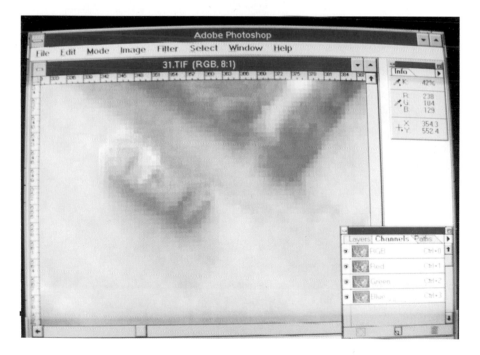

Fig. 7.4 Photoshop 3.0 *Info* and *Channels* drop-down menus, with air photo of road scene.

Fig. 5.9 Outdoor portrait taken with a DC-40 digital camera, printed on HP glossy paper with the HP 560C (inkjet) colour printer (Photo: Ron Graham).

Fig. 5.12 DCS-420 colour image of a difficult (high dynamic range) subject. The text can easily be read in the original (dye-sublimation) print (Photo: Ron Graham).

VIII

Fig. 5.13 Kodak EOS.DCS-5 digital camera. Interior 'off-the-cuff' portrait, under fluorescent lighting. Printed on Kodak dye-sublimation printer (Photo: Ron Graham).

Fig. 6.7 Scanned image from an original aerial photograph of Hastings (Courtesy Brian Gulliver). Original taken on Kodak Ektar 200 colour film at 2500 feet with a 50 mm lens, and scanned with a Kodak RFS 3570 film scanner at 2000 dpi to produce a 17.1 Mb colour file. Printed by Kodak KDS 8650 dye-sublimation printer.

X

(a)

(b)

Fig. 7.1 Typical example of image enhancement using Photoshop 3.0. (a) Raw TIFF image taken from 1500 feet with DCS-200 camera. (b) Enlarged and enhanced version with: (i) improved colour balance and contrast. (ii) Gaussian blur (to minimise aliasing), (iii) unsharp masking (to gain better definition) and (iv) fine adjustment of brightness (Photos: Ron Graham and Jon Mills). Note: The photograph in (b) has been 'manipulated' as explained on pages 121 through 125.

Fig. 10.8 Two DCS-200 digital images forming part of a colour mosaic of the village of Raskelf (North Yorkshire) Flown with Thruster aircraft at 1560 feet at an estimated ground speed of 30 mph (into wind). Photo-scale 1 : 17 000 with a forward overlap between 50 and 55%, and a base/height ratio of 0.25. Photo-interval (ΔT) $\approx$ 5 seconds. Image processing (sharpening, contrast, brightness adjustment, colour balance and matching) conducted under Aldus Photostyler 2. Printed on A4 HP Glossy paper at 1 : 850 scale (Ron Graham and Jon Mills).

XII

Fig.10.10 Remote sensing images of a farming area near Lake Baringo, Kenya. Multispectral composite images from DCS-420 (monochromatic) cameras with red and infrared filters. Images merged and processed in Photoshop 3.0 to provide a false-colour infrared composite. Images courtesy of Dr Rick Curr RSGIS Unit, Bath Spa University College.

Fig. 10.11 Large scale aerial image taken with a Kodak DCS-420 CIR (false-colour infrared) camera, part of an on-going remote sensing programme undertaken by the RSGIS Unit at Bath Spa University College. Images courtesy of Dr Rick Curr and Dr Alex Koh.

Fig. 10.12 Remote Sensing image taken with the Kodak DCS-420 CIR camera. The bright red cluster of plants near the centre of the frame is an illegal plot of cannabis plants. Image courtesy of US Forest Service and Dr W.S. Warner.

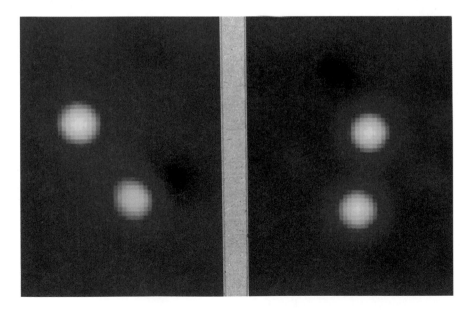

Fig. 10.15 Binary star Capella recorded in two successive CCD images, and image processed by the COAST system. The two resolved bodies (separated by 55 milliarc seconds) are shown rotating around each other. Images courtesy of J. E. Baldwin, Cavendish Laboratory, Cambridge University, and AstroCam Ltd, Cambridge Science Park.

Fig. 10.13 Husthwaite village, north Yorkshire. One of a series of overlapping mapping photographs taken with the DCS-460 C camera in June 1997. The flying height was 2600 feet. Photo scale 1 : 25 000. From these images an accurate orthophoto map was produced. Photo: Dr Jon Mills, Universiy of Newcastle-upon-Tyne.

Fig. 10.14 Rievaulx Abbey, north Yorkshire. One of a stereoscopic pair of remote sensing photographs taken with the DCS-460 CIR in June 1997. Photo: Dr Fiona Strawbridge, RSGIS Unit, Bath Spa University College, Somerset.

5.6 Scanned Linear Array Systems (Type 4)

Scanned linear array systems have been with us for some time in the form of aerospace imaging sensors. Called push-broom imagers, they generally employ a single linear array of pixels for monochromatic records, and three or more linear arrays for colour or infrared false-colour recording.

SPOT Push-broom CCD aerospace imagers

Designed by the French Space Agency, SPOT was the first earth observation satellite to employ linear CCD sensors. Since 1986 two versions of SPOT have been launched into space where they are engaged in remote sensing of the earth. The satellite completes 14 earth orbits per day at an altitude of 830 km (at the equator) and carries two HRV (*haute resolution visible*) imaging telescopes.

As the satellite sweeps forward in its orbit, the 2.5 m long telescopes receive scattered radiation from the earth which is received by the linear arrays of sensors in the focal plane of the telescopes. The linear arrays have 6000 CCDs per scan line, each pixel being 13 μm square. As each scan line corresponds to a swath of terrain perpendicular to the ground track, and as each pixel covers 10 m of ground, the total swath width is 60 km.

The telescopes are designed to operate in either of two imaging modes in the visible and near infrared portions of the spectrum.

• Mode 1: a monochromatic (Panchromatic) mode intended to provide a high ground resolution of 10 m in the 510 to 730 nm band.

• Mode 2: a multispectral mode consisting of three narrower spectral bands, each with a ground resolution of 20 m and a swath width of 60 km: band (i) 500–590 nm (green); band (ii) 610–680 nm (red); and band (iii) 790–890 nm (near infrared).

SPOT imagery is transmitted directly to a number of receiving stations on earth, from which an internationally available source of data allows users to obtain either hard copies or computer compatible tapes. Many earth scientists, such as geologists, agriculturists, foresters, town planners and cartographers can obtain a wealth of important, and constantly up-dated, information from SPOT, and image-maps at scales of 1 : 50 000 or even 1 : 25 000 can be made from these data files.

The Agfa StudioCam

Aimed at the professional studio operator, the Agfa StudioCam is intended for still life product photography of table-top dimensions. Its chief applications are with direct mail catalogues, product brochures and other rapid turn-around documents. It is a custom-built camera incorporating a 36 bit trilinear CCD sensor capable of capturing a wide dynamic range of colour to afford increased detail in shadow and highlight zones. The system sensitivity is 100 to 400 ISO.

The StudioCam employs one-pass scanning with the aid of a precision stepping motor, and covers a 36 × 29 mm area with an effective 4500 × 3648 pixels, by scanning parallel tricolour CCD linear arrays, each with 3648 pixels and a bit depth of 12 bits per RGB colour. Maximum file size is 24 bit, 50 Mb or 36 bit, 100 Mb (software interpolation is not required). Image capture takes place with scan times in the range of 1/200 to 1/30 second per line, and a total recording time between one and ten minutes.

StudioCam is available for both Mac and PC platforms, and the Mac software package includes Agfa FotoLook, a Photoshop scanning plug-in; FotoTune colour matching profiles; FotoFlavor colour enhancement plug-in; Photoshop 3.0 LE and Canto Cumulus archiving software. The package also includes a Nikon 35-80 AF (auto-focus) lens, all for a total price of around £8500 + VAT.

The Zeiss video colour camera: VOS 80 C

The VOS 80 C is a high-resolution digital video colour system, designed for real-time ground data collection from aircraft. Intended for environmental control and surveillance, this camera is suitable for both military and civilian applications. The detector (Kodak KLI-6003) features three parallel CCD linear arrays, each with an individual colour filter (RGB). In all there are 3 × 6000 pixels, each 12 mm square, and the line-spacing is 96 mm. The maximum data rate is 230 Mb/second, and the maximum line rate is 1.6 KHz. A Zeiss Planar 80 mm, $f/2.8$ lens is fitted as standard.

The system is push-broom, with the resolution in the flight direction dependent only on the aircraft's velocity. In order to gain square ground pixels, the correct line rate for detector read-out is calculated from the aircraft's altitude and ground speed, and the focal length of the lens.

5.7 Scanning CCD Backs for Studio Cameras (Type 5)

A description of some of some types of camera back has already been given under Type 3 systems. But here we are concerned with scanned linear arrays such as the so-called *slip-in* digital camera backs.

The Phase One, PhotoPhase Plus

Phase One is a Danish company, and was the first to place a slip-in scanning back on the market with the PhotoPhase FC70 back. Designed for use with 5 × 4 inch studio cameras like the Sinar P2, the back is directly connected to the computer. The PhotoPhase scanning software requires no more than 24 Mb of RAM and is designed to produce a 24 bit RGB TIFF file that can be imported into Photoshop.

A pre-scan provides a low-resolution image that allows the operator to check framing and exposure, together with the line-scan speed set which can vary from 1/15 to 1/125 second. Scanning speed depends upon the processor used, with a maximum of around 30 Mb/minute using a 9500 Power Macintosh.

PhotoPhase Plus can be relied upon to produce very high-quality colour images with a good dynamic range. Current price is around £15 000.

The Dicomed 5 × 4 inch slip-in camera back

Inserted just like a conventional 5 × 4 inch film slide, the Dicomed uses a Kodak KLI-6003 chip with three (RGB) parallel linear arrays each with 6000 pixels. The scanned resolution is 6000 × 7520 pixels over a 72 mm × 90 mm area, and the system applies a one-pass colour scanning time determined by exposure and resolution settings. This is a 36 bit system with user selectable image resolution up to 83 pixels/mm, and independent LUTs for real-time 24 bit file storage. In addition, image contrast, colour balance and dynamic range can be optimised for each scan.

The Dicomed scanning back can be used with any 5 × 4 inch camera, with full 'camera-movements' included. There are also optional adaptors for use with the Mamiya RZ67 and RB67 cameras. A typical price for this back is in the region of $22 000 (USA).

5.8 Single Exposure, Single Area-array Camera Backs (Type 6)

In this concept the single-shot digital camera back represents the best of all worlds for those professional photographers who simply wish to exchange film for CCD as the imaging medium. Just as film has always allowed medium and large format cameras to be employed in a large range of work, including subjects in motion, so is the need for a CCD system to do likewise, without any restrictions such as an on-line computer.

Kodak DCS-465 multi-format camera back

Fitted with an M-6 CCD chip (Kodak KAF-6301) providing a resolution of 6 million pixels, the DCS-465 camera back can be supplied for 5 × 4 inch or 120 size cameras. It has also been designed for exclusive attachment to a number of professional studio cameras such as the Sinar, Horseman, Mamiya and Hasselblad. In every case the camera can be used as with film, either in the studio or on location. Each image provides 18 Mb of data with 36 bit colour, conveniently stored on PCMCIA-ATA type IV cards (both flash-memory and hard-disk cards).

For location work, power is provided by a nickel-hydride battery sufficient for an hour, and a capacity to shoot 100 images, while in the studio the system can be operated from the a/c mains. Image capture takes 12 seconds from either source, depending on the removable media used. If a typical 105 Mb PCMCIA card is employed, the operator can store 17 full-resolution (18 Mb) images, and cards with larger capacities are always available. A useful extra is the built-in voice recording which can be made directly onto the storage disk using the DCS-465 incorporated microphone.

Although the uncompressed file size is 18 Mb, compression to 6 Mb is used when images are sent to the PCMCIA disk. When used in the studio, however, images may be downloaded directly to the computer. Prices vary of course, depending on the camera. But it is reasonable to expect a typical Sinar or Horseman DCS-465 to be in the region of £25 000 or more.

5.9 Future Developments

Although digital camera developments are fast (and almost impossible to predict) there are some indications that a new class of image sensors, known as complementary metal oxide semiconductors (CMOS), will be strong competitors to CCD within a year or two. Their main advantage is economy, since they are cheaper to manufacture, and they also tend to have fewer defects. Unlike CCDs, which must transfer their charge through neighbouring pixels, each CMOS pixel has its own amplifier and output, which means it can be read out independently and so permit variable frame-rates.

Another development utilises conventional CCDs, but employs optical *diffraction* (see Chapter 1) to increase apparent resolution by a factor of 4. The Japanese Pixera Corporation have invented a method where low-priced, medium-resolution CCD arrays, can be turned into high-resolution devices by shifting a single pixel element onto four different areas of a CCD sensor. Evidently this technology can be employed with CCD *and* CMOS systems and, again, the main thrust is in producing better image quality at much less cost to the consumer. From what is known, all Pixera products rely heavily on software since raw pixel data go direct to the computer for image processing.

6 Scanning Methods

For many people and institutions, digital imaging means *scanning* available images rather than using a digital camera. And as billions of photographs already exist, either in private collections or photo-libraries there is a ready supply of images that can be selected for further use. Setting aside all questions of copyright, morality and ethics (being outside the scope of this book) it can be said that a suitable scanner, image software and a good printer are all that is needed for many people working in a wide range of industries, who use images in desk-top publishing to produce publications: advertising and promotion, short-run leaflets, illustrated reports, in-house journals, etc.

Scanners can digitise photographs either in monochrome or colour, and from originals that are either prints or diapositives (transparencies); in addition they can digitise artwork and text. Once scanned these images can then be manipulated and merged according to requirements.

It can be said that current scanner technology focuses around four basic types: hand-held, flatbed, drum and dedicated film scanners. But apart from that, and the fact that they all make use of CCD arrays or, to a lesser extent, photomultiplier tubes (PMTs), scanners also come in a wide variety of designs. Most of the popular low-cost scanners are of the flat-bed type, and offer monochrome and colour reproduction from either prints or diapositives. They also provide for optical character recognition (OCR), and many of them are sold with their own bundled software.

Today, most computer work stations include a scanner as an indispensable tool for importing text, or image files, that can be manipulated and/or merged with the aid of graphics software. In many ways the scanner resembles and often takes on the role of a photocopier but, apart from the fact that both can copy flat two-dimensional images, any similarity stops there. The important difference between a scanner and a copier is that the former is digitised and works through a computer, allowing software to manipulate the image before going to the printer. In this respect a scanner is little different from the digital camera.

Most scanners come with their own software, which is usually sufficient for most of the basic image manipulations, but if more sophisticated processing is required it is a simple matter to transfer the scanned file to another program, such as Photoshop.

The large variety of scanning hardware and software make it impracticable to do full justice to the subject in a single chapter but, since much of the technology has already been covered, emphasis will be restricted to scanning principles, parameters and applications.

However, before discussing scanners in any detail it is essential to define the types of original they scan, and the important peripheral they serve: the printer. Although printers are mainly discussed in chapter 7, it is essential to consider printing technology at this point, since a number of issues important to scanners are dictated by the final output device.

6.1 The Original and its Reproduction

It is important to be precise when discussing the type of image (document) that is being scanned, mainly because there is much confusion in the terms employed. And in an attempt to clarify matters the following printing terms and processes are explained here.

Text. Where text is mentioned, this refers to alphanumeric characters which, unless qualified further, will mean black characters on a white ground.

Line art. Any artwork, such as a line drawing, created in black and white (one bit).

Grey scale. Any art work comprising shades of grey in the image. This multi-bit expression is also common usage for defining *monochrome* photographs, as opposed to colour photographs.

Monochrome. The term, generally accepted by the photographic industry, defines a non-colour photograph. Very often referred to as *black and white* photography, or *continuous tone* photography.

Resolution. Because most printed images are made up of dots formed by lined printing screens, it is traditional to discuss printed resolution either in dots per inch (dpi) or lines per inch (lpi). As a consequence all scanners and output devices (such as laser or inkjet printers) have their resolution specifications quoted in these terms. Typical resolution figures for desk-top printers are of the order of 300 to 800 dpi.

Halftone. The *halftone* image is a printing term reserved for the reproduction of a continuous tone (or colour) photograph by breaking up image tones into evenly spaced dots of different sizes. This is done by photographing the original through a fine screen (*halftone-screen*). Dark areas of the original then translate into dense patterns of dots, whereas lighter areas translate into fewer and smaller dots. For colour, three (CMY) or four (CMYK) halftones, are laid on top of each other but at different screen angles in order to avoid moire effects. When halftone images are viewed, the dots confuse to provide an impression of continuous tone or colour.

Screen frequency. Halftone screens are line-grids with a pattern frequency ranging typically from 85 lines per inch (lpi), through 133 lpi screens and higher. Whereas the former are used for relatively coarse newspaper images, the latter are employed for quality illustrations. When a negative is screened to a positive material, the resulting halftone comprises dots with a size proportional to the received exposure. Thus, for an 85 lpi screen, there could be 84 dots ranging in size from the just visible to a diameter of 1/84 inch.

A basic 300 dpi printer, such as a laserjet or inkjet, generally produces a halftone screen frequency of 53 lines per inch (lpi), and a 600 dpi laser printer would usually achieve a screen frequency of 75 lpi.

Resolution and screen frequency are interlinked parameters and, as we have seen from the above examples, screen frequency is always less than the resolution. For (one bit) *line art* scanning it is important that the scanner gets as close to the printer resolution as possible but, as we shall see, for photographs this is not as important as the screen frequency.

Diffusion dithering. Because digital printers (such as those discussed in chapter 8) can only form a single dot size, they employ a simulated form of halftone printing known as *diffusion dithering* where, instead of clusters of black and white dots, they are distributed throughout the image in a fashion similar to a fine *mezzotint*. In general, dithering can be used any time a halftone can be used, and is a process well suited to printing on low- to medium-resolution devices. The process is also known as *representative halftone* and is used to simulate true halftones by the process of *bit-mapping*.

Bit-mapping. Shades of grey can be simulated by using a predefined group of black dots (pixels) called a screen-cell. A typical 4×4 screen-cell is shown in Fig. 6.1, where a total of 16 pixels are possible. As described above, this *dithered* system of (n) pixels can create a number of grey tones since the eye confuses their number to an average value. Screen-cells can be of different sizes; 4×4, 6×6, 8×8 or 16×16, to provide a potential number of grey values (GV) according to Eq: 6.1.

$$GV = n^2 + 1 \quad \text{(grey tones/screen-cell)} \quad (6.1)$$

In the limit there are 16 dots possible in the 4×4 screen-cell shown in Fig. 6.1a, and if the entire matrix is empty there are none, giving a possible 17 tones (from white to total black) within the cell.

Since the printer can only print a single dot, it prints a number of them within the screen-cell to simulate a tone. Naturally, the larger the screen-cell

1	9	3	11
13	5	15	7
4	12	2	10
16	8	14	6

a

h

Fig. 6.1 A 4×4 dithered screen-cell, capable of producing $n^2 + 1$ grey tones per cell.

the larger the number of grey levels – but only at the expense of resolution, since each screen-cell now represents the unit of image resolution. The numbers shown in the screen-cell of Fig. 6.1a, form 16 grey levels (above white), with each number mapping a grey tone in the original to a similar tone in the print. Level 4, for example, will have dots in all the small cells from 1 to 4 (a 25% grey tone), and if level 8 were signalled, then every level from 1 to 8 would be filled making this screen-cell a mid-grey (50% grey tone) as shown in Fig. 6.1b.

The numerical matrix shown in Fig. 6.1a, is only one of many cell patterns available, and they all operate in the same way, but the positions of the numbers vary within the cell.

Obviously fine detail and adequate tonality are a compromise; small screen-cells might provide for better resolution, but only with limited grey values. Screen-cell size (n), and screen frequency (S_f) are related to printer resolution R_p (dpi), by:

$$S_f = R_p/n \quad \text{(lpi)} \tag{6.2}$$

For a 4×4 screen-cell ($n = 4$), and printer resolution of 300 dpi, $S_f = 75$ lpi, and from Eq: 6.1 we calculate 17 possible shades of grey. But if an 8×8 screen-cell is employed then we trade improved tonality (65 possible grey levels) for a reduced screen frequency of only 37.5 lpi.

Screen frequency is used to define quality standards where, for example; newsprint will employ screens in the range 65–80 lpi, medium-quality books and reports are usually 80–130 lpi, and high-quality books and journals in the range 130–150 lpi.

6.2 Scanner Principles

Basic to all two-dimensional scanners is the requirement for a linear array of CCD sensors to scan an illuminated original either by running the sensor array past the original, or by keeping the sensor static and passing the original (or its image) over the array. Other methods can be used, however, particularly for three-dimensional scanning, and progress is such that 'painting' techniques (using solid-state inertial sensors) that allow the scanner to be freely moved around the object could be introduced by the late 1990s.[33]

For the main part we are concerned with two-dimensional subjects, and the various methods used for scanning are best explained as we look at the principles involved with each device.

Scanner parameters and specifications

Regardless of type, all scanning devices are qualified by the following parameters:
- scanner resolution,
- dynamic range,
- bit-depth,
- scanning speed.

Each of these will be discussed in turn.

Scanner resolution

When talking about scanner resolution, and particularly with respect to flat-bed scanners, we must qualify exactly what kind of resolution we mean. If we are talking about the *optical resolution* of a scanner this simply relates to the scanner itself, but if we talk of *interpolated resolution* (which is greater) then we are looking at enhancement. When purchasing a flat-bed scanner it is sensible to take more account of the optical resolution since interpolation usually means a drop in image quality.

It is also well to remember that the final product may be sent to a professional printing house, where an image file is likely to be screen printed by an *imagesetter* with very high resolution. For, while the average desk-top, laser, inkjet or thermal printer may have a resolution between 300 and 800 dpi, an imagesetter can be anything between 1225 to 2450 dpi.

For desk-top scanners optical resolution in the horizontal direction is simply a question of how many CCD elements there are to the inch (dpi). But in the vertical direction optical resolution is determined by the stepping motor's gearing, where resolution depends on the fine incremental steps that shift the original (or its image) past the linear CCD array. As a consequence vertical resolution is given in terms of lpi. As an example, typical optical resolution figures for a monochrome/ colour flat-bed scanner, such as the Canon IX-4015 are: mono: 400 dpi × 1200 lpi, and colour: 400 dpi × 800 lpi.

Interpolated resolution is simply a question of putting some *artificial* pixels in between the dots of the optical resolution. In this fashion it is possible to increase a nominal 300 dpi to something like 10 000, but only at a cost in quality. Interpolation can be made while the image is still in the scanner (output resolution), as the data are passed to the computer (driver interpolation), or while the image is inside the computer (software interpolation). For scanning monochrome images the extra 'resolution' gained from interpolation can easily be justified since it usually reduces the jagged edges often found in curved shapes, but where colour is concerned its benefits can be doubtful (except for software interpolation as mentioned in chapter 5), and particularly if interpolation is carried too far. In any event, the best results are gained by scanning at the same resolution as the printer, which is usually in the region of 300 dpi.

A fair number of scanners are sold with bundled software, and some of these, such as OFOTO-V.2, provide resampling algorithms that maintain pixel resolution when resizing the image.

In practice, all considerations of image resolution should refer to resolution in the final output device, that is, at the printing stage. For, if an image is scanned at a resolution higher than that used for printing, then time and disk space are wasted on redundant data. This is particularly important when a scanned image is to be production printed, and an empirical expression promoted by the printing industry suggests that scanning resolution (R_{scan}) should take into account the printing screen frequency (S_f) and the magnification between original and the final print (M_p) as:

$$R_{scan} = M_p \times k(S_f) \quad \text{dpi} \qquad (6.3)$$

110 where k is either $\sqrt{2}$ (1.414) for the minimum scanning dpi, or 2 for the maximum allowed dpi.

As an example we can take the case of an original that is to be printed for a quality magazine using a screen frequency of 133 lpi. And if the overall enlargement is ×2.5, then from Eq: 6.2, we calculate the minimum scanning resolution to be: 2.5 × 1.414 × 133 = 470 dpi, which is a resolution easily handled by a number of flat-beds without recourse to interpolation.

As a general rule it can be said that anything lower than the minimum scanning resolution may result in *pixelisation*, where the square-shaped pixels are visible in the final image. On the other hand, anything higher than the maximum resolution will result in larger files without any improvement in image quality. For screen rulings up to 133 lpi, the factor k in Eq: 6.2 should be 2, whereas for screens above 133, it can be reduced to $k = 1.414$.

Dynamic range

The dynamic range of a scanner is its capability to absorb the *density range* (ΔD) of an original, either print or transparency. For conventional, paper-based originals we talk of reflection densities (D_p) with a maximum range $\Delta D_p < 2.0$. For transparencies, either negative or positive, transmission densities (D_n) have a much higher range that easily extends to $\Delta D_n > 3.0$.

Most of the modern scanners can accommodate a density range of 3.0, which is sufficient for most applications, but high-quality dedicated film scanners generally need more than this. The Leaf 45 model, for example, is capable of accepting transparencies with $\Delta D_n = 4.8$.

Bit-depth

In colour terms, dynamic range is a question of *bit-depth*, and a scanner with say 36 bit-depth will have a much better capability to deal with high contrast originals than a 24 bit device. The standard bit-depth for an economic colour scanner is 24, which allows for 256 levels per red, green and blue colour, but the more expensive types (rated at 30 or 36 bits) are more suited to the scanning of colour transparencies.

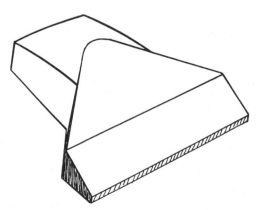

Fig. 6.2 Typical form of hand-held scanner.

Scanning speed

One of the most important parameters for professional users is the time it takes to scan an original, and this is not lost on advertisers who never lose an opportunity to take advantage of a fast scanning specification. Scan speed depends upon a number of factors, including the original, scanner resolution and type.

Flat-beds, such as the Canon IX-4015, might scan an A4 printed document in 10 seconds, but will take considerably more time with a detailed colour photograph. And, even with the same original image, one scanner can take five times longer than another – with similar specifications.

Drum scanners can be an excellent way to reduce scanning time, since it is possible to tape a number of transparencies to the drum, which can then be batch scanned automatically.

6.3 Hand-held Scanners

Although the first hand-held scanners could only be used with small originals, some of the current models are able to cover originals that are larger than the scanning head, simply by scanning in swaths and then stitching them together with software. Most hand-held scanners have a four inch linear CCD array housed in a T-shaped head and have an appearance similar to that shown in Fig. 6.2. They are useful for small jobs and are both cheap and simple to operate. Usually these scanners are powered directly from the computer and employ coloured LEDs (light emitting diodes) to illuminate the document being scanned.

Typical examples in the hand-held range are those from a major manufacturer of the type: Logltech. The Logitech ScanMan 256 is a well-known monochromatic model, with a scanning window of 105 mm and a choice of four resolutions that can be switched from 100 to 400 dpi. The scanner comes with an interface board, and two programs of software are available: ScanMan and FotoTouch. To operate the device one simply rolls the scanner gently across the document at a rate of something between 1 and 5 cm/s, taking care not to pause or move the scanner in anything but a straight line. If the original being scanned is larger than the scanner window then multiple scanning can be done (by overlapping adjacent swaths by about 20 mm) using the *AutoStitch* facility within the ScanMan software to produce a single image. A more advanced model, the ScanMan Colour Pro, uses a 16 bit interface card and is TWAIN 32 compliant. Using enhanced software resolution the device gives excellent results up to 800 dpi, and has a street price in the region of £113 + VAT.

A similar device is the MUSTEK TWAIN-SCAN which can be connected to a PC either by a 16 bit expansion card or, more expensively, via a parallel port connector. The TWAIN 32 driver making it compatible with Windows 95. Maximum resolution is given as 400 dpi, and the scanner comes bundled with IPHOTOPLUS software. With expansion card the device is an inexpensive £75 + VAT, but with a parallel port interface the price is increased to £124 + VAT.

A recent product in the hand-held range is the ScanMate Colour Deluxe which, at £91 including VAT is very good value. With up to 3200 dpi interpolated resolution, this 24 bit TWAIN compliant scanner is bundled with PhotoFinish 3.0, and

SmartPage Direct OCR software, and comes with a jumperless interface card for easy installation.

Although hand-held scanners have tended to be dismissed as amateur devices, they can be employed for professional work when used with care, as Fig. 6.3 makes clear.

Aerial photography represents one of the most exacting fields of imaging there is, mainly because the subject demands so much in terms of resolution of detail, dynamic range, contrast and subject discrimination. For these reasons aerial photographs make ideal subjects for comparative studies of image quality, and are used extensively in this book.

The monochrome aerial photograph shown in Fig. 6.3a is an original print, and its ×2 scanned copy is shown in Fig. 6.3b. Scanned with a hand-held GENISCAN GS-B10 5GX, this 3.54 Mb file was printed on a Canon BubbleJet BJ-10ex printer at 360 dpi, and image processed in Aldus Photostyler with two applications of *sharpen heavily*. It can be seen that the scanned copy yields just as much fine detail as the original, including the domestic power line that zig-zags over the gardens.

Fig. 6.3 Scanned imagery from an aerial photograph. (a) Original aerial photograph (monochrome print).

Fig. 6.3 (b) Scanned copy (×2) of original, using the hand-held GENISCAN GS-B10 5GX scanner, image processed in Aldus Photostyler (v.1.1) with two applications of *Sharpen Heavily* and printed by Canon BubbleJet BJ-10ex printer at 360 dpi.

6.4 Flat-bed Scanners

Flat-beds are the most popular and generally useful scanners available, and because of intense market competition are reasonably priced nowadays.

A monochrome scanner will usually employ a single linear array of CCDs which are scanned in a single pass, but colour scanning is more complex.

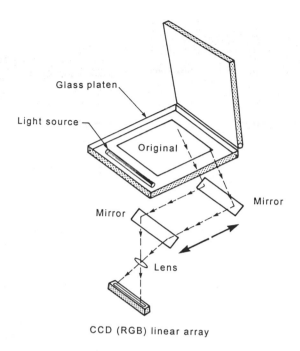

Fig. 6.4 Typical flat-bed scanner, with tubular light source and linear CCD sensor.

One method of colour scanning is to scan three times, using a different colour filter (red, green, blue) for each separate pass. Another technique is to employ only one pass, but illuminate the original with three different coloured light bars that flash in rapid sequence and are linked to the CCD timer so that the scanner knows which colour is being recorded. The most common technique is to use three linear arrays, each with its own red, green or blue filter, to provide a full colour sensing device.

Although nearly all scanners differ in one or two respects most of them follow the arrangement shown in Fig. 6.4, where a glass platen supports the original (face down) to be illuminated by a tubular light source. Most scanning methods employ mirrors that move up and down the original in fine incremental steps, so that each vertical scan-line can be imaged via a lens onto the CCD sensor.

Whereas horizontal optical resolution is defined by the number of CCD elements per inch, vertical resolution depends upon the fine gearing of the scan mirrors.

My own scanner is a Canon IX-4015 flat-bed which, with 24 bit colour and TWAIN driver, was bundled with the excellent OFOTO V.2 software package for less than £1,000. Optical resolution is quoted at 400 dpi (H) and 800 lpi (V) for colour, and 400 dpi (H), 1200 lpi (V) for monochrome scanning. Nominal scanning speeds are 20 seconds for an A4 colour original, and 10 seconds for A4 monochrome.

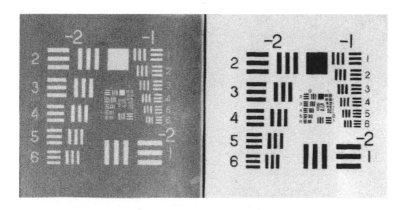

Fig. 6.5 USAF three-bar resolution targets (transparent negative and positive versions), scanned images from a Canon IX-4015 flatbed scanner, using a white paper backing.

Like many flat-beds the Canon is not a dedicated transparency scanner, but it can do a reasonable job of scanning transparencies simply by backing the original with a sheet of white paper. The USAF three-bar resolution chart shown in Fig. 6.5 is a transparency original shown in both negative and positive form, and was scanned on the Canon IX-4015 by simply using a white paper backing. Printed onto HP Glossy paper by the Hewlett Packard DeskJet 560C printer, Fig. 6.5 indicates an overall resolution in the region of 2 line-pairs/mm (observed in the original scanned image). The formula for finding the reproduced resolution of the USAF chart[34] follows Eq: 6.4, where G is the group number and n the pattern number of the resolved frequency (k).

$$k = 2^G (2^{n-1})^{1/6} \qquad (6.4)$$

In both charts of Fig. 6.5, we can just resolve pattern 2 of group 1 ($n = 2$ and $G = 1$), so that $k = 2^1(2^{2-1})^{1/6} = 2 \times (2)^{0.166} = 2 \times 1.1224 \approx 2$ l.p./mm, which is approx 51 line-pairs/inch or 102 dpi. Not a first-class resolution perhaps, but for a non-dedicated transparency scanner it remains a useful resolution for many applications in education and commerce.

A number of flat-beds can be supplied with a special transparency adaptor as an optional extra. Among them are the Microtek Scanmaker E3, and the Umax Vista S6E. The Microtek Scanmaker E3 is a single-pass, 24 bit colour scanner, with a 300 × 600 dpi optical resolution that can be interpolated up to 2400 × 2400 dpi. Included in the price (£279 + VAT) is bundled software consisting of OmniPage LE for OCR, and ImageStar for basic retouching. There is an excellent TWAIN driver, and among the options available is a transparency adaptor for an extra £299.

The basic Umax Vista S6E has a street price of £299 + VAT, and is also a 24 bit single-scan device. It has an optical resolution of 300 × 600 dpi which can be interpolated up to 4800 × 4800 dpi, and the optional transparency adaptor is priced at £495 + VAT. Umax also offers the Pro version of the S6E, which with the transparency adaptor and full Photoshop 3.0 has a street price of around £700.

116   With suitable image processing software, a flat-bed scanner can usefully copy an original and either improve, merge or modify it for further reproduction or display purposes. A case in point is the original photograph of an aphid, shown in Fig. 6.6a, where detritus on the leaf tends to draw the eye away from the subject. Yet with slight retouching in Photoshop, the scanned image can be enhanced, as shown in Fig. 6.6b.

6.5 Film Scanners

Dedicated film, or transparency, scanners are the professional route to scanning films, and their resolution is much higher than that required of a conventional flat-bed. Film scanners come in various sizes, from those suitable for 35 mm film to those dedicated to scanning large format air films (23 × 23 cm).

(a)

(b)

Fig. 6.6 (a) Original photograph of an aphid. (b) Scanned image of (a) using the Canon IX-4015, and some retouching in Photoshop 3.0 to remove detritus matter on leaf. (Photo: Ron Graham).

Well known in this field is the Kodak Professional RFS 2035 Plus, 35 mm film scanner. Dedicated to 35 mm films, this unit can scan colour or monochrome (negative or diapositive) with a choice of scans: either 1333 dpi (8 Mb), 1600 dpi (11.5 Mb) or 1800 dpi (14.6 Mb), all at 12 bits per RGB colour. The 2035s CCD sensor is a 2048 × 3072 area-array chip, and it takes about eleven seconds to scan a full frame 4.6 Mb image, using an Apple QUADRA 850 computer with 32 Mb of RAM. The TWAIN acquire modules interface to Future Domain SCSI host adaptor boards, and to SCSI host adaptor boards, such as Adaptec, that support the ASPI specification. This scanner features automatic colour correction, with correct colour balance, density and contrast, and takes both mounted or unmounted slides and film. Current price is around £5900.

For scanning films and transparencies from 35 mm up to 70 mm (6 cm × 6 cm format), the best option is Kodak's Professional RFS 3570 film scanner. The 3570 incorporates an area-array, 36 bit colour CCD sensor, and can provide a full-frame 18 Mb image in under one minute. Calibration and focus are fully automatic, and in most respects this scanner is much the same as the RFS 2035 except for the larger format facility.

In Fig. 6.7 (see colour section), we again demonstrate quality with a scanned image taken from an aerial photograph. In this case the original (courtesy of Brian Gulliver)[35] was taken on a 35 mm Olympus camera, using Ektar 200 colour film. The vertical photograph of Hastings was made from a height of 2500 feet with a 50 mm lens, and the colour negative scanned in an RFS 3570 film scanner at 2000 dpi to produce a 17.1 Mb, 24 bit colour file. After a little processing in Adobe Photoshop 3.0, the image was then sent to a Kodak KDS 8650 dye-sublimation printer to provide an A4 print. There can be no doubt that this two-stage (film and scan) route is a viable alternative to direct digital (camera) imaging, particularly in this type of application.

Other film scanners include the Minolta Quickscan 35, Polaroid Sprintscan 45, and the Nikon LS-20 Coolscan II. The Nikon LS-20, for example, incorporates a 2592 linear CCD array and is dedicated to 35 mm negatives and diapositives in monochrome or colour. The light source is a RGB light emitting diode (LED) array, and scanning is accomplished from a single pass with 8 bits per colour channel. The LS-20 is usually bundled with Photoshop LE (limited edition) and sold at about £900.

The most dedicated film scanners are those designed for scanning monochrome and colour diapositives produced by large format mapping cameras. These cameras (capable of providing 500 exposures on a format of 23 cm × 23 cm) provide overlapping images which can then be viewed stereoscopically in various types of plotting machine. But modern methods now routinely scan the films, and their digital files are submitted to photogrammetric analysis through computer software.

The Zeiss PS1 PhotoScan is a universal high performance scanner for digitising monochrome and colour aerial photographs with high geometric and radiometric accuracy. The maximum scan area is 26 cm × 26 cm and the minimum scan pixel size is 7.5 mm. In this instrument the transparency to be digitised is

118   placed on the photocarriage and moved across a stationary CCD linear array of 2048 pixels. Coloured filters can be inserted in the illumination path for the digitisation of colour photographs, in which case the scanning process is repeated for each RGB colour. An image can be scanned at various resolutions, with pixels selected from a range: 7.5, 15, 30, 60 or 120 μm. In my experience a 7.5 μm aperture is ideal for matching photographic quality. Scanning rates for a 23 cm × 23 cm frame are quoted as 20 minutes for a 7.5 μm pixel, 10 minutes for 15 μm, and 3 minutes for the coarse 120 μm pixel.

Leica produce a desk-top digital video plotter (DVP) which can utilise imagery from any scanner capable of scanning 256 grey levels at 600 dpi, from diapositives or prints, and is an ideal entry level into digital photogrammetry. The Leica DVP performs a useful service for many applications when used with several well-known GIS (geographic information systems) software, such as Arc/Info and MicroStation.

6.6 Drum Scanners

Drum scanners are now rather specialised devices, having been largely overtaken by the modern flat-beds which are less difficult to manufacture and therefore less expensive. Nevertheless, drum scanners still provide the highest quality.

The drum system basically comprises a hollow perspex drum onto which a transparency or reflection print is taped. For transparencies, a focused light source moves up the inside of the drum while the image sensor (mounted on the outside of the drum) moves with it. In this case the sensor is a photomultiplier tube (PMT), because PMTs have a greater sensitivity than CCDs and are capable of recording a much higher density range with better shadow detail. For reflection prints, both light source and sensor are located on the outside of the drum.

In operation the drum is rotated at high speed (usually 1000 to 1600 rpm) while the PMT scans the image. A top quality drum scanner can scan up to 12 000 dpi without interpolation, and will have a dynamic range approaching $\Delta D = 4.0$, but at a price!

Drum scanners have a price range running from the Imapro QCS 4100 (£13 000 + VAT) to the Dainippon Screen SG-7060 (£82 000 + VAT). The Imapro QCS 4100 is a small (A5) desk-top scanner capable of recording transparencies and reflection prints, and offers RGB 12 bit colour with a resolution of 4000 dpi. By comparison, the Dainippon Screen SG-7060 has a 12 000 dpi resolution and can take originals up to 21 × 24 inches in size, with automatic focus, aperture, and light source selection.

In the intermediate price range, Scanview produce the Scanmate 3000 (£17 900), Scanmate 4000 (£22 900) and Scanmate 11000 (£34 900) models, all capable of producing high-quality images.

7 Image Processing

If, for a moment, we ignore built-in system processes such as image compression and adjacent pixel colour interpolation, we could say that most of the widely used image processes fall into four distinct categories: *enhancement, manipulation, transformation* and *analytical processing*. All but the last of these processes are as common to conventional photography as they are to digital imaging, although the first three are generally known as 'after treatment' or 'darkroom techniques' and are of course much slower! The exception, analytical processing, adds a further dimension to image processing in that it allows the operator to employ proprietary software to analyse image data, and even supplement this by interfacing his/her own programming to the installed software. Image files such as BMP, TIFF etc., may then be analysed to provide data for scientific, industrial, commercial or social research.

7.1 Practical Applications of Image Processing

Image enhancement means improving the quality of an image; *manipulation* is concerned with making changes to its content while *transformation* takes care of any required geometric and dynamic changes.

On the other hand, *analytical processing* evaluates spatial and radiometric image components, which are then put to algorithms specially computed to provide either programmed solutions, or to discriminate or emphasise various aspects of the image in terms of tone or colour.

Although I have a number of software programs, including the rather modest Desktop Imager, Aldus Photostyler 2 (now unavailable), Picture Works Photoenhancer (bundled with Kodak's DC-40/50 cameras) and the analytical mapping software Arc-View, all the images shown here have been transferred (as TIFF) and processed in Adobe Photoshop 3.0. The reason for this is to avoid confusion, particularly when comparing images, and also to take advantage of Photoshop's general popularity and comprehensive facilities, which include some analytical components as well.

It is generally accepted that image processing increases an image file considerably, and in order to have a comfortable margin the computer should have a RAM capacity at least three times the expected image file size. Currently I have 48 Mb of RAM but, like many others, I find this should be improved by a factor of two or three at least, if only to speed up operations let alone accommodate an ever increasing number of files and programs.

Image enhancement

The most common enhancement procedures are: *contrast and brightness control, colour balance and correction* and the use of filter algorithms to provide *image blur and anti-aliasing, despeckle,* and *dust and scratches removal.* These are a few of the facilities incorporated in high-quality software such as Micrografx Picture Publisher, Apple PhotoFlash, and of course current and future versions of Photoshop.

Before any form of image processing it is always good practice to inspect the *histogram* for any given image. Regardless of the software employed, all histograms exhibit the same kind of display; a simple distribution of vertical lines arranged across a horizontal axis that represents dark tones at the left, through midtones in the centre, to highlights at the right of the diagram. The histogram shows the tonal distribution of an image (grey tone or colour) and helps to determine how these values can be adjusted to improve quality. Usually a good image will have a well-distributed display, with most of the pixels occupying the mid-tones and with less at the shadow and highlight ends. Typically, a low-key image will show most of the pixels crowding the left-hand side of the histogram, whereas a high-key image will tend to crowd the right-hand side of the histogram display.

The histogram palette is also a very useful guide for indicating the contrast of an image. As we know, a low-contrast image appears grey, with hardly any shadows or highlights. In this case the histogram will be crowded in the centre, with few or no pixels at either end. On the other hand, a high-contrast image will have few mid-tones and most of the pixels will be at each end of the display.

Digital enhancement has already been mentioned in Chapter 5 where, for example, Fig. 5.8 is an original colour image enhanced and printed in monochrome (by using the green-channel palette option in Photoshop 3.0) to create a greyscale image for printing. And in Fig. 5.9, where we have a DC-40 outdoor portrait which (after transfer from its native KDC file to TIFF) has been enhanced with improved colour balance and contrast, some Gausssian blur (to remove aliasing) and some unsharp masking to provide sharper image detail. These enhancements are done routinely with digital images, mainly because of the character of the medium, but also because it is a simple procedure that can be accomplished on the computer screen much more efficiently than with traditional darkroom printing techniques.

More obvious enhancement is illustrated in Fig. 7.1 (see colour section), where the typically flat appearance of the aerial photograph shows little contrast (because of haze) and poor colour discrimination. Recorded in the evening at 1500 feet with a DCS-200 camera, the raw (TIFF) image shown in Fig. 7.1a has had no further treatment.

Image processing in Photoshop 3.0 has made a considerable difference, as shown in Fig. 7.1b, and if we ignore the obvious manipulations, we can list the enhancements made to Fig. 7.1a, as follows:

Improved colour balance and contrast

These improvements are made from the *IMAGE* menu found on the Adobe Photoshop screen header. Using the left-hand mouse button the operator can click-on (c/o) this menu to view a pull-down list of functions, from which a (c/o) *Adjust* leads to yet another list, and then (c/o) *Auto Levels* automatically finds the best colour balance and contrast (clips the histogram at the black and white points ±5%).

Gaussian Blur

Found under the *FILTER* menu, *Blur* is selected and then (from the following menu) *Gaussian Blur*. Although the term has statistical connotations (a normal distribution of pixels), in practical terms the process feathers the edges of an image to minimise the effects of aliasing. Control of Gaussian blur is accomplished by selecting the pixel radius, in this case 0.5 pixels.

Unsharp Mask

Found once again under the *FILTER* menu, we first (c/o) *Sharpen,* then (c/o) *Unsharp Mask* in the following drop-down menu. Here we find three controls: *Amount, Radius* and *Threshold,* and in Fig. 7.1b, these were given the values 150%, 1.6 Px , and 8 levels, respectively.

Unsharp masking was first undertaken with conventional photographic processing by making an unsharp diapositive contact print (of low contrast), and then registering this with the negative to provide a new negative of lower density range. Not only did this provide a density range that could be printed onto a contrasty grade of paper, but because the fine detail in the diapositive was lost (due to the unsharp positive image) the fine detail in the negative was retained to yield a sharper final image. This process is an excellent method for gaining better image definition, and in some places is still used in aerial photography laboratories, but is very time consuming. What can take a few hours by traditional methods takes only a few seconds on the computer!

Fine adjustment to brightness

From the *IMAGE* menu *Adjust* is selected then *Brightness/Contrast*, where a slider is moved (with the mouse) until the image looks suitably brighter. In this case an extra 28% of brightness was added to the image.

Manipulation

Image manipulation takes much more skill than enhancement procedures, nevertheless it can easily be learnt and the process is great fun! Unlike darkroom manipulations, digital work can be accomplished in more comfortable surrounds and with greater efficiency and subsequent quality than with traditional methods. But most importantly, on-screen manipulations are far quicker, and the operator's handiwork is immediately evident at each iterative improvement.

In Photoshop for example, most manipulations are undertaken with a number of *tools* found in the Toolbox column provided on the left-hand side of the screen, as shown in Fig. 7.2(a, b). And for the obvious changes shown in Fig. 7.1b, five tools were employed along with some assistance from the menus shown at the top of the screen in Fig. 7.2.

As may be seen from Fig. 7.1b, and Fig. 7.2b the image has been enlarged and cropped and, apart from obvious enhancement, the four cars parked down the road have been removed, and one of them relocated to crash into a larger vehicle that has backed out of its drive.

It might seem that some artistic ability is required to accomplish such modifications. But the reader has no reason to be concerned since I, who am quite

(a)

(b)

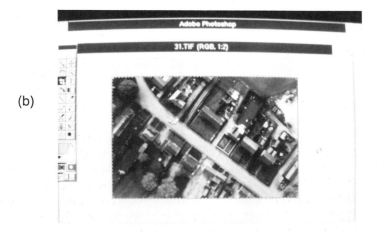

Fig.7.2 Photographs taken from monitor, showing the Photoshop Toolbox for manipulation of the image shown in Fig. 7.1b.

clumsy in this respect, managed reasonably well with hardly any practice!
     The manipulation procedure was as follows:

Enlarging the image

To make the retouching tasks easier it is necessary to enlarge the screen image, and this is done by (c/o) the *WINDOW* menu, then (c/o) *Zoom-in* and selecting a 1 : 2 enlargement.

Image rotation

This is a transformation function and can be found under the *IMAGE* menu, where three *Rotations* are possible. There are two 90° rotations, *CW* (clockwise) and *CCW* (counter clockwise) and an *Arbitrary Rotation* which allows for any degree in either direction. Image rotation is necessary so that the selected image area to be surrounded by the *Marquee* (see below) can be oriented correctly. For Fig. 7.1a the first vehicle to be moved (by the *Marquee*) required a CW rotation of 60° so that the rectangular *Marquee* could fit closely to the shape of the vehicle.

Moving image components with the Marquee

The *Marquee* tool can be found at the upper left of the Toolbox (Fig. 7.2) and is shown there as a rectangular icon. But it is possible to select an elliptical *Marquee* with a double (c/o) the *Marquee* tool with the mouse cursor. This releases the *Marquee Options Palette* and allows the operator to select the required shape (including squares and circles). To move the rectangular *Marquee* to the subject, in this case the vehicle, all one had to do was (c/o) the tool and drag the *Marquee* over to the vehicle, then surround it as tightly as possible by pressing the mouse button and dragging diagonally from corner to corner. Next all that had to be done was to press the mouse button and drag the enclosed vehicle to the required position. Another (c/o) by the side of the *Marquee* and the vehicle was now relocated and the *Marquee* removed.

     A similar procedure was adopted for one of the cars on the road, this time positioning the car to suggest a collision. After which the image was rotated to its correct position once more.

Pipette, Paintbrush and Pencil

The next task was to wash over the white spaces left by the moved vehicles and remove the remaining three cars on the road. This is a very simple procedure involving the *Pipette* (to sample the correct wash colour from the image), and either the *Paintbrush* or *Pencil* (to either wash over, or wash out the required image area). For larger areas it is convenient to use the *Airbrush* tool but, as the corrections to Fig. 7.1 were small, accuracy demanded smaller tools.

     First, the *Pipette* (or *Eyedropper*) was dragged over to the road adjacent to a white space and after (c/o) a suitable area, the mouse cursor was brought back to the Toolbox to (c/o) the *Paintbrush*; the latter was then applied to the white marks (left by the moved vehicles) to cover the road with brush-strokes of an identical colour. The *Pipette* had to be dragged over a number of times in order to match the road colour of course, then by use of *Paintbrush* or *Pencil* the cars were washed out completely. The five tools used in this exercise are shown in Fig. 7.3.

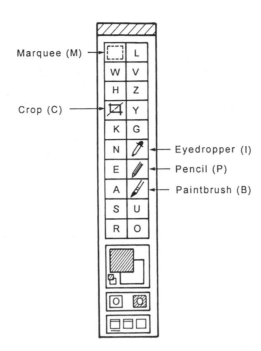

Marquee (M)

Crop (C)

Eyedropper (I)

Pencil (P)

Paintbrush (B)

Fig.7.3 Photoshop 3.0 Toolbox, showing the five tools employed in modifying Fig. 7.1b.

These are only five of the twenty available in the Photoshop Toolbox.

The cropping tool

As may be seen in Fig. 7.2b, the selected area for cropping is shown by a dotted line within the image space. This was first drawn by (c/o) the *Cropping Tool* with the mouse cursor, then dragging over to the image where the desired cropping was outlined. A further click on the inside of the cropped area and the tool now appears as *Scissors*, indicating that cropping is complete.

Transformation

Image transformations are generally found under the Photoshop *IMAGE* menu, and include commands such as: *Rotations* (already mentioned above), *Image Size, Flip* and *Effects* commands, with the latter including facilities such as: *Scale, Skew, Perspective* and *Distortion*. These commands allow for geometric changes and, if re-sizing or rotating for example, will usually require an increase in the number of pixels by the process of *Interpolation*. This does not mean an increase in image resolution, however, but is simply a means to an end. Interpolation in Photoshop is discussed below.

Re-size the image

The *Image Size* command is found under the *IMAGE* menu, and in Fig. 7.1b the image was re-sized to a width of 6.5 inches. This command was then directed to the Hewlett Packard 560C inkjet rinter, where Fig. 7.1 (a, b) was printed on HP Glossy paper.

Interpolation

Photoshop has three interpolation modes that can be pre-selected by the operator. It is through interpolation that Photoshop determines the DN (digital number) value of pixels to be added or depleted whenever an image is re-sized or rotated, or given any of the other transformation commands. Photoshop offers the following modes: *Nearest Neighbour*, which is the fastest but lowest quality mode; *Bilinear*, which offers medium quality and speed, and *Bicubic* which is of the highest quality, but also the slowest mode. Bicubic is also the default mode and the one employed for the digital images shown here. All three interpolation modes can be selected from *Preferences* found under the *FILE* menu.

Analytical processing

Although analytical processing suggests some kind of mathematical or computerised process, it must not be forgotten that subjective methods remain the most common, and in many respects the most valuable when in the hands of experienced image interpreters. Those of us with experience in either military air-reconnaissance, air-mapping, or remote sensing readily appreciate the simplicity of the Mark I eyeball, but as satellite imagery and digitised aerial photographs are now common forms of aerospace imagery, analytical processing by computer is a logical addition to conventional methods.

Analytical photogrammetry has been with us for many years now, and similarly computer analysis of satellite imagery for remote sensing has progressed ever since Landsat data were available in the early seventies. Today, there are a number of software programs dedicated to the analysis of aerospace imagery, most of them designed for desk-top image stations. Among these we have software such as: R-Wel Desktop Mapping System (photogrammetry); Meridian Image (image analysis for resource mapping), Arc-Info and Arc-View (cartography); ERDAS IMAGINE (Geographic Information Systems, GIS; and military reconnaissance); PCI EASI/PACE for Windows 3.1 (remote sensing and GIS); and AeroSys Version 2.0 for Windows (photogrammetry).

A typical example of such software is the R-CHIPS system produced by IS Ltd, who sell a 'basic user system' for £5000. R-CHIPS can be installed in any PC 486 machine and upwards with a recommended 120 Mb hard disk capacity. The software includes such items as: histogram equalisation, automatic contrast stretch, overlay operations, density slice images, image statistics, plot profiles, image mathematics, file classifications, image transforms, image registrations and many other functions.

Notwithstanding the high cababilities of these dedicated systems, our old friend Photoshop has a number of useful functions that allow it to be used for processing air-mapping imagery, as will be explained further in Chapter 10.

Astronomical records are usually made with CCD cameras today and, as can be expected, the subject has its share of analytical software. AstroCam software provides for customised image analysis, not only for astronomy, but also for a wide range of scientific applications backed up by a family of CCD imaging systems in support of microscopy and spectroscopy.

Hamamatsu offer the Argus-20 image processor to provide quantitative analysis via a chilled three-chip CCD camera. This system is mainly devoted to microscopy.

Logical Vision Ltd. market the WiT software which allows for custom user interfaces, with over 150 different processing functions, and the user can interface with either C programming language, or Visual Basic.

For industry, medicine and research, PC Image is a Windows program for image analysis and processing, with a wide range of tools to count and measure objects, enhance image quality and analyse and display data.

7.2 Image Analysis with Photoshop 3.0

Photoshop incorporates some useful analytical functions which can be found under various menus. These commands not only provide a means for measuring the x, y location of an image point, but can also show histograms, monochromatic and colour channels, photometric data, and the characteristic curves of images, which can then be adjusted either in full colour or independently for any single red, green or blue channel.

Rulers

To reveal the *Rulers* dialog box (c/o) the *WINDOW* menu, then *Rulers*. The rulers come as strips along the top and side of the image and can be ruled in various units selected from the *Preferences* sub-menu, found under *FILE*. Once in *Preferences* it is possible to (c/o) *Units* and select any of the following rulers: *Pixels, Inches, Centimeters, Points* and *Picas*.

When the image file 31.TIF was opened up (see Fig. 7.2a) it came on screen at the reduced scale of 1 : 3, as shown. If *Rulers* are selected with *Pixels*, the entire resolution of the camera (DCS-200) is exhibited with rulers reading from zero to 1524 horizontally, and from zero to 1012 vertically.

Info

The *Info* box can be brought on screen by (c/o) the *WINDOW* menu, then (c/o) *Show Info*. At this command the *Info* box appears. If the mouse cursor is placed upon a certain point in the image then the info-box will display the photometric data and the (x, y) image coordinates of that pixel (in units selected under *Rulers*). The top panel of the info-box is designated K, and gives the percentage reflection of the image (at the cursor) with white as zero and black as 100%. Under this panel lies another, where it is possible to select either RGB, CMYK or HSB (hue, saturation, brightness), then in the bottom panel we find the (x, y) image coordinates.

Channels

The *Channels* command is useful since it allows the operator to display, and analyse independently, each of the red, green and blue channels that make up the

full colour image. *Channels* can be splayed by first (c/o) *WINDOW,* then *Palettes,*
then (c/o) *Show Channels.*

An example

In Fig. 7.4 (see colour section) we have a raw (air photo) image taken with a DCS-200 camera. This is the same image as that shown in Fig. 7.2a, except that the Toolbox has been removed (by hitting the Tab key), and the screen image has been 'zoomed-in' to a scale of 8 : 1. The *Rulers* have been selected with *Points* to gain the highest accuracy. Inspection of Fig. 7.4 reveals a pixelated image of a red car with the cursor (a cross) located on the bonnet. And if we now look at the *Info* box we see the following values:

K = 42%; R = 238, G = 104, B = 129 (DN), and the coordinates
are $x = 354.3$, $y = 552.4$.

An analysis of these values provides the operator with information concerning reflecance and metrication.

Reflectance
The reflection factor K is given as 42% black (total black would be 100%), but in photometric terms a value of 100% is reserved for a perfect white. Therefore we translate K to mean an overall reflectance value of 58% ($\rho = 0.58$), and from this we can calculate the reflection density (D_p) according to Eq: 7.1 (see Box 2 in Chapter 2), where:

$$D_p = \text{Log}_{10}(1/\rho) \tag{6.1}$$

Obviously, the *Info* box doubles as an on-screen densitometer, and if we substitute 0.58 for ρ in Eq: 6. 1, we get a reflection density of 0.21.

Colour
Leaving the cursor at the same location, we gain yet another value for overall reflectance by calculating the RGB average. From the *Info* box R + G + B = 471 DN, and the average comes to 157 DN. Since we are dealing with an 8 bit colour system (from 0 to 255) this amounts to an overall reflectance (ρ) equal to 157/255 = 0.61, which is close to the value taken from K.

By clicking-on the RGB pipette we get a drop-down menu that allows us to select HSB, which reveals values of H = 349°, S = 56% and B = 93%. These values give us a complete analysis for the colour at the image point under inspection. At 349° the hue is a good red (as shown by the colour wheel in Fig. 7.5), with a saturation of 56% and brightness of 93%. That the brightness is so high can be understood from the RGB figures; with green and blue pixels as high as 104 and 129 respectively, they indicate a high specular reflection of white-light coming from this part of the car bonnet.

Metrication
The selected image point shown in Fig. 7.4, has coordinates $x = 354.3$, $y = 552.4$, and, although individual pixels may not be too obvious here, they are perfectly visible in the original print. As a consequence, it is possible to measure any point

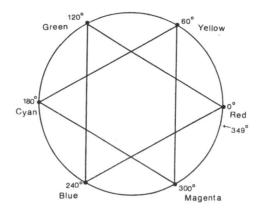

Fig. 7.5 Photoshop 3.0 colour wheel, showing hue position (349°) of bonnet on car in Fig. 7.4.

in the image with considerable accuracy, and with known ground measurements (ground truth) scale subjects within the frame.

Curves

The *Curves* command provides a useful graph which allows the operator to adjust input-to-output relationships for any given area of the reproduction. Intuitively one can adjust shadow, mid-tone or highlight areas by dragging any point of the curve with the cursor. The output can be viewed immediately and changed if not considered suitable. The *Curves* dialog box can be gained from *IMAGE,* then c/o *Adjust* and *Curves,* to reveal the drop-down box shown in Fig. 7.6 (a, b). In Fig. 7.6a we have the example of a rather dark colour-image, with its RGB curve shown as a straight line at 45° indicating that the image has not been altered. By dragging the curve upwards (in the mid-tone area) we get a much lighter result, as shown in Fig. 7.6b, and to save this image all one needs to do is (c/o) OK.

Further analysis of an RGB image can be done by (c/o) the *Channel* panel at the top of the box, to reveal another menu which allows one to sample either the red or green or blue component of the RGB image. In this fashion it is possible to adjust and view a particular channel by (c/o) the *Preview* symbol. By (c/o) any part of a curve we get an *Input/Output* analysis (in terms of pixel brightness), which is displayed just below the curve. A number of sampled points are shown on the curve of Fig. 7.6b, and the *Input/Output* data for one of these points are displayed at the bottom of the box.

7.3 Spatial Filtering

Image processing is controlled by software and, as we have seen, is accomplished by resampling the digital number (DN) ascribed to various pixels, either by interpolation or by filtering in the spatial domain. A number of different resampling methods can be used to assign the appropriate output DN and, as we know, three

(a)

(b)

Fig. 7.6 Photoshop 3.0 *Curves* drop-down menu. (a) Screen record of outdoor portrait, without change to RGB curves. (b) Screen record of image in (a), now modified by changing RGB curves.

forms of convolution (*Nearest Neighbour, Bilinear* and *Bicubic*) are available for the task. Spatial filters are also employed, mainly for improving edge-definition, increasing sharpness and noise reduction.

As we have seen, standard software such as Photoshop includes a number of filters for image processing, but these offer only a fraction of the possibilities available from software devoted to scientific analysis. These programs usually allow the user to apply mathematical inputs that will enable them to improve or extract certain image features.

Principles of spatial filtering

Digital image processing is facilitated by the quantisation of pixels into a binary scale (see Appendix A), usually to a capacity of 8 bits, that is, with image brightness levels (grey scale or colours) on a scale of 0 to 255.

Quantisation, from input to output, allows the image to be modified, improved and compressed, and spatial filtering is one of the mathematical processes for achieving these ends. Known as *local neighbourhood processing,* this particular transformation depends not only on the DN value of the pixel being processed, but also on the DN values of the pixels in its immediate neighbourhood.

Spatial filtering uses a technique where a filter matrix (*kernal*) is employed as an operator to produce a convolution with an array of DNs in the image. These *operators* are known as *filters* and they can be in a 3 × 3 matrix, 5 × 5, 7 × 7 or any other odd number geometric array. The standard matrix is 3 × 3 as shown in Fig. 7.7.

There are many different types of filters, each one designed for a specific process, but the most common ones are those used for *sharpening, smoothing (noise reduction),* and *edge enhancement.* In operation the filter starts at the top left corner of the image and processes a 3 × 3 *window* of that portion of the image according to values within the *kernal.* The objective is to change the central pixel within the 3 × 3 window.

The smoothing filter: an example

In Fig. 7.7, the kernal represents an averaging (smoothing) filter which, starting from the top left of the image, will operate on the nine image elements shown in Fig. 7.8a, in accordance with Eq: 7.2.

$$g(x, y) = 1/M \sum f(i, j) \qquad (7.2)$$

where, i and j are the respective rows and columns in the image window, and M is the product of i and j.

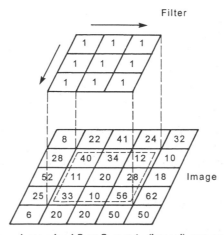

Fig. 7.7 Spatial filtering. A standard 3 × 3 matrix (kernal) moves over the entire pixel array to modify the image digital numbers (DNs). This kernal acts as a *smoothing* or *low-pass* filter, useful for reducing image noise and speckle.

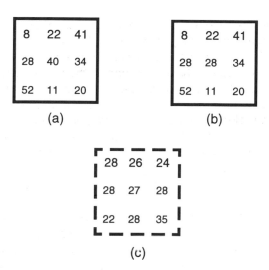

Fig. 7.8 The effects of the low-pass filter shown in Fig. 7.7 (a) Original pixel values (top left 3 × 3 array of Fig. 7.7). (b) After smoothing the 3 × 3 array in (a) is changed, with the centre pixel now DN = 28. (c) After smoothing *all* pixels in (a), we have a completely new set of pixel values, with a lower dispersion of DNs.

Taking each row of pixels in the window we have the sum and average of the convolutions, as:

$$\Sigma(8 \times 1) + (22 \times 1) + (41 \times 1) \qquad = \quad 71$$
$$\Sigma(28 \times 1) + (40 \times 1) + (34 \times 1) \qquad = \quad 102$$
$$\Sigma(52 \times 1) + (11 \times 1) + (20 \times 1) \qquad = \quad \underline{83}$$
$$\Sigma f(i, j) = 256$$
$$g(x, y) = 256/9 = 28$$

As a consequence, the centre pixel shown in Fig. 7.8a has now changed its DN from 40 to 28, as shown in Fig. 7.8b. Naturally the process does not stop there! It moves on to the right, and downwards, pixel by pixel, until every DN in the image has been averaged. For the centre 3 × 3 image window shown in Fig. 7.7 this smoothing operation results in a new window of DNs as shown by Fig. 7.8c.

By comparing the DNs of Fig. 7.7 with those of Fig. 7.8c, it is obvious that the filter has smoothed out the original image DN values to a large extent.

Smoothing, or *low-pass,* filters are generally used for the smoothing out of over-enlarged images, and for removing noise and speckle. In contrast we employ *high-pass* filters for sharpening or edge enhancement purposes, a well-known and much used example being the *Laplacian filter.*

The Laplacian filter: an example

Using the same image input as before, the *Laplacian* kernal shown in Fig. 7.9, is operating on the same window as that shown in Fig. 7.7, but this time the effect is quite different.

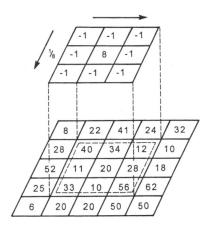

Fig. 7.9 Laplacian Operator. This kernal produces greater image contrast, and edge-enhancement.

In a fashion similar to that following Eq: 7.2, the Laplacian operator takes the sum of the DNs in each of the three rows shown in Fig. 7.8a, but instead of averaging it divides the total by 8 to obtain the centre pixel value, as:

$$\Sigma(8 \times -1) + (22 \times -1) + (41 \times -1) \quad = \quad -71$$
$$\Sigma(28 \times -1) + (40 \times 8) + (34 \times -1) \quad = \quad 258$$
$$\Sigma(52 \times -1) + (11 \times -1) + (20 \times -1) \quad = \quad \underline{-83}$$
$$\Sigma f(i,j) = 104$$
$$g(x, y) = 104/8 = 13$$

The centre pixel of Fig. 7.8a, is now replaced by the new DN of 13, as shown in Fig. 7.10a. And by convoluting the entire centre window of Fig. 7.7 with the Laplacian kernal, we have the completely new pixel array of Fig. 7.10b.

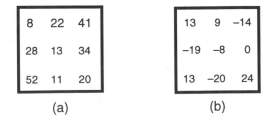

8	22	41
28	13	34
52	11	20

(a)

13	9	−14
−19	−8	0
13	−20	24

(b)

Fig. 7.10 Laplacian Operator. (a) Original DNs shown in Fig. 7.8a, now have a new centre DN = 13. (b) By convoluting the entire centre window of Fig. 6.7 with the Laplacian kernal, we have a new *edge-enhanced* pixel array.

If we compare the results of the two operators on the same image window, then a statistical analysis of the *smoothed* pixels shown in Fig. 7.8c, reveals a standard deviation from the mean of $\sigma = 3.36$. And for the *Laplacian* $\sigma = 14.96$, which indicates a much sharper contrast between the adjacent pixels of Fig. 7.10b, compared with those of the smoothing filter.

Laplacian edge-enhancements are not the only ones available however; others include *gradient* filters and *shift and difference* filters but, whereas these are directional in nature, *Laplacian* operators reveal edges in all directions.

Obviously image processing is a very complex business and, although only touched upon in this text, further information can always be found in the software manuals devoted to scientific data processing and in various papers and textbooks, particularly those dealing with remote sensing[36][37][38][39].

7.4 Image File Formats

A *file format* is a structure which defines how information is stored in the file, and how that information is displayed on the monitor or printer. There are a number of graphics file formats available but not all of them can be used universally. With some programs only a specific format can be employed whereas with others, such as Photoshop, a large variety can be used.

Typical of the many well-known file formats that can be used on either Macintosh or PC platforms are: TIFF (tagged image file format), BMP (Windows compatible bit-mapped graphic image), DIB (device-independent bit-map), PICT (Mac supported), EPS (encapsulated PostScript), Photoshop and JPEG.

Possibly the most well-known format, TIFF, was jointly developed by Aldus and Microsoft in 1986 and in its many versions is a standard file format for bit-mapped graphics images. The TIFF standard also defines *data compression* techniques and provides for monochrome and colour images. The TIFF is readily supported by Mac, PC/Windows and many other platforms.

Developed by Microsoft, the BMP format was designed to be used under DOS, Windows, Windows NT and OS/2, and can save both monochrome and colour images up to 24 bit. The bit-map DIB format was introduced as a refinement to BMP, and today all Windows and OS/2 BMP files are assumed to be in DIB.

PICT is a general-purpose format supported by Macintosh and used for storing either *bit-mapped* or *object-oriented* images (see Box 4, Chapter 5). PICT bit-maps can provide for grey scale, monochrome or colour with up to 32 bits per pixel (at 32 bits per pixel JPEG compression options are available). PICT format can be saved, opened, or imported by most Macintosh programs and also in some Windows applications, including Photoshop.

EPS is the file format of the PostScript page description language, and is device independent, which means that images can readily be transferred from one application to another. However, an EPS file can only be printed on a PostScript compatible laser printer. EPS can store either bit-mapped or object-oriented images. Using this format one can place images into programs such as Adobe PageMaker, CorelDRAW and Adobe Illustrator, which is why EPS is a popular format for exporting grey scale and colour images to page layout and illustration programs.

Photoshop file format is native to Adobe Photoshop in its various versions and, when working in Photoshop 3.0, files can be opened and saved much more quickly than with any other format. It is also the preferred format for moving Photoshop files between Macintosh and Windows platforms. Photoshop supports JPEG compression in several ways.

JPEG (Joint Photographic Expert Group) is the name of the committee that developed the file format for storing compressed images. The format is based on the discrete cosine transform (DCT) algorithm which analyses 8×8, or 16×16 pixel arrays (cells) within an image (independent of resolution), and performs an averaging of each cell, dramatically decreasing image size. JPEG employs *lossy compression* techniques that result in some loss of original data and is considered as a baseline standard for this type of image compression.

7.5 Image Compression

Digital image files are often very large, and typically a good quality colour image (with at least 8 bits per RGB channel) can consume something like 18 to 25 Mb of memory (depending on picture size). And as we have seen (Chapter 5), many digital cameras usefully compress their images before downloading them to the host computer.

The basic idea is to compress the number of image bits to a point where the image is still acceptable, and obviously there are degrees of acceptance here. For some images, with large areas of common tone or colour, a compression ratio of perhaps 20, or even 30 to 1, would not be unacceptable since much of the information is redundant! But if the image were filled with fine detail that must be preserved, then the compression limit might well be set at only 2 to 1!

Compression techniques look at the following redundancies as a means of reducing the size of an image file[40]:

- Repetition of data.
- Redundancy in the way the data is coded.
- Redundancy between adjacent pixel values.
- Psycho-visually redundant information.

The first three of the above techniques are *lossless* methods that do not change the original image at all, but the compression ratios are relatively small, usually 2 : 1 or 3 : 1. The fourth method is known as a *lossy compression* and can be as high as 30 : 1. Obviously the amount of compression has to be balanced with desired quality.

The most well-known example of *lossy compression* techniques is JPEG, as mentioned above. Other *lossy* examples are fractal transforms, and Kodak's RADC which allows for compressions of 16 : 1 and 32 : 1 (see Table 5.2) when used with their DC-40 camera.

JPEG was specifically designed to discard information that is not easily perceived by the eye and makes use of known facts concerning human vision. To start with, the sensitivity of the human eye decreases as spatial frequency (of image detail) increases[41][42][43]. Secondly, we can detect small changes in luminance (brightness) more easily than small changes in colour[40][44]. And thirdly, it has been shown that in photographic prints at least, monochromatic detail is best discriminated in the lower mid-tones where ΔD_p is of the order of 0.03[43][45]. Finally, research with a reference print has shown[43][45] that for a continuous-tone image containing 6 bits of luminance, about 3 bits contain 80% of the total intelligence.

With the aid of a discrete cosine transformation (DCT) the JPEG algorithm removes visually redundant information by quantising image data in the frequency domain. It then converts it back again (*decompression*) with its inverse function (IDCT). For colour images this process is carried out separately for the three RGB channels.

Recent research[40] has identified a number of distortions common to JPEG compression, among them *blocking* (where a block pattern occurs at high compression, caused by the independent processing of pixel blocks), severe degradation of edges, loss of fine detail, and shifts in tone or colour.

As may be expected, compressed or uncompressed image quality is dependent upon viewing conditions as well as the nature of the image itself.

JPEG image compression with Photoshop

Photoshop automatically decompresses a JPEG file as soon as it is opened, and when *Save* is selected from the *FILE* menu, JPEG is one of the format choices. A dialogue box then allows one to choose an *Image Quality* level: Low, Medium, High or Maximum. If 'Maximum' is selected a larger file of higher quality will be produced, and if 'Low' is the choice, then a smaller file of lower quality will be provided.

Lossless compression

A number of software products can compress images using *lossless compression* techniques. Among those suited to the Macintosh are: StuffIt Delux, DiskDoubler, now Utilities and Compact Pro. Each of these can compress Photoshop images as well as other files.

The standard for PC platforms is PKZIP, which is a shareware DOS application published by PKWare. For those who prefer to use Windows rather than DOS, there is WinZip which features PKZIP to compress files and PKUNZIP to decompress archives.

It must always be remembered that lossless compression ratios are much lower than those gained from lossy compression! On the other hand, lossy compression and decompression, as with JPEG for example, is a slow process (depending on the speed of the computer's processor) because of the amount of computation required.

<u>136</u>   *Wavelet compression*

Wavelet compression transforms signals into a sum of small overlapping waves for analysing, storing and transmitting information. This method is mainly used for scientific applications.

8 Digital Printers

Like all image processes it's the final result that counts, and without a good printer even the finest image file cannot produce a good print!

Over the past decade we have witnessed a number of digital printing innovations and now, it is safe to say, decent quality prints can be produced at reasonable cost from even low-end digital cameras, as shown by Fig. 5.9. Quite apart from printing images, the desk-top printer is undoubtably the most useful peripheral one can buy for a computer, but choice is becoming more and more difficult as different types and standards of printer prolificate.

A number of different kinds of printer are available, including that earliest of models, the *dot matrix* which, though generally thought to be out of date, still enjoys a good market despite the fact that decent *inkJet* and *laser printers* can be purchased for as little as £200 these days.

In general, electronic printing can be put into two main groups: *impact* and *non-impact*. Impact technology creates an image by literally hammering ink dots onto paper and, although still around in the form of Dot Matrix, its popularity has waned due to poor colour handling, low resolution, low speed and noisy operation. On the other hand, non-impact printing has developed extremely well since 1991 and has managed to overcome all the problems associated with impact types. Other than photographic printing, non-impact methods include *liquid ink, electrostatic, direct thermal,* and *thermal transfer.* Current technology favours non-impact printing and, apart from direct thermal (which is generally reserved for calculators, since image quality is poor and tends to fade), all of the non-impact methods are to be found among the popular digital printers of today.

8.1 Dot Matrix Printers

The dot matrix impact printer uses columns of small pins and an inked ribbon to create text and images. Although it is mainly used for black and white text, single and even four-colour ribbons are available. Dot matrix printers are available in 9, 18 or 24 pin configurations, but they are not generally recommended for image production because of their poor quality.

8.2 Inkjet Printers

The inkjet printer is fitted with an array of tiny nozzles which spray coloured ink

138 droplets onto paper to produce a full colour image. Most of these printers use liquid inks, but some use sticks of solid inks that liquify at the point of imaging. By employing piezo or thermal methods, anything up to 10 000 droplets per second can be applied by each inkjet nozzle.

Inkjet printers (and laser printers) work by printing a fine pattern of dots with a standard of not less than 300 dpi (dots per inch), now often found as high as 600 dpi. Both monochromatic and colour inkjets are available, but since the colour models do both jobs they are the most obvious choice for imaging purposes. Colour printers such as the HP 500 series usually employ two separate ink cartridges, a tri-colour (cyan, magenta, yellow) cartridge, and a black one. Although a composite of CMY should produce black (see Fig. 2.11b in colour section) in practice the printed colour usually comes out as a muddy brown or green, so the black ink (K) is added to provide a good CMYK image.

The HP Deskjet 870Cxi uses a combined colour cartridge rather than separate CMY ink reservoirs, but with no loss of quality, although running costs are slightly higher. Somewhat less expensive, and certainly a better bargain for many, is the HP Deskjet 820Cxi which can run on either Windows 95 or Windows 3.11. The 820Cxi prints black at 600 × 600 dpi, and colour at 600 × 300 dpi in best mode, dropping to 300 × 300 dpi in normal mode. Overall print performance is good (although it cannot match the 870Cxi) and paper weights up to 135 g/m^2 can be used. The 820 Cxi uses two cartridges; as a result the black is excellent (as good as any laser printer output).

The basic inkjet system is roughly drawn in Fig. 8.1, where it can be seen that an ink reservoir feeds each nozzle through a heated capillary. As the ink heats up it forms a minute vapour bubble at the end of the nozzle then, when the heat is turned off, the bubble is released as a fine droplet which is squirted onto the paper with high precision. The system works on what is known as *drop on com-*

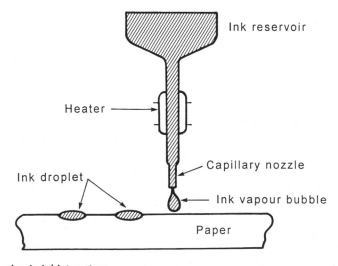

Fig. 8.1 The basic inkjet system.

mand technology where, as soon as the droplet is ejected, a vacuum is formed within the capillary that attracts fresh ink to replace the lost droplet.

Another method is to employ a piezo electric crystal to the rear of the ink reservoir. When a drop of ink is commanded, an electric current flows through the crystal which then flexes (rather like a loudspeaker cone), to force a drop of ink through the nozzle.

With conventional inkjets the print-head will take about half a second to traverse an A4 sheet of paper (8.31inches), and with a resolution of 300 dpi this means a possible 2450 dots across the page, with the print-head switching on and off about 5000 cycles per second. And since the system is one of *drop on command,* the print-head has to respond in 1/5000 second! This is truly a wonderful piece of technology, particularly since each nozzle in the print-head has a diameter approaching that of a human hair, with up to 256 nozzles per system, and a heating/cooling cycle that runs many thousand cycles per second.

I use two thermal inkjet printers: an HP 560C (CMYK) inkjet, and a Canon BJ-10ex (monochrome) bubble jet, and have never had a single problem with either of these printers in over three to four years of continuous use.

Inkjets are sensitive to paper quality, however, and for optimum image quality (monochrome or colour), coated papers are essential. A number of manufacturers market suitable papers for inkjets, among them: Ilford, who produce Ilfojet; Hewlett Packard, who make the Premium Inkjet Glossy Paper and Transparency Films; and the Swiss-based manufacturer, Folex, who market no less than 17 different polyester films and papers, all with special inkjet receptive coatings that provide good resolution and improved colour saturation.

When inkjets deposit ink onto conventional media the ink dots swell and create prolonged drying times which, if one is not careful, lead to smudged prints. Folex, however, manufacture a special microporous coating on their products which draws ink into the surface of the media by capillary action, to facilitate an instant drying and smudge-resistant bonding. The Wiggins Teape PlusJet paper also gives excellent results at a very economic price.

Quite apart from the well-known and well-tried HP 500 series of inkjets, Hewlett Packard offer inkjets in a wide range of prices, from the HP Deskjet 400 (£151 + VAT) to the Deskjet 1600C/CN/CM models priced at £1150, £1450 and £1690 respectively (all excluding VAT).

Epson market a variety of units ranging from the inexpensive Stylus Color 200 at £174 + VAT, to the Stylus Pro XL at £1295 + VAT. The Stylus Pro produces a 720 × 720 dpi output using an advanced piezo print-head with a unique micro-dot ink delivery system. Epson claim their new system reduces the size of a typical inkjet dot by 30%, to a diameter of only 30 µm (half the diameter of a human hair), which is a major factor in optimising the 720 × 720 dpi resolution. From examples of colour prints that I have seen, the Epson Stylus Pro offers a new standard for inkjets, with outputs that are almost photographic in quality, and certainly just as acceptable when printed from a high quality digital image file.

According to Tinsley[46] the finest quality in inkjet printing is provided by the expensive (£17 000 and upwards) *continuous inkjet* printers. These units force ink under pressure through fine nozzles, one ink for each of four colours, to create a stream of droplets onto paper wrapped on a rotating drum. Continuous ink technology is capable of printing images close to photographic quality, and although capital oulay is expensive they are cheap to run and tolerant of paper quality.

8.3 Laser Printers

For the main part laser printers are restricted to monochrome outputs, this is not to say that laser printers cannot work in colour – it's just a question of their very high price! Whereas a good monochrome laser printer can be purchased for less than £1000, most colour lasers cost over £5000, and to date are difficult to find for less than £3000.

Laser printers use a multi-stage process to turn an electrical signal into an image on paper. And the process starts with the printer taking its instructions from the computer in a language that specifies either size and position for text, or graphic information for images. The usual languages are either Postscript or PCL (as used by Hewlett Packard compatibles).

If we look at a monochrome laser printer first, it will give some idea of the complexity of design and the reason why they are so much more expensive than, say, inkjets.

As soon as data are received from the computer, the laser printer's internal processor converts these instructions into a bit-map where memory maps every dot of the image. Some laser printers are designated *Windows printers* and don't have their own internal processors, which means the computer has to create the bit-map itself and then write this directly to the printer's memory.

The printing engine is a drum with a coating that allows it to hold an electrostatic charge. The entire surface of the drum is charged by rotating it past an array of high voltage electrodes, and selectively discharged as the drum (which has the same area as the paper onto which the final image will appear) is scanned by a laser diode beam. Every point on the drum is mapped to a point on the sheet of paper passed under it, and selective discharging is done by switching the laser on and off as it scans the drum. Obviously this is a complex process employing optical relays, with printing resolution directly proportional to the size of the laser beam. However, many laser printers are actually LED printers, since they use a row of hundreds of light emitting diodes across the width of the drum, which are then selectively switched on and off (according to image instructions in the printer's memory) as the drum rotates.

The image medium used in laser printing is a *toner* which, for monochrome printing, is a fine black powder. As the drum rotates it picks up the toner at points where its surface remains charged, and since the selective discharge process was mapped according to a *negative* image, a black *positive* image is left on the drum, ready to be transferred to paper. Heat and pressure are now applied to the paper in order to fuse the toner onto the sheet. Finally, after each sheet of paper has been printed, the drum is cleaned off and the process can start again.

It can be seen that such a system will require four drums for CMYK colour, passing the paper from one drum to another! Alternatively, a single drum can be employed with four changes of coloured toner. It's therefore not surprising to find that laser colour printers are highly expensive!

8.4 Dye-sublimation Printers

There can be no doubt that *dye-sublimation* printers produce some of the best digital images and, for professionals at least, at reasonable cost. Indeed, usually a dye-sublimation print cannot be distinguished from a conventional silver halide photograph, particularly in colour.

Dye-sublimation printers require expensive ribbons and special papers, so each print is relatively expensive when compared to that of an inkjet, but then again the quality is far superior, as may be seen from inspection of Fig. 5.13. Currently (1997) a decent dye sublimation printer, such as the Kodak XLS 8600 costs in the region of £6000, which puts it firmly in the professional category. Nevertheless, despite its near photographic quality dye-sublimation prints cannot match the archival permanence of a conventional colour print, and with this in mind Kodak have recently introduced an 'Extra-Life' ribbon which coats the print surface with a transparent protective layer.

Sublimation is a process where a direct transition from solid to vapour can take place without any liquid phase being involved, and the basic principle of a dye-sublimation printer is to use a heated press to drive an image from one material into another. Some dyes and printing inks are able to undergo sublimation, and after being driven into a material as a vapour, can solidify to form an image beneath its surface.

With a dye-sublimation printer the thermal printing head heats a dye ribbon containing a stable base layer and a dye layer. The ribbon actually contains three or four successive dye panels (CMYK), and during operation the dye ribbons are passed sequentially over the thermal head and vapourised as the print-head (heated to 400 °C) passes over each panel. During the contact printing process the dye sublimates, and the gaseous pigment is then absorbed by the polyester resin coating on the printing paper. The temperature of each microscopic pin in the print-head varies the amount of dye used (each dye can be addressed by 2^8 different temperatures, which results in a possible 16.7 million colours) and colours are fused into the paper with a slight bleeding to allow the dots to merge and so create a dither-free image.

Dye-sublimation papers are specially coated with a gloss or semi-gloss finish, but in order to safeguard the final print, Kodak's 8600 printer automatically applies a final pass through the Ektatherm XtraLife donor, which is a protective laminate on the donor ribbon to guard against moisture, fingerprints, PVC sleeves (which, if damp, can easily strip a colour print of its image layers) and light.

Specifications for the Kodak XLS 8600 quote a 300 pixel per inch resolution and printing speeds (A4) of 78 seconds for CMY colour reflection prints, and three minutes for colour transparencies. With the addition of XtraLife these figures are

101 seconds and 2 minutes 36 seconds respectively. Monochrome printing speeds (with XtraLife) are 58 seconds for prints and 71 seconds for transparencies.

Although dye sublimation (correctly known as dye diffusion thermal tansfer, or D2T2) may be too expensive for most people, there are always those images that really justify this quality of printing, and in these cases it is a simple matter to send the image file to a printing bureau. Nevertheless, we can expect dye-sublimation printers to come down in price, and the Fargo PrimeraPro (thermal wax and dye-sublimation) printer is available for £1649.

8.5 Thermal Wax Transfer Printers

Similar in many ways to the dye-sublimation printer is the *thermal wax transfer* system, which uses a CMY coloured wax ribbon with a width equal to the printed paper. The waxed ribbon passes over the print-head containing thousands of heated pins which melt the wax onto the print in proportion to their heat (70 to 80 °C). The three colours are printed sequentially, with the print paper passing through the print-head three times in perfect register (four times for CMYK). On contact with the paper the wax then solidifies to its final colour.

Although not up to the same standard as dye-sublimation printing, thermal wax has the advantage of being cheap in terms of materials and is also reasonably quick.

The hybrid, dual function, FargoPro wax thermal/dye-sublimation printer delivers laser quality text, and can be used with either CMY or CMYK dye-sublimation ribbons. But as a thermal wax printer it also offers colour print quality at least as good as most of the small colour inkjet printers. In the thermal wax mode CMY printing is first made with the yellow wax ribbon, followed by magenta and finally cyan. If a CMYK ribbon is used then black follows the cyan. Using a three-colour thermal wax ribbon a 300 × 300 dpi image takes four minutes to print, including computer time to assemble the file. According to Tinsley, print quality is best using Fargo's own paper, and although photocopy paper can be used there is serious loss of quality.[47]

8.6 Thermo-autochrome Printers

A relative newcomer to the printing scene is the Fujifilm Fujix NC-500 A4 printer, which uses dyes formed within the actual print paper. In this respect *thermo-autochrome* (TA) is a process rather similar to conventional photographic colour printing, but now the three (CMY) colour layers are coated on a conventional base with a protective heat-resistant layer on top of the sandwich. Said to give results equal to those of dye-sublimation printers, the NC-500 is priced around £5000 and has relatively low running costs since the only consumable is the TA paper which, at £1.50 + VAT is very reasonable.

Windows and Macintosh compatible, the NC-500 is bundled with an Adobe Photoshop Plug-In module and is computer connected via a SCSI interface. Operating requirements for the Macintosh suggest a minimum 2.5 Mb of available memory (12 Mb recommended), and at least 30 Mb available on the hard disk. For Windows these requirements are 8 Mb and 50 Mb respectively.

Printer resolution is quoted as 300 dpi on either TA paper or overhead pojector (OHP) film, with a printing time of 140 seconds for the paper and 165 seconds for the transparency film.

The major points of interest with TA technology are the complete absence of printing inks and ribbons, and the fact that the printer uses RGB files directly, cutting out the need for RGB/CMY conversions; as a result the printer is a much simpler device and media costs are less. The TA paper is the heart of the system, and acts very much like photographic colour print material, with a yellow dye layer on top, followed by magenta, and a cyan layer next to the base. Each colour layer is filled with one micron diameter colour generating capsules, with CMY dyes formed from diazo compounds and colour couplers. Processing is accomplished by applying a constant level of heat from the thermal heads (for different time periods) to each colour layer. The colours of the top two layers are then fixed by ultra-violet radiation.

8.7 Pictrographic Printers

If there is a challenge to dye-sublimation printing then it has to be either TA technology or, better still, *pictrography*. Currently both of these systems are being promoted by Fuji, and both provide quality equal to photographic products. However, with pictrography this is not too surprising since the final print is actually made on silver halide material.

Pictrography uses red, green, and blue laser diodes to make a single-pass exposure from a digital image file onto a photographic donor material. A latent image is formed in the dye layer of the donor, which is then brought into contact with the final paper or film (with the aid of a little moisture) for thermal development transfer from donor to print.

The Fujix Pictrography 3000 printer is capable of 400 dpi resolution, and can produce the first print from a file in two minutes, after which further prints are produced at a rate of one every 70 seconds. The prints are of photographic quality, but this can be expected from a printer that currently (1997) costs in the region of £18 000.

Pictrograph images can be printed on a variety of materials, such as glossy and matt papers, or OHP transparencies, all with the usual range of 16.7 million possible colours. Fuji make a particular point of stressing the importance of this printer for scientific applications, where resolution and dynamic range are essential, and for printing from Photo CDs.

9 CD-ROM and Photo CD

The acronym CD-ROM stands for compact disk - read only memory, a technology that was introduced by Philips and Sony in 1984. Today, most desk-top, and many laptop computers come with a CD-ROM installation, and it is estimated that about 75 million CD-ROM drivers are installed worldwide.[48] CD-ROMs not only facilitate the creation and use of a huge database, allowing the storage of multimedia encyclopedias such as the 1996 Grolier (Windows 3.1 or 95), but they can also provide for a very comprehensive encyclopedia of stock photography. In the latter category, Comstock Inc, offer over 2100 digital stock photographs on a single CD-ROM which, for £50, gives the potentional buyer an excellent catalogue of 'thumbnail-image' choices. From these 24-bit colour images a client may then select a full resolution file, for use with the appropriate copyright release (see Appendix C).

As a storage medium CD-ROM acts rather like a second hard disk, and is particularly useful for storing image files that would otherwise take up excessive amounts of hard-disk space. Currently a typical CD-ROM can hold around 650 Mb of data, but we can expect this to be increased in the near future. Normally all information stored on CD-ROM is permanent. However, the new *rewritable* CDs will allow users to erase and rewrite information onto their CD, much the same as with a hard disk.

9.1 CD-ROM Drives

All CD-ROM disks are read from a CD drive (usually the 'd' drive) and most of today's computers – PC, Mac, desk-top, laptop and even notebooks – come with a built-in CD-ROM drive of at least 'Quadra-Speed' standard. As recently as 1995 a standard PC would be fitted with a double-speed CD drive, but by 1997 we had 6, 8, 10 and even 12-speed drives! Speed of access is important of course, particularly when one is searching for information within an extensive data store, or extracting a large image file for processing and printing.

For those who don't have a CD-ROM drive integral to the computer, it is a simple matter to connect an external drive unit to the computer via a SCSI socket. A wide variety of drive units are available, with speeds in the range of ×4, ×6, ×8 and ×10, and prices extending from £33 to £170.

9.2 CD-ROM Writers

A CD writer can be installed via the usual SCSI chain to a computer, and should be located on a vibration-free platform. Products range from about £400 upwards, and are mainly priced according to their speed of operation (a double-speed writer takes about 30 minutes to record 600 Mb of data).

A good example of a dual purpose read/write CD unit is the quad-speed CD-R writer and CD-ROM drive from TEAC. Currently (1997) available at a basic price of £671 (internal fitting), an external device is also expected soon. Associated software comes on a hybrid Mac/ISO 9660 disk, including Toast 3 (Macintosh) and WinOnCD 3 (Windows 3.11 and 95). Specifications give a write time of 15 minutes for 650 Mb, and 220 ms access time as a CD reader.

At a similar price, the CD-R Shuttle PS is a double-speed CD writer which reads at quad-speed. The Shuttle PS writes at 352 Kb/second, and reads at 600 Kb/second, using an SCSI or parallel port, and supports CD-ROM XA, CD-DA, Photo CD and Multimode ISO 9660. It comes with drivers for DOS, Windows 3.11 and 95, and Electroson Gear 4.0 CD authorising software.

The Kodak PCD Writer 225

The PCD Writer 225 is a desk-top CD writer and reader that allows users to output their data (including digital audio) on custom CDs, but also includes a bar-code reader to take advantage of the unique identification number on Kodak's 'Writable CD Media with Infoguard protection'.

This professional reader/writer device is shipped with 2 Mb of RAM, expandable to 32 Mb, enabling the device to write disks more reliably by reducing the risk of buffer underrun, and is currently (1997) priced at £2850 + VAT.

Kodak recordable CDs are marketed as 'Kodak Writable CD Media with Infoguard Protection Systems'. Each polycarbonate disk has a thickness of 1.2 mm, a diameter of 120 mm, and 580 Mb or 682 Mb Mode 1 capacity. The Kodak disk is compatible with all leading CD writers and readers and the Infoguard protection is said to give a lifetime of 100 years.

Generally speaking a writable CD (CD-R) can record up to 650 Mb of information, and fresh image files can be added at any time – up to maximum capacity. They should be of ISO 9660 standard (meaning they can be read by virtually all CD readers) and cost about £7 each.

The Kodak Aerial Writable CD

Second only to the hard disk on a computer, writable CD is now considered to be the most common form of storage for geographic information systems (GIS), completely cutting out previous storage systems such as magnetic tape. Air mapping, remote sensing and GIS rely on air films for their primary data, and although a small part of the acquisition is now being gained directly from digital cameras (see Chapter 10), most of the aerospace imagery used in computers is transferred from film (by film scanners) and stored on CD-ROM for RS and GIS applications.

As a consequence Kodak, with a long-standing interest in the air film market, now produce an appropriate CD-R disk in the form of the Kodak Aerial Writable CD, which operates at ×1 to ×6 speeds, and also incorporates INFOGUARD for the benefit of its scratch resistant overcoat.

9.3 CD-Rewritable Drives

Adding a new dimension to CD technology is the CD-rewritable drive, which allows users to erase and re-write information to a CD. Although in its infancy at time of writing, this new form of CD technology will undoubtably be known as *read, write and erase* within a year or two.

9.4 Kodak Photo CD

Photo CD is a Kodak specification that allows users to record and display photographic images on compact disks. For those who wish to transfer exisiting photography into their computers, Photo CD opens up exciting new possibilities for industries such as advertising and desk-top publishing.

Computer manipulation of images is now commonplace, as reflected by the growth of photo-libraries and digital imaging bureaux that service the publishing industry. In addition, many amateurs now send their cherished negatives to bureaux where, on transfer to CD, they can be imported to software for further image manipulation.

Eastman Kodak's Photo CD began life in late 1992, and was designed to offer an inexpensive route for creating and accessing digital images. The concept is simple: exposed 35 mm film can be dropped off at a Photo CD outlet then, within the space of a few days, the client receives a CD with five scans of each photograph. These images can be connected to almost any television set, or read by a Photo CD compatible CD-ROM drive connected to the computer (where they can be manipulated with software such as Photoshop).

The Photo CD disk holds 650 Mb of image data which are recorded by burning a series of pits into the dye layer beneath the gold surface. The image information is then read by a laser diode in the CD drive.

For those who simply wish to see their holiday photographs displayed on television, Kodak provide a range of Photo CD players (some with image manipulation features). The PCD 5850 model, for example, allows the user to enlarge, pan, rotate and display up to 500 photographs, or play audio CDs for up to six hours!

Kodak Photo CD Media formats allow for a number of different applications, but the most common are the Photo CD Master Disc (35 mm film only) and the Pro Photo CD Master Disc (35 mm to 4 × 5 inch films).

Kodak Photo CD Master Disc

The Photo CD Master Disc can store up to 100 colour images at full resolution using YCC, a device-independent colour space described by two chrominance

values and one luminance value. YCC colour space allows for high levels of visu- **147**
ally lossless image compression, and also provides a wide range of colour space
for both negative and positive originals. Photo CD uses a proprietary, compressed
image format developed by Kodak called Image Pac.

All Photo CD images contain five different levels of resolution, each suited to a
different application, as shown in Table 9.1.

Table. 9.1 Photo CD Master Disc Resolution Table

Base	Resolution (pixels)	Application
Base /16	128 × 192	Thumbnail for photo-indexing
Base /4	256 × 384	Thumbnail for photo-indexing
Base	512 × 768	TV monitor viewing
Base ×4	1024 × 1536	High definition TV
Base ×16	2048 × 3072	Photographic-quality digital printing
Base ×64	4096 × 6144	Pro Photo CD Format

Each of the five Photo CD scans is contained in a single image file, called an
Image Pac which is compressed to about 4.5 Mb with lossless compression. These
images can be negative, positive colour or monochrome. If monochrome, up to
150 images can be stored within the 650 Mb disk. One of the advantages of the
system is that you can add images at any time, until the disk is filled.

In computer operations all that has to be done is to view the *Thumbnails* and
select the required image, then open the full resolution image and save it as a
TIFF, PICT or EPS file for further processing. Kodak have released a number of
software packages, such as Photo CD Access, PhotoEdge and Kodak Shoebox.

Those wishing to use Photoshop 3.0 make use of Kodak's Colour Management System (KCMS) and simply choose *Open* under the *File* menu. The required Photo CD image is then opened, and as soon as the dialog box appears
the required resolution and film type are selected from the pop-up menu.

Kodak Pro Photo CD Master Disc

The main difference between Photo CD, and *Pro Photo CD* is that the latter can
scan formats up to 4 × 5 inches (with higher resolution), and that bureaux will
naturally charge more for this service. With Pro Photo CD the maximum number
of stored images depends on file size and resolution, but is generally within the
range of 6, 25 and 100 (35 mm).

9.5 CD ROM Advantages and Applications

After a somewhat slow start, CD-ROM imagery (including Photo CD) has now
become a standard method for archiving and displaying images in a variety of
disciplines. In terms of storage and display the CD is very convenient, and although the disk looks delicate it is amazing how much handling it can take. Small

148   photo-libraries can absorb a large number of disks, and with a possible 100 images on each they can provide a substantial photo-library for research and education, particularly when disks can be used as a source of hard copies.

A significant application of CD-ROM imagery is in geographic education where, under terms of the National Curriculum, young students can be introduced to geography through a CD-ROM that holds a number of terrestrial and aerial photographs of a given local area. In a series of CD-ROM disks entitled *The Physical Landscape of Britain* a host of photographs illustrate a given area, and are backed up by suitable explanations concerning each image. These excellent, self-learning packages are each supported by a small information booklet, and users are allowed to make hard copies on site, or can request photographs from the supplier. Produced by Photoair Software (who also take the aerial and ground photographs), in conjunction with Bedfordshire Education Service(for details see Appendix C).

One of the earliest users of Kodak's Photo CD was Landcare Aviation Inc., of Marcy, New York who, as specialists in small format aerial photography,[49] have flown SFAP for many years and have collected an extensive 35 mm photo library suitable for low cost map revision within the USA. Making full use of this provision, and more recent cover that has the additional accuracy of GPS (global positioning systems) technology, Landcare now offer their GPS-ACCUPHOTO system with high location accuracy (see Appendix C).

As early as 1992, Landcare arranged to put 12 complete counties (about 15 000 square miles) worth of 35 mm aerial photographs on Photo CD; this imagery became their first file coverage base in digital form. This base is still in use, providing clients with both soft- and hard-copy coverage of upstate New York.[50] Each image is 3072px × 2048px, and has a file size of slightly less than 5 Mb for 24 bit colour. As more clients acquire suitable CD-ROM computing facilities, the more use there will be of Landcare's highly acclaimed software for such things as map intensification, mosaicing and GIS applications.

Part Three

Applications

10 Digital Imaging Applications

Just as photography has become an indispensable tool for science, industry, medicine, commerce, research, entertainment, exploration and warfare, so its digital counterpart will provide equal service, but much faster, and with increasing importance and application.

Digital cameras and scanned photographs give the greatest advantage from the computer. Not only can digital images be manipulated much faster than photographs, but they can be analysed much faster too. An important example is the airborne military photograph which, exposed in a hostile environment at some considerable risk, requires the very fastest processing and interpretation. And, although human intelligence will never be replaced, items such as prior knowledge, comparisons, coordinates, image manipulation, background information, metrication and statistics can be interfaced with image data to provide essential answers.

Apart from the wealth of proprietary software available (much of it capable of dealing with just about any subject) there are increasing numbers of customised programs dedicated to supporting imagery with specific applications, such as earth sciences, mapping, astronomy, medicine, physics, etc. The TAL SoftwareWedge™ is a particularly useful package that allows a two-way input/output (I/O) via the RS232 serial port found on all computers. SoftwareWedge can capture data from all manner of laboratory and industrial instruments, and can add serial data acquisition and instrument control to any Windows application without additional programming. With this type of software any image can be supported with graphs, charts and tables, with information taken directly from the image itself.

There can be no doubt that tomorrow's users of photography will use digital cameras exclusively; just as publishers now expect their authors to supply manuscripts on disk, so will they expect photographs on the same medium. Nevertheless, we can expect conventional methods to remain for a long time yet, mainly because film currently offers one or two advantages over digital systems, but in general the future belongs to the digital camera.

The amateur photographer will seek his/her choice of medium according to interest. But it is already obvious that many are taking a fresh interest in their hobby, as digital cameras and software become less expensive.

The professional (commercial) photographer has already seen the writing on the wall, and few would argue they could continue business outside of the new technology. But for the most part it is the professional (non-photographer) who sees the digital camera for its true worth. As the industrial and scientific photographer has steadily found less work over the past twenty years (mainly because of increased technology) only the medical photographer seems to have survived as a technical specialist within the profession. Today everyone is a photographer, yet very few have seen the inside of a darkroom, let alone exposed a black and white photograph! Nevertheless, within a few days they can master digital technology and experiment with their own creativity (in colour or monochrome) to produce prints with a quality limited only by cost. For this reason, the following list of digital imaging applications includes many professions other than that of the professional photographer.

10.1 Press Photography and Photo-journalism

Press work is perhaps the most readily understood area of photography, mainly because it intercepts everyone's life at some stage or other, and also because it's a major source of news gathering. Press photography is extremely competitive of course and, although the work can be interesting, it is also very demanding. The practitioner has to be prepared for any environment – interiors, exteriors, harsh or benign – the accent is always on speed of image capture and speed of transmission to the editorial desk.

With photo-journalism there is perhaps less demand for speed, and more demand for image quality. But in both fields everything and anything is to be expected. For this reason it is important to select the right tool for the job.

Traditionally the camera (or rather the equipment) has to include a number of lenses, a flash gun, filters, rolls of film, and (sensibly) a portable tripod. All of these can easily be realised with most high-quality digital units because they are based on conventional 35 mm cameras, and they can certainly offer comparable quality. But this misses the point entirely!

The prime advantage of handling digital images is speed! Subsequent to exposure, images can be immediately downloaded to a laptop computer where they can be cropped, enhanced, modified and re-sized, then transmitted via a modem and digital mobile telephone to the newsdesk. Such methods are already being used of course, and even packaged as a complete system for this purpose,[51] mainly with cameras like the Canon EOS DCS-3, the Nikon E2s, Fujix DS-505/ 515, Kodak DCS-420 and Kodak EOS.DCS-5, all of which offer professional 35 mm camera quality, good shutter speeds, fast burst rates and high ISO speeds. High ISO speeds are very important for press work and, although all of these cameras allow for an ISO equivalent of at least 400 (colour) and some of them up to 1600 (monochrome), the more inexpensive DCS-410 has a sensitivity limited to only ISO 100, which effectively removes it from the list. As with film, the digital equivalent ISO speed is important for press work, since fast subject movement can only be arrested with high shutter speeds, and if the problem is compounded with low light levels, the press camera needs all the 'film speed' it can muster.

Satisfactory dynamic range is desirable in all digital cameras, and since circumstances might dictate recording an image such as that shown in Fig. 5.12

(where text, colour and deep shadows prevail), it is prudent to check this quality in cameras selected for press or photo-journalism.

Yet another desirable feature is an internal microphone, such as that incorporated in the DCS-420, and EOS..DCS-5, which provide 'telephone quality' voice recording to annotate images as they are recorded. Above all, quality is paramount for photo-journalism and with these cameras it is assured, even for snapshot portraits such as that shown in Fig. 5.13.

10.2 Commercial and Industrial Photography

Although perhaps wanting for a better definition, commercial photography has long been understood to include work such as that carried out by high street photographic studios, fashion and advertising agencies and, in some establishments, industrial photography.

Just as high-street photographers have been offering wedding videos for many years, so they now offer CD-ROM images taken from either conventional film or digital cameras. One particular company of interest is the London based Multimedia Factory which offers the 'Forever Yours' service consisting of a 50-image wedding CD, complete with customised captions and music. Any established wedding photographer wishing to offer this service to his/her clients can do so by acting as an agent for 'Forever Yours' on a commission basis.

A number of studios specialising in high-quality catalogue and brochure photography are now seeing the advantage of digital cameras, and have invested in expensive systems such as the Phase One Studio Kit, and the Leaf Lumina, with images processed in Photoshop. For the main part it has meant a considerable capital outlay, new lighting and fresh expertise, but financial advantage comes from increased efficiency, time saving and improved products.

An increasing number of manufacturers and industrialists are using digital cameras for various tasks ranging from simple data recording to sophisticated research systems. Examples in the former category include the use of a Kodak DCS-420 for providing a spare-parts database in the transport industry[52] and for log tracking in forestry.[53] In the research field, simple CCD video cameras are now being used with frame-grabbing and JPEG compression, in order to record holographic interference fringes in non-destructive testing rigs.

10.3 Holographic Interferometry

Although holography normally requires extremely high-resolution photographic plates to form a three-dimensional image, holographic interference fringes can be recorded with far less resolution, even with the inferior quality of a frame-grabbed video image of 512×480 pixels, provided that a reference hologram of the subject is already available. A particular system of interest is that employed for the vibration testing of propeller blades used on cruise missiles, and for detecting cracks in space shuttle heat shield tiles,[54] where a typical holographic interferometric arrangement (see Fig. 10.1) is recorded by a digital system rather than a holographic plate. Commercial users of these systems include Boeing and

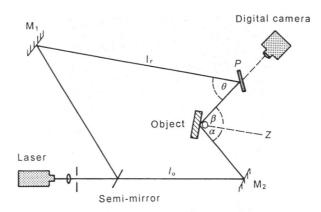

Fig. 10.1 Holographic arrangement suitable for optical interference recording. Although not elaborated in the diagram, the laser beam is expanded by the lens and spatial filter placed immediately in front of the beam-splitting semi-mirror.

McDonnell-Douglas among many others who use interferometry for routine non-destructive testing.

Although true holograms (three-dimensional images, exhibiting parallax) are constructed on the principle of optical interference, with primary fringe spacing recorded at the micro-resolution level (< 1 μm), a holographic interferometer only looks at the secondary fringes, which have spacings large enough to enable fringes to be counted by the human eye, as shown in Fig. 10.2. These secondary fringes can then be recorded by a relatively low-resolution CCD imager.

A basic interferometric layout is shown in Fig. 10.1, where a 30 mW HeNe laser has split-beams I_r (reference beam) and I_o (object beam) meeting at the holographic plate P. An object under test is placed at O and angles α and β measured from the motion vector OZ.[55][56]

With the object (O) in position the reflected object beam (I_o) interferes with the reference beam (I_r) to create primary fringes, and when subsequently developed the hologram reveals a 3-D image of the object when placed in its original position at P and illuminated with the same reference beam. With the object beam blanked-off, the hologram's virtual image is revealed and by careful adjustment this can then be accurately superimposed upon the object. If the object is now changed in shape by any means, and re-illuminated by I_o, then hologram and object differences are revealed as a system of secondary fringes, as shown in Fig. 10.2.

In Fig. 10.2, we have an overloaded 2 μF (275 V) paper capacitor with fringes recorded by 'time-lapsed' (or double-exposure) interferometric holography using the set-up shown in Fig. 10.1 (not to scale). First, a record was made with the subject unloaded, then another exposure was made with the capacitor overloaded to 500 volts.[54] The resulting double exposure then gave secondary interference fringes due to changes in the skin of the capacitor.

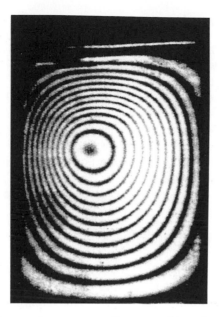

Fig. 10.2 Coarse interference fringes are easily recorded by a low-resolution CCD imager. This subject: a 2 μF (275 V) paper capacitor under voltage overload (Photo: Ron Graham).

Referring to Fig. 10.1 and Fig. 10.2, the measured change in state is taken along the motion vector (*OZ*) and has amplitude ΔZ given by:

$$\Delta Z = n\lambda/(\cos \alpha + \cos \beta) \qquad (10.1)$$

where:
n is the fringe order number,
λ is the wavelength of the laser (HeNe = 632.8 nm).

To find the value of n, the count must proceed from the zero-order fringe ($n = 0$) which can usually be found by scanning across the reconstructed image (thus varying β) causing the fringes to move except where $n = 0$. For Fig. 10.2, the zero order was found to be at the edge of the capacitor and counting into closed fringe contours, n was observed to be 13. With $\alpha = 20°$ and $\beta = 26°$, Eq: 10.1 then gave a displacement value of 4.45 μm.

With the digital variant of this system, the only difference is that the subject's second exposure is recorded by a low-resolution CCD imager, and analysed through a computer. Whereas the method just described is known as *time-lapsed inter-ferometry*, similar systems (using the same optical set-up) are known as *real-time interferometry* (where fringes are observed and can be recorded in real-time), and *time-averaged interferometry* (where vibratory deformation can be exposed while the object is actually vibrating). For the non-destructive testing of vibrating pro-peller blades, the method used is time-averaged interferometry.

<u>156</u> *The Minolta Dimage V camera*

A novel digital camera produced by Minolta incorporates a rotating detachable ×2.7 zoom lens that will certainly be useful for recording otherwise inaccessible areas in industrial photography.

The Minolta Dimage V has a built-in 1.8 inch colour LCD (liquid crystal display) monitor, and a removable SmartMedia memory card of 2 Mb capacity. The CCD sensor is a full-frame 640 × 480 pixel chip and up to 16 images can be stored in fine JPEG compression mode. Computer interface is via RS232C, and an integral flash unit (Guide Number of 10) supports a 100 ISO sensitivity. However, the most important aspect of this camera is the detachable zoom lens which, extended on a 1 metre cable, is capable of looking around corners and into areas normally impossible to photograph.

10.4 Medical Photography

There are few scientific disciplines that employ photography and digital imaging more than medicine, where it is used for patients' records, teaching, surgery, pathology, research and diagnosis. For over 100 years, photography has served medicine well, and has allowed clinicians to evaluate medical images exposed under an EMR (electromagnetic radiation) extending from X-rays to the near-infrared, with instruments ranging from the humble camera to the electron microscope.

Owing to the size of subjects ecountered in medical imaging, much of the work is table-top technology that comes under the general heading of macro-imaging. And, for smaller than macro-sized specimens, special tools such as the optical microscope and endoscope are required. All teaching hospitals and medical research centres rely on medical imaging, and usually have specially qualified staff dedicated to this work.

Digital imaging is not only an extension of well-established photographic techniques, but also a very useful method for putting images into patients' files along with related data. Wherever a photographic camera can be put to a task, so can the digital camera – even to fluorescent microscopy!

One of the first departments to use digital imaging (1993) was the Medical Illustration Unit at the Institute of Child Health, Great Ormond Street, London, where they pioneered the inclusion of digital images in patients' medical records.

Since the Patients' Charter came into effect (allowing all patients access to their medical records) it has become more and more important to keep these records up to date, and digital imaging is ideal for this purpose. At Great Ormond Street for example, a large proportion of the patients are recorded digitally, using the Kodak EOS.DCS-3 camera and Kodak 8600 printer. One of the main attributes of the digital camera system is speed, particularly since the Patients' Charter states that information has to be turned around as quickly as possible. At the City Hospital, Truro, Cornwall, where they employ the Kodak DCS-420, they find that turn-around with a digital system is between 6 and 12 hours, whereas with film it can be up to three days!

Digital imaging extends throughout the entire medical scene, including opthalmology, dentistry, anatomy, physiology and X-ray; it is now common to use digital cameras to record X-ray screened images.

Digital cameras are also invaluable in the ambulance service, where paramedics use digital cameras to record accident scenes. These images are then transmitted to hospital via digital mobile telephone, so that doctors can see the extent of injuries incurred and allow treatments to be planned in advance.[57]

Face scanning

An interesting medical innovation that has also proved itself in fields other than medicine is a scanner system for digitising human body surfaces. Developed by Dr Alfred Linney (Head of Medical Graphics) and his team at the Department of Medical Physics and Bioengineering, University College London, the system records facial surfaces and is based on the principle of triangulation.[58]

Motivated from an idea that computer graphics might be used to simulate and predict facial surgery, the optical face scanner is widely used in reconstructive surgery to correct badly deformed faces, and for a variety of forensic and anthropometric studies.

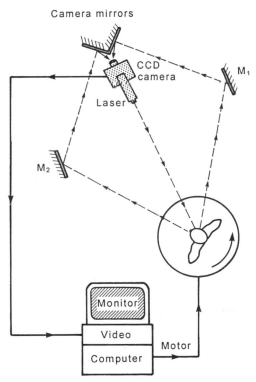

Fig. 10.3 Face scanner system with CCD imager, developed at University College London.

158   The basic principle of the scanning system is shown in Fig. 10.3, where a line of laser light is seen to be projected on to the facial surface. Viewed obliquely, the line appears distorted, reflecting the shape of the surface anatomy. This distorted line is then recorded by a CCD camera connected to a computer via a customised interface board. The mirror arrangement shown in Fig. 10.3 allows the line to be viewed by the camera from two opposing directions, which is necessary to avoid loss of data caused by the occlusion of parts of the facial surface by the prominence of the nose. Using a video camera and frame-grabber (Panasonic 6200), camera signals are pre-processed by the interface board. For each TV frame a set of digital numbers is generated, representing the mid-point of the pulses on the video scan lines produced by the projected laser line. A calibration programme converts these numbers into spatial coordinates of points lying along the laser line illuminating the surface.

To scan the surface of a face (or body), the subject is rotated on a platform under computer control and, for a face, the platform is usually rotated through 200° in a 15 second period, but both speed and extent of rotation may be varied according to subject. Up to 256 profiles may be recorded per scan, and the angles at which these are recorded may be programmed according to the detail required. Something between 30 000 and 60 000 three-dimensional coordinates of points lying on the anatomical surface are usually collected in a single scan, the points being recorded with a precision better than 0.5 mm.

For low-cost medical reports, images are produced in TIFF and faces can be reproduced with any desired view as shown in Fig. 10.4. Used in conjunction with X-ray computed tomography and other medical imaging systems, the optical scanning system shown in Fig. 10.3 assists in a number of applications including; surgery, diagnostic radiology, prosthesis and implant design, clinical growth studies,

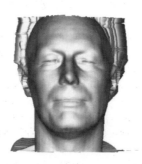 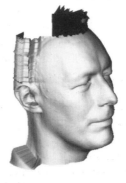

Fig. 10.4 Two views selected from the digitally imaged scan of a subject's face. From the scan file of any face, it is a simple matter to reconstruct selected viewpoints from the system's software, and print hard copies, as shown here. Images courtesy of Dr A. Linney, Medical Physics and Bio-Engineering Department, University College London.

forensic science, archaeology, psychology and training. In addition, the system also generates the data necessary to drive a numerically controlled milling machine to cut out a three-dimensional model of any image displayed on the monitor.

10.5 Forensic Science and Police Work

The camera has always been a useful tool in forensic science and, from examples taken from other disciplines, it seems natural to assume that digital cameras may offer considerable advantages to Scenes of Crime Officers and forensic scientists, where images and audio records could be made quickly, and where a satisfactory result could be confirmed before evidence is lost through difficulties such as bad weather, or other uncontrolled situations. Nevertheless, the digital camera has yet to be employed by UK Scenes of Crime Officers and, although one can expect the situation to change at some time in the future, there are significant problems associated with digital recording in this particular field.

Unlike most imaging applications, forensic records are always open to argument in a court of law where, if an image is to be accepted, it must be above legal criticism. For most purposes we have seen that digital images can equal photographic quality, either monochrome or colour. Indeed, we have seen (Fig. 2.9) that digital cameras exhibit tonal linearity unequalled by silver halide imagery, so in this respect they have a great advantage. But in certain areas digital systems are flawed by their very character.

Although conventional silver halide materials can be considered isotropic (exhibiting physical properties independent of direction), a CCD array (with an x, y matrix of pixels) is a non-isotropic medium that can introduce aliasing problems in some images. As a consequence there is a natural reluctance to employ a system that could be questioned in a court of law. Indeed, this problem has already been investigated with respect to fingerprint records where, according to Roy Thompson of the Home Office, Police Scientific Development Branch,[59] there is evidence that digitised records of fingerprints exhibit prohibitive aliasing errors, and for this application digital cameras and scanning techniques are not recommended. For a full sized fingerprint (about 2 cm wide) a scanning resolution of 500 dpi is recommended, but most prints lifted from a scene of crime are only a fraction of this size, and so a resolution of at least 1000 dpi is considered necessary! These are very stringent conditions of course, and ones that will require a degree of 'overscanning' to avoid Nyquist limitations (Eq: 3.10). Even so, it's possible that high-resolution cameras such as Kodak's DCS-460 may prove useful in this respect.

The laser scanning system shown in Fig. 10.3 is also used in forensic work where, not infrequently, a skull is found in suspicious circumstances and needs to be identified. To perform a reconstruction of the face the skull is scanned, and a scan is taken of a face of an individual of similar type to that inferred from the skull. The facial surface is then adapted to the skull using accepted tables of mean soft tissue thicknesses.[60] Aquaintances of missing persons are then asked to view the reconstructed facial image.

160   The 3-D dataset produced by the optical scanner has also been used to confirm identification of suspects recorded on security cameras, where the shape and proportions of the face of the accused can be compared with those found in the security images. A single optical scan may then be used to provide good silhouettes of the face as depicted from all of the viewpoints shown in the video recording.

Turning to less esoteric applications, up to a dozen police forces within the UK are already using digital cameras for tracking millions of drivers along British roads. With the help of sophisticated software, these cameras can read a passing numberplate and automatically check it against a police database of known or suspected offenders. A digital camera placed above and behind the traffic flow, can read several plates at once using the Racal Talon system, which has successfully been tested on major motorways since 1993.

Other agencies employing digital surveillance cameras include HM Customs, who similarly log every vehicle entering the UK.

10.6 Military Applications

All military photographers are trained at the Joint School of Photography at RAF Cosford and, whereas this course was initially for Royal Air Force personnel only, it has been the main source of photographic instruction for all three armed forces for a number of years now. All photographers are trained in conventional photographic techniques, and digital cameras form an important part of the training.

Army personnel will, on completion of their course, be transferred to the Royal Logistics Corps of Photographers, and some could end up at the Public Relations Office at HQ Land Command, where their work is based around digital imaging systems. As photo-journalists, the modern Army's two-man public relations teams carry all their kit in a suitcase containing a Nikon E2 or DS-515 digital camera, PCMCIA cards, modems, Apple Mac computer, Powerbook 5300ce scanner, and small satellite telephones plus a portable generator. The advantage of digital is of course speed, particularly when military news events need to be transmitted as quickly as possible, but the majority of work is still done with colour film, which is processed in a portable darkroom before being scanned.[61]

The RAF (and other Air Forces) also employ digital cameras for general work, but their main interest is in the more serious role of airborne reconnaissance. Naturally little is known about these applications, but some idea of their importance can be gained from known use of these cameras in aerial mapping and remote sensing.

Current investigations by US military forces include trials with a modified Kodak DCS-100 camera for reconnaissance in low threat areas such as Bosnia and Somalia.[62] Known as the tactical airborne digital camera system (TADCS) this camera, complete with 105 mm lens, has been operated by the Radar Intercept Officer of US navy F-14 aircrews for tasks suited to pre-strike reconnaissance, and from P-3 aircraft for monitoring shipping and counter narcotics operations. According to this report, image quality does not equal that provided by conventional photo-recce cameras carried in the usual F-14 pods, but TADCS imagery can be relayed back to ship, or land base, in under 30 seconds by a line-of-sight UHF data link effective up to 300 km. The TADCS allows up to 24 images to be taken in a single burst, all of them being stored in the system's hard disk. Up to 150 images can be stored on the hard disk and, once clear of the operational area, aircrew are able to review and select images on a tactical information display screen. From here it is a simple matter to compress image data and relay it back to base via an encryption unit.

10.7 Aerial Surveys and Remote Sensing

Conventional topographic mapping is done with large format cameras, and when we say *large* we are talking about a 23cm × 23cm format air camera that costs anything up to £400 000 for a top-of-the-range unit complete with navigation interface, navigation sight and various other bits of advanced technology.

Useful air mapping can also be done with good-quality 35 mm cameras, but obviously there are limitations, or why do we use such large and expensive air cameras?

Small format aerial photography (SFAP) has come of age at a time when large format air cameras have never been more sophisticated or expensive. As a consequence, survey missions using large format must reflect these costs which, for many clients, are totally prohibitive. Naturally SFAP can only satisfy those requirements that do not demand photogrammetric cover extending over large areas, but this still leaves a number of tasks that require neither metric accuracy nor extensive survey, and it's in these areas that SFAP is both useful and economic.[63]

The main reason for using 23 cm format is because it covers a larger area (footprint) on the ground, whereas a 35 mm camera (for the same photo-scale) covers only 1.6% of the same area. Needless to say a digital camera is even more restrictive, and for equal scale the DCS-420 (9.2 mm × 14 mm format) covers only 0.24% of the large format footprint. Nevertheless, by using wide angle lenses (28 mm or less) the digital camera has proved to be an effective means for remote sensing, and for mapping small areas.

Digital mapping with the Kodak DCS-200 camera

In cooperation with the Department of Geomatics, University of Newcastle-upon-Tyne, I have an on-going programme investigating the use of various digital cameras and aircraft for topographic mapping.

Initial trials involved a Cessna 337 survey aircraft (courtesy Photoair) and the Kodak DCS-200ci camera to make a survey run over St Neots (Cambridgeshire) at a photo-scale of 1 : 40 000. The camera was fitted with a standard 28 mm lens and the flying height was 3600 feet. Although the mission was intended to provide a conventional 60% forward overlap of successive images, only 41% was achieved because of a longer than anticipated recycle time. As a consequence there was insufficient frame overlap to provide stereoscopic cover for height measurements, although planimetery was plotted with satisfactory accuracy.[64]

Fig. 10.5 Kodak DCS-200 image of St Neots (Cambridgeshire) taken from 3600 feet with a 28 mm (calibrated) lens. Camera scale approx 1 : 40 000 printed to a scale of 1 : 2000 at 300 dpi. Image processing (Aldus Photostyler 2) provided extra contrast and sharpening. (Jon Mills and Ron Graham, 1994).

A typical frame taken from this mission is shown in Fig. 10.5, where the image has been reproduced at a scale of 1 : 2000 and printed at 300 dpi in monochrome. Image processing with Aldus Photostyler 2 gave extra sharpening and contrast.

The DCS-200 was calibrated (for photogrammetry) in cooperation with the department of Civil Engineering, City University, London, where a total of six images were taken from four camera stations exposing 41 circular retro-reflective targets. The procedure was carried out using a free network, self-calibrating bundle adjustment, as explained by Fryer.[65] Future calibrations can be carried out at the University of Newcastle-upon-Tyne because it has since set up its own test field, where work is continuing into the assessment of both the radiometric and geometric stability of digital cameras.

Calibration values for the DCS-200 are shown in Table. 10.1, where f is the principal distance, p_x and p_y are coordinates of the principal point offset from image centre, and k_1(radial), and t_1 and t_2 (tangential), are distortions.

Table 10.1

Calibration parameter	f(mm)	p_x(mm)	p_y(mm)	k_1(μm)	t_1(μm)	t_2(μm)
Calibrated value	29.3045	0.0335	0.1933	−169.540	0.025	−.043
Standard error	0.0433	0.0706	0.0576	6.952	0.029	0.023

RMS error values of x, y image coordinates (calculated by Dr Jon Mills, University of Newcastle-upon-Tyne) were found to be in the region of 1/9 pixel.

The first stage of turning the DCS-200 imagery into metric form was to create fiducial marks, which were made by using a template image (the same size as the DCS-200 image) which had marked pixels to represent the fiducials. The position of the fiducials were deduced by extrapolation from the known coordinates of the calibrated principal point. This template was then overlaid as a transparent layer onto the image being rectified in Photoshop.

The second stage was to remove the radial and tangential distortions from the image, which was done in Photoshop by using the *Displace Filter*. Displacement maps were then produced using a C++ program written specially for this purpose. Finally, with the camera calibration data entered into the program, each pixel in the DCS-200 array was interrogated, its centre being determined relative to the calibrated principal point, and its displacement (Δx and Δy) being calculated according to the following equations:

$$\Delta x = x(k_1 r^2) + \{t_1(r^2 + 2x^2) + 2t_2 xy\} \qquad (10.2)$$

$$\Delta y = y(k_1 r^2) + \{2t_1 xy + t_2(r^2 + 2y^2)\} \qquad (10.3)$$

where x and y are the image coordinates and r is the radial distance from the calibrated principal point to the pixel centre.[64]

From the first mission a large scale (1 : 1650) map of part of St Neots was produced using soft-copy photogrammetry in a Leica DVP plotter, as shown in Fig. 10.6. Ground control was provided from a 1 : 1250 Ordnance Survey Superplan mapsheet.

Flight details: St Neots mission
Image quality was excellent, mainly because of a shutter speed of 1/250 second with a short focal length lens plus good sunlight and reasonably long shadows, but the mission was spoilt by lack of sufficient forward overlap (p) which needs to

Fig. 10.6 Large scale map of St Neots. Processed by soft-copy photogrammetry to a scale of 1: 1650. The image was first edited in AutoCad, then in CorelDraw, before plotting on a Leica DVP to provide revision to a 1:1250 Ordnance Survey sheet. Image processing by Dr Jon Mills, Department of Geomatics, University of Newcastle-upon-Tyne.

be at least 55% to get the required stereo cover from adjacent photos. Although this is easily planned (equations 10.4 to 10.7), the lack of a reliable interval timer, and an image-download period longer than the specified 3 seconds, resulted in a forward overlap of only 41%, which is not sufficient for heighting measurements.

The important calculations for a line-overlap survey are those which determine scale number (m_b), ground coverage (S), base (b), for a given forward overlap (p), and the time interval between exposures (ΔT) for a given ground speed of the aircraft.

$$m_b = H_g/f \qquad (10.4)$$

where H_g is the height above ground, and f is the focal length of camera lens.

$$S = m_b S' \qquad (10.5)$$

where S is the length of side of ground covered, and S' is the side of image format.

$$b = S(1 - p/100) \qquad (10.6)$$

where b is the base (ground distance between centre of one image and the next), and p is the percentage of forward overlap.

$$\Delta T = b/V_g \qquad (10.7)$$

where ΔT is in seconds, and V_g is the ground speed of the aircraft in metres/second.

In calculating for St Neots, the flight plan anticipated a ground speed of 48 m/s with the Cessna 337 flying at 100 mph and, with $f = 28$ mm, the required flying height was 1120 meters (3600 feet). Unlike a mapping camera, the DCS-200 has a rectangular format of 14 mm × 9.2 mm and so it was decided to place the camera with the longer edge leading (to give better allowance for side-lap errors, when flying adjacent lines). In this way our calculation for S (Eq: 10.5) had to be made using the shorter edge for S', giving a value of 368 metres. Putting this into Eq: 10.6 provided a base value of 147 metres for a nominal 60% overlap, and from here we could calculate the inter-frame interval (ΔT) as: 147/48 = 3 seconds. If this sounds very convenient (since the nominal download time for the DCS-200 is 3 seconds) it must be mentioned that a 1 : 40 000 scale was selected on the basis of the camera's download period.

In the event, we found that the DCS-200 required something like five seconds and was the main reason for not getting the required 60% overlap.

Obviously the only way to get a better overlap would be to (a) use a shorter focal length lens, (b) use two cameras with staggered time-intervals, (c) fly higher (smaller scale), (d) fly over the designated flight-line twice, using staggered start points to gain the required overlap, or (e) fly slower. Since we only had a single calibrated camera, options (a) and (b) were out and, although option (c) was possible, ideally we wanted a scale of 1 : 20 000 so flying higher was not desirable. Whereas option (d) is feasible, and was seriously considered, it meant flying with great accuracy and since we didn't have a drift-mount, wind vectors would have been a problem in keeping a steady overlap. Happily, option (e) was possible by using a microlight.

Fig. 10.7 (a) DCS-200 digital camera situated in a simple aluminium mount fitted to a Thruster microlight aircraft. Note: the 9.3 mm edge of the image frame is leading in line-of-flight. The electrical shutter release cable can be seen in front of the mount, leading to the pilot's position (b) Thruster aircraft showing location of crew (Jon Mills and Ron Graham). Aircraft from Baxby Airsports, North Yorkshire. Camera from University of Newcastle-upon-Tyne.

Flight details: Raskelf mission

Using a Thruster (3-axis) microlight and flying at 30 mph it was possible to provide an appropriate exposure interval (ΔT) equal to 5 seconds when flying at 1550 feet above mean ground level. This time, the DCS-200 was mounted on a semi-rigid aluminium mount suspended behind the pilot, but with the shorter edge leading, as shown in Fig. 10.7.

With this arrangement we photographed the village of Raskelf (North Yorkshire) at a scale of 1 : 17 000 with good overlap (approaching 60%) as shown in Fig. 10.8 (see colour section). Although winds were slight, drift problems were avoided by flying into wind, which also helped to keep the ground speed down without stalling. Two adjacent runs were made with an average of 24% side-lap, and from these a small colour mosaic was made.

With the aid of GPS (global positioning system) ground control, and using the Softcopy Photo Mapper module of the Desktop Mapping System (DMS) by R-Wel Inc., Jon Mills made an excellent 1 : 1250 scale map (complete with heightings) from the 1 : 19 000 scale imagery (see Fig. 10.9).

The principal benchmark for any new air mapping or reconnaissance system is resolution. One of the main questions to be answered from these trials was what we could expect from an off-the-shelf airborne digital camera. According to Eq: 5.3, we can expect an image resolution of 48 μm for the M5 colour chip (21 LP/mm) which, when translated to the ground (via the scale number of 17 000), gives a ground resolution of 82 cm. This means that two similar objects (such as a three-bar target) separated by a distance of 82 cm would be resolved. But it is well known in aerial survey and military reconnaissance that we can detect and recognise ground detail much smaller than that predicted by expressions such as Eq: 5.3.

For one thing, small differences in colour are seen much better than those in monochrome, and lineaments are seen much better than complex subjects. As a consequence, it is now common to quantify spatial resolution in satellite and remote sensing imagery in terms of the ground sampled distance (GSD) which, although lacking scientific rigour, provides a convenient figure of merit and one that seems likely to be adopted for digital aerial imaging.[63] Rather than quantifying resolved *image* detail, GSD is a measure of the resolved *ground* detail, and is calculated from the product of image spread function (ISF) and scale number, as:

$$GSD = (ISF)m_b \qquad (10.8)$$

Applying Eq: 10.8 to the DCS-200 imagery under discussion we can, with some reservations,[66] replace the ISF with pixel size, to give a fair approximation as:

$$GSD \approx (Px)m_b \qquad (10.9)$$

which results in a GSD of 9.2 μm × 17 000 ≈ 16 cm.

It was possible to check this value from the colour images shown in Fig. 10.8, where a broken barn roof shows a 15 cm beam, clearly resolved in the original inkjet print. This is a very satisfactory result and one that can be expected to prevail for all cameras using the M5 chip, such as the DCS-410 and DCS-420.

It's interesting to note that Kodak now market a special version of the DCS-420, which comes complete with a GPS interface and is known as the DCS-420 GPS camera. Digital imagery and GPS data can be captured in tandem, making this camera an ideal device for many SFAP applications including map intensification, geographic information systems (GIS), digital orthophotography and remote sensing.

Airborne remote sensing with digital cameras

With a spectral sensitivity equal to that of silver halide materials (see Fig. 5.4), CCD cameras are particularly well suited to the role of remote sensing since much

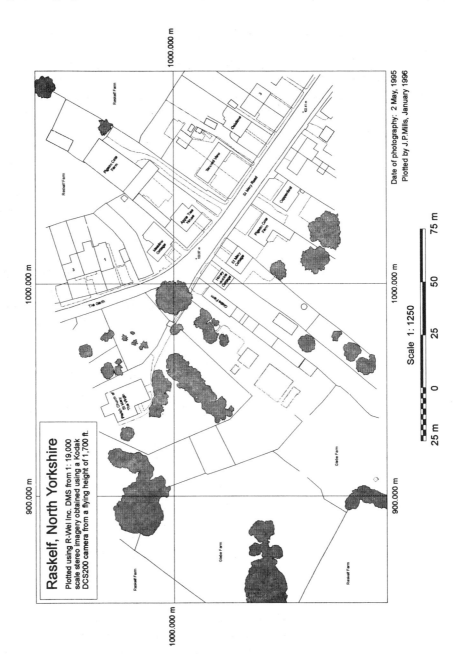

Fig. 10.9 Map of Raskelf village plotted from images shown in Fig. 10.8. Photogrammetry undertaken with Softcopy Photo Mapper module of Desktop Mapping System (R-Wel Inc). Map scale 1:1250. Mapping accuracy (against GPS ground control) gives RMS errors as: 0.1 m in x and y (0.7 px) and 0.24 m in z (1.5 px). Plotted by Dr Jon Mills, Department of Geomatics, University of Newcastle-upon-Tyne.

of this work is done over relatively small areas, and images can be accessed very   <u>169</u>
swiftly.

Whereas large area remote sensing is adequately covered by satellite imagery
(and has been since 1972 with the launch of LANDSAT 1), with continuing cover
from LANDSAT's 4 and 5, plus the 10 metre resolution SPOT imagery, it is often
necessary to supplement satellite data with airborne remote sensing in order to
gain better detail for a particular surveillance.

The basic principle behind remote sensing imagery is to sample specific terrain features and crops with various bands of EMR. Using various types of film
(colour, infrared, panchromatic and false-colour infrared) in conjunction with nar-
row-band filters and an array of cameras, multispectral photography (MSP) provides a valuable remote sensing technique, particularly when applied in a multi-
temporal mode.[67][68]

For most purposes a panchromatic film with a Kodak narrow-cut red no. 29
red filter, and monochrome infrared film with a no. 87 infrared filter will suffice.
Analysis is mainly a question of comparision between the red and infrared records:
where infrared is strongly absorbed by moisture, and highly reflected by healthy
organic matter (chlorophyll), the red record can then be used as a control. I found
this simple two-channel technique to be both economic and satisfactory in studies such as disease in wheat crops.[67]

Multispectral photography with DCS-420 cameras

The Remote Sensing and Geographic Information Systems (RSGIS) Unit, Bath
College of Higher Education, is a small but very experienced group who use digital MSP techniques both abroad and within the UK. Headed by Dr Rick Curr, the
RSGIS Unit employs two monochrome DCS-420 cameras and a DCS-420 CIR
(colour infrared) model for research and development in this area. Most of the
imagery is processed in Photoshop from images stored in PCMCIA (Type III) cards,
where MSP images are merged to produce false-colour products and mosaics.

The RSGIS camera assembly was put together by Alex Koh, and incorporates
a drift mount with timer for sequenced line-overlap surveys. The two monochrome
DCS-420s are ganged together to provide red and infrared records via narrow-cut
(10 nm) interference filters. One of the advantages of CCD sensors is their sensitivity, which allows the use of narrow-cut filters without under-exposure.

A typical MSP composite image is shown in Fig. 10.10 (see colour section); it
is of a farm in the alluvial plain west of Lake Baringo, Kenya. This MSP composite
used three DCS-420 mono-cameras, one with an infrared filter (in red display),
and the two red filtered images in green and blue display. Image processing and
the merging of all three images was done in Photoshop, and printed with a Kodak
dye-sublimation printer. Analysis of these images gives considerable information
about river drainage and the effects of overgrazing, which have resulted in sparse
vegetation cover of acacia trees and poor grasses. It was also interesting to note
that RSGIS quote a GSD of 15 cm!

The Kodak DCS-420 CIR camera

A recent acquisition by the RSGIS Unit is the DCS-420 CIR (colour infrared) camera. Early trials with this device show great promise, as images can be processed much faster than with the mono-camera composites. A typical example from this camera is the large scale aerial photograph of a riverside scene shown in Fig. 10.11 (see colour section).

The DCS-420 CIR records spectral data in the green, red and near infrared simply by changing from the normal (interpolated) colour filters found in the conventional model to a composite which includes an infrared filter, it being remembered that the spectral response of the M5 chip extends to 1000 nm! The camera also comes with a tri-port adaptor for plugging in the shutter cable release and also a GPS receiver.

The DCS-420 CIR camera is an interesting device, and will certainly be of interest to many who require a reliable MSP system that can be processed quickly, even in flight! The development of this camera is said to have started at the suggestion of the US Forest Service, who requested Kodak to produce a digital equivalent to the well-known false-colour infrared film they market. Since then it has been used for numerous forestry and riparian projects, as well as for applications more related to law enforcement than earth sciences. This point is made clear by Fig. 10.12 (see colour section), where a helicopter-borne DCS-420 CIR has been used to record an illegal plot of cannabis hidden within a forest. The bright red cluster of plants near the centre of Fig. 10.12 is easily detected.

The Kodak DCS-420 C/CIR camera

Currently the best digital camera available for mapping and remote sensing is the DCS-460 C/CIR model. The C stands for colour and CIR for the integrated colour infrared option. This camera is specially designed for Kodak's Aerial Systems division and can be purchased only against a special order.

It has a 27.6 mm × 18.4 mm sized chip and this larger format covers a greater footprint than the 420 series, given the same 28 mm lens and flying height. Although image capture is rather slow (one frame per 12 seconds) this period can be reduced if the best quality PCMCIA card is used. The DCS-460 C/CIR has only one exposure-speed rating and that is 80 ISO.

There is no doubt that the DCS-460 C/CIR can provide image quality equal to that of many colour films and although the M6 chip (Kodak Sensor KAF 6301) has the same 9 µm square pixels as the M5 used in the 420 series, the improved CFA interpolation used in the 460 C/CIR facilitates much higher image resolution.

Mapping and remote sensing with the DCS-460 C/CIR camera

In a recent air survey project I was privileged to join a highly experienced group of mapping and remote sensing experts who, through the courtesy of Kodak Ltd. UK (Trevor Miller), were able to use the DCS-460 C/CIR for a number of airborne trials. In this project the group used a Thruster Microlight aircraft at a nominal ground speed of 40 mph to map the north Yorkshire village of Husthwaite at a scale of 1 : 25 000 using the DCS-460 in its conventional colour (C) mode, and take spot photographs of selected sites on the north Yorkshire moors, with the camera in its false colour infrared (CIR) mode for the purpose of remote sensing.

Mapping at 1 : 25 000 with the DCS-460 C (ISO 80)

The camera exposure for the mision was 1/500th at *f*/4 and the 28 mm lens was taped to its infinity setting before fitting to the camera mounting (the same mounting as for the Raskelf mission). The flight plan called for a flying height of 2600 feet above mean ground level and, as before, the aircraft wss flown into the wind to avoid problems of drift. The three adjacent flight lines required accurate navigation to afford a 30% lateral overlap of photographs and so a GPS unit with pre-prepared way-points and camera start/stops entered for each flight line was strapped to the pilot's knee. Forward overlap of each photo was planned to be around 70% and the camera intervalometer was set to provide a fresh photograph every 12 seconds (equal to the minimum download period for each image).

For the first trial I took the role of pilot/camera operator in the hope that one person could keep altitude, track and ground speed in order to establish the wind vector and indicated air-speed for immediate re-flights. In addiion I operated the camera Intervalometer (an excellent device specially made by Dr Alex Koh of the RSGIS Unit, Bath Spa University College). After flying a single test line, the aircraft was landed only to find that no photographs had been taken. It was soon established that the fault was due to vibration and the camera's PCMCIA card did not like it! Nevertheless, this first flight was by nature a test to determine the wind vector and air speed for the set ground speed of 40 mph (set by the GPS). It also showed that single crew operation was possible, provided we could get around the problem of camera vibration. A second flight with a more flexible mount arrangement was undertaken by Dr Koh who concentrated on the camera and GPS (with fresh way-points arranged according to the newly found wind vector) and the rest was left to the pilot who now flew on a heading of 100° magnetic to bring the aircraft into the wind.

Once again the camera refused to cooperate. On the third flight the camera operator held the DCS-460 out of the side of the open cockpit. Since this meant that the operator (Dr Jon Mills, Department of Geomatics, University of Newcastle-upon-Tyne) would need to concentrate upon holding the camera vertical and steady, the GPS was now transferred back to the pilot. All three flight lines were then flown with great success, as was shown on the computer as soon as the images were uploaded after the flight. A typical image of the village (printed on a Kodak dye-sublimation printer) is shown in Fig. 10.13 (see colour section).

Remote sensing with the DCS-460 in CIR mode

Once we had eliminated the vibration problems (if only temporarily) we flew a remote sensing mission, leaving the question of an improved camera mount until a later date. Dr Fiona Strawbridge (RSGIS Unit, Bath Spa University College) now took the camera work and flew over the north Yorkshire moors at 2300 feet. The camera was set in CIR mode (by placing a Kodak filter in front of the 28 mm lens) and the exposure was 1/250th second at *f*/5.6 (including the filter factor of 1.7). An excellent false colour infrared image of Rievaulx Abbey (Fig. 10.14; see colour section) was obtained, showing the potential of this camera for serious remote sensing applications.

172 *DCS-460 C/CIR camera calibration*

All air cameras used for photogrammetry must be calibrated. This was done by Dr Mills the following day. Using a special target projected onto a laboratory wall, 16 images from various camera stations were taken and then uploaded into the EOS Systems Photomodeler software for automatic camera calibration.

After camera calibration, the images were subjected to further analysis using softcopy photogrammetry software such as R-WEL DMS and WuDAMS VirtuoZo, both of which were run on a Silicon Graphics O2 R5000 workstation equipped with 64 Mb RAM and 13 Gb of hard disk space. Demonstrations of the VirtuoZo system were provided by Jon Mills and stereo pairs of the images shown in Fig. 10.13 and Fig. 10.14 were displayed to ilustrate how quickly these systems can produce heighting and planimetric data suitable for mapping using either 'crystal eye' shuttered glasses (VirtuoZo) or anaglyph spectacles (R-WEL DMS) to view the 3-D image on computer monitor.

10.8 Applications in Astronomy

Perhaps astronomy should have been mentioned first in this list of applications, since it was here that CCD imagers were first put to serious use in the mid-1970s. There are few keen amateur astronomers today who haven't put a CCD camera at the end of their telescope (particularly since these can now be purchased for something like £300), and the use of CCD cameras in professional astronomy is universal. Many of these CCD cameras have exceptional sensitivity, and can record the image of a nebula or galaxy as much as 30 times faster than photographic film.

CCDs are now the most widely used optical sensor at all major astronomical observatories and, as low-light-level detectors, they are both sensitive and stable with signal sensitivities almost at the single electron level. The CCD is now an essential component of modern astronomical instrumentation, as may be appreciated when one recalls that the Hubble Space Telescope uses CCDs to achieve high-resolution images from space. Indeed, one of the most remarkable properties of the CCD camera is its ability to penetrate into deep space and turn the telescope into a virtual time machine, as witnessed by CCD images such as those of *Abell 2065 in Corona Borealis*, where a cluster of galaxies are so remote their light takes over a billion (10^9) years to reach the camera.[69]

In recent years we have seen the arrival of affordable astro-CCD cameras and sophisticated computer-driven telescopes, and what was too expensive for the keen amateur astronomer only a few years ago is now within the financial means of many, although this still remains a highly expensive hobby!

Like the professionals, many amateurs have now replaced their film cameras with CCD imagers, mainly because they don't have to wait until the film is developed, but also because CCD offers something like the equivalent of 20 000 ISO speed, and its linear response allows accurate luminance measurements to be evaluated. Yet another advantage with CCD sensors is their lack of reciprocity failure, a problem common to photographic film, particularly in astronomy where long time exposures are necessary for recording faint stellar images.

A camera exposure of 1/50 second at f/11 provides the same exposure as 1/100 second at f/8 and, similarly, 1/30 sec at f/11 should give the same exposure as 1/1000 sec at f/2. This follows the so-called *reciprocity law,* which states that the product of radiation intensity (I), and exposure time (t), equals a constant.[70] This can be formally stated as:

$$It = \text{const.} \qquad (10.10)$$

But photographic materials are well known to deviate from this law, particularly colour films, either when exposure times are too short (<0.001 second), or too long (>30 seconds), with reciprocity limits depending on the type of film employed.[71][72] Fortunately CCD sensors obey the law pretty well in this respect.

A number of special CCD imagers are now available for astronomy. Some are designed for star tracking and others for recording; the latter are usually cooled to provide negligible dark current and low noise. It is important to remember that, in astronomy, exposures are usually counted in minutes or hours, and so system noise (dark current) has to be removed as much as possible.

Although modern telescopes can be connected to a computer that will find a given star on command, astrophotography requires accurate tracking as the earth moves during exposure. This can be done by following a reference star (in a field offset from the main field of interest) with a 'guidescope', and a drive corrector to keep this star centred while the telescope tracks on its equatorial mount.

For professional work accurate tracking can be accomplished with a CCD controller using fast framing rates, where the reference star is image-processed to allow the telescope to be controlled automatically over long exposure periods.[73]

AstroCam Ltd (a company specialising in astronomical cameras: see Appendix C) offer a large range of cooled CCD imagers which, although originally designed to meet the stringent requirements of astronomers recording faint stars and galaxies, are now being used for other applications in science.

Since cooled CCD systems enable extremely small differences of light intensity to be detected, details of very low contrast phenomena can be studied against much brighter backgrounds, without saturation of the higher intensity areas. As a consequence, cooled CCD cameras far surpass most other imaging systems in their ability to detect low contrast images with high sensitivity and wide dynamic range.

AstroCam produce a family of cooled CCD cameras in their Capella and Antares range of imagers which, apart from all the traditional benifits of cooled CCD systems, offer high-speed readout capabilities at very low noise levels. The Capella and Antares products differ mainly with respect to the read-out rates at which they operate, with the Capella range being the faster system.

Three models in the Capella family are available, providing a choice of grey-level resolution and speed:

- the basic Capella system provides a 12 bit resolution (4096 grey levels) at pixel rates from 500 KHz to 8 MHz,
- Capella Beta gives 14 bit digitisation (16 384 grey levels) at up to 2 MHz,
- Capella Beta+ gives 14 bit digitisation up to 5 MHz.

Typically, each Capella system comprises three basic components: a cooled CCD camera head, an electronics unit, and Imager 2 camera control with software. Two types of cooled head are available: air cooled or liquid cooled. The air cooled system employs thermoelectric (Peltier) primary cooling with air cooled heat exchangers, and the liquid cooled system is the same, except that it uses water cooled heat exchangers.

Peltier cooled camera heads consist of a number of junctions between two dissimilar materials so that, when a current is passed in the correct direction through these junctions, localised cooling occurs. This has the effect of cooling the CCD imager mounted within the sealed cooling compartment.

It is common practice to cool astro-CCD imagers in order to reduce the amount of thermally generated dark current as explained in Chapter 4 and quantified by Eq: 4.10. Accumulation of dark current severely limits the performance of uncooled systems but, by lowering the temperature of the sensor, dark current is reduced by a factor of about 10 for every 20 °C drop in CCD temperature. However, cooling below −140 °C gives no further advantage since at these temperatures CCDs no longer function properly.

The AstroCam TE3/A camera head incorporates a Peltier/Air cooling system, whereas the TE3/W incorporates a Peltier/Liquid system, both of which offer a limiting luminance sensitivity of 10^{-9} lux. Both of these systems can be attached to either Pentax or Nikon cameras, by either screw or bayonet mounts.[74]

For the ultimate in sensitivity and dynamic range, a liquid-nitrogen cooled CCD head is the best answer. With these systems dark current can be reduced to less than one electron per pixel per hour by cooling to approximately −140 °C, and dynamic range can be extended to $10^5 : 1$ within a single exposure. The AstroCam Compact LN/C head can meet these specifications and also provide a limiting luminance sensitivity as low as 10^{-11} lux. Liquid-nitrogen cooled heads contain the imager within a vacuum sealed housing to minimise heat loss, with the CCD chip connected by a *cold finger* to a container filled with liquid nitrogen. The user can then select and stabilise the operating temperature within the range −60 °C to −140 °C.

CCDs for astronomy

A good variety of CCDs is available for astronomical work, and can be selected according to the user's requirements. Well known suppliers are AstroCam,[75] Hamamatsu,[76] SBIG,[77] Celestron[78] and Starlight Xpress,[79] all of which supply cooled imaging units and guidance systems.

The Santa Barbara Imaging Group (SBIG) have combined imaging and auto-guidance in their ST-7 and ST-8 self-guiding imaging cameras that contain two CCD detectors: one for guiding, the other for collecting the image. This allows the imaging CCD to integrate while the PC uses the guiding CCD to correct the telescope. Both these models use a Kodak CCD detector with 9 μm square pixels, and carefully guided exposures of one hour are possible, enabling a standard Celstron C-8 telescope to capture 19th magnitude stars.* Specifications for these models are shown in Table: 10.2.

* Apparent stellar magnitudes are based on an empirical system where a magnitude of six is just visible to the naked eye. Stars that are below the visible threshold
have a magnitude greater than six. This system was evolved many years ago (2nd
century BC) when stars were categorised with brightnesses on a scale from 1 to
100, in six brightness groups. In this logarithmic system, a 2nd magnitude star
such as the North Star (Polaris) is 2.51 times fainter than a 1st magnitude star,
and so on. Stars brighter than zero magnitude (Vega), have a negative value,
such as Sirius (−1.42) the brightest star in the sky.

Table. 10.2

	SBIG Model ST-7	SBIG Model ST-8
Resolution	765 × 510 pixels	1534 × 1020 pixels
Total pixels	390 0001	1,500,000
CCD area	6.9 × 4.6 mm	13.8 × 9.2 mm
Celestron C-8 f.o.v	12 × 8 arc minutes	24 × 16 arc minutes
Software	Windows and MSDOS	Windows and MSDOS
Colour filter wheel	CFW-8	CFW-8

AstroCam supply a range of CCDs with a great variety of pixel numbers, pixel
sizes and sensitivities. Standard CCDs all show similar spectral sensitivities between 400 nm and 1000 nm. However, special techniques can be used to increase the spectral sensitivity.

Thinned CCDs

Thinned CCDs are treated so that the side away from the electrodes is mechani-
cally and chemically etched to an overall thickness of only 10–15 µm. The device
is then mounted so that incident radiation falls on the rear surface of the CCD,
and doesn't have to pass through the covering electrodes (as with the configuration shown in Fig. 4.8). As a consequence blue-wavelength sensitivity is enhanced,
and sensitivity to other wavelengths improved. Thinned CCDs may also be coated
with AstroCam's Astrochrome 90, which further enhances ultra-violet sensitivity
down to 180 nm or, without the standard fused silica window, down to 90 nm!
Astrochrome 90 is available for all types of CCD.

There are a good number of CCD manufacturers and these are heavily represented in astronomy where it can be argued the CCD has had the greatest impact
in terms of opening up new research possibilities. Characteristics of some of these
CCDs are listed in Table 10.3.

Table 10.3

CCD	CCD15-11[a]	KAF - 1600	CCD 442
Manufacturer	EEV	Kodak	Loral
Pixel format ($H \times V$)	256 × 1024	1536 × 1024	2048 × 2048
Sensitive area (mm)	6.9 × 27.6	13.8 × 9.2	30 × 30
Pixel Size (µm)	27 × 27	9 × 9	15 × 15
Typical full well capacity (electrons)	600 000	85 000	400 000
Typical read noise (electrons) at 40 kHz	4	8	6
Typical dark signal (e⁻/px /s)	0.03 - 0.3	0.05	10[b]

[a] Standard or thinned. [b] Dark signals will be reduced when using thermoelectric cooled heads.

CCD astronomy in practice

The CCD is clearly an essential component of modern astronomical instrumentation, as proved by both professional and amateur alike. In the professional theatre we have the Hubble Space Telescope using CCDs to achieve high resolution from space, and ground-based astronomers developing techniques of 'adaptive optics' whereby distortions introduced by the atmosphere can be corrected in certain instances to allow a dramatic increase in image sharpness.[79]

A good example of what can be done with modern optical techniques is the new Cambridge Optical Aperture Synthesis Telescope (COAST), which is designed to generate diffraction limited images with a resolution as good as one milliarc second. Consisting of four telescopes on separate foundations, COAST feeds beams from the same object to a central laboratory where the beams are combined.[80]

For the four beams to interfere with optimum fringe visibility each telescope must be accurately and continually aligned to remove apparent first-order shift of the images caused by the atmosphere. These adjustments must be made at rates in excess of 100 Hz, and are realised by using a fast detector system namely the EEV CCD15-11 (EEV Ltd., Chelmsford, UK).

A good example of COAST imagery can be seen in Fig. 10.15 (see colour section) which shows successive CCD records of the binary star Capella. An interesting subject, and one of the brightest stars visible (apparent magnitude 0.08), Capella is nearly 50 light years away and can be found in the constellation of Auriga (RA 5 h 16.6', dec +46° 00'). In Fig. 10.15, Capella's two resolved bodies (separated by 55 milliarc seconds) are shown rotating around each other in successive exposures.

The COAST system is obviously very professional and also very expensive, but serious work continues to be done by amateurs using relatively inexpensive equipment. Many examples are shown regularly in magazines such as *Astronomy Now*, where numerous CCD images are printed with full details. Typical examples include deep-sky subjects such as galaxies, which are regularly exposed by amateur

astronomers using off-the-shelf equipment such as the Starlight Xpress SXL8 CCD
camera.

The Starlight Xpress SXL8 is a frame transfer CCD imager with a 7.7 mm^2 sensitive area providing an array of 512 × 512 pixels, each 15 μm^2. This camera-head can be supplied in either Standard Grade (with a few minor blemishes) or Super Grade which is essentially perfect. However, published results taken with the Standard Grade imager show that this low-cost version (£790) is suitable for most workers. Images of planetary nebula, such as the Dumbell (M27), are easily recorded using a 160 second exposure with an f/4.3, 330 mm telescope. Similarly, it has been shown that, with the same system, very faint subjects like the Hercules globular cluster (M13) can be successfully recorded with only an 80 second exposure. Some idea of the light grasp involved can be appreciated when one considers that M13 is at the limit of naked eye visibility (with an apparent magnitude of 5.9), and is only obvious on a clear night. Found in the northern hemisphere, M13 is approximately 17 arc minutes in diameter and 23 000 light years away.

10.9 Scientific Laboratory Applications of CCD Imagers

Just as photography has long been an indispensable tool of science, so we find digital cameras are now taking over from film in a number of areas. This isn't to say that film has been discarded – far from it – but CCD imagers fit nicely into a number of high-tech systems now being introduced into modern laboratories, particularly where high resolution is not of paramount importance.

Among a variety of laboratory applications, the CCD camera can be found as an integral part of a number of screened-image systems. The camera then records the screen display and sends it direct to computer store, from where it can be processed with various types of software.

Hamamatsu, AstroCam and Kodak are among many firms that supply scientific CCD cameras for this expanding market. From Hamamatsu there is the Cooled C4880 series of cameras which couple high sensitivity with low noise and high dynamic range. A signal-to-noise ratio of 60 dB is claimed for this camera, with over 20 different models within the series. From Kodak there is the Megaplus Camera Model 1.4, which has been specially developed for scientific image capture, including time-lapse photography, machine vision and diagnostic imaging. Full details on all these cameras can be obtained from the suppliers listed in Appendix C.

X-Ray recording

Typical X-ray screen applications include the recording of X-ray diffraction images, formed from an X-ray image intensifier (with beryllium window); X-ray fluoroscopy (via an X-ray scintillator screen); Neutron radiography (where the neutron image is made visible by a neutron scintillator screen); and X-ray film imaging (simply recording conventional X-rays made on film). With all these applications a CCD imager has the distinct advantage of both linearity and wide dynamic range, which are essential attributes for recording images that can host a density range (ΔD) as high as 5 or more.

Conversion from X-rays to visual photons is accomplished by scintillation screens, which commonly are made of zinc cadmium sulphide, or gadolinium oxisulphide, which are then imaged by a cooled CCD head fitted with fast (f/1.0) lenses.[81]

Since CCDs are sensitive to X-radiation it is also possible to employ CCD cameras for direct X-ray recording. In this case the imager has a Be (beryllium) window, and images in soft X-ray regions (100 eV and higher) can easily be acquired. In addition, X-ray energy can be determined by measuring the charge generated by a single quantum of X-radiation.

Spectrography

Spectrography embraces most sciences and is routine procedure in many laboratories. The CCD camera is ideal for recording spectrographs since it offers a full spectral range, high sensitivity and linearity. In addition, the camera system is directly coupled to computer and software for data storage and analysis.

AstroCam supply a number of cameras and CCD chips for this purpose, employing their usual range of Capella and Antares systems. In addition they also market a specialist system dedicated to spectrography, known as the Prisma, which comes with a wide range of cooling options and choice of CCD chips. Prisma also has its own software (PrismaSoft) which operates in Windows 95 and offers complete spectral analysis and databasing functions.

For high-speed spectroscopy *frame transfer* chips are recommended (see Fig. 4.11) because no mechanical shutter is required, and the time needed to operate a mechanical shutter can easily limit fast frame rates. Small shutters, as used in the AstroCam TE3 heads, cannot be used for exposures smaller than 10 ms, whereas frame transfer CCDs can always be gathering light during the period when the stored charges are read out. However, with the Capella family of AstroCam imagers only the EEV CCD37 is available in frame transfer mode; it can be operated with one microsecond parallel transfer times. With a *fast read* Capella head, the system is capable of recording up to 127 transient spectroscopic events (images) at intervals of 8 µs, using the EEV CCD37 chip.

Perhaps one of the most significant advances in CCD spectroscopy is due to the researches of Professor David Batchelder (Leeds University), who constructed a CCD system for Raman spectroscopy in the early 1990s. In the past a typical Raman spectrum (due to light being scattered by vibration of atoms in a sample) would take several hours to obtain, but with new optical filters, improved optical design, and CCD detectors, measurements take only seconds for most semiconductor and polymer applications.[82]

Optical transmission microscopy

Transmission microscopy covers traditional options such as brightfield, darkfield, phase contrast, interference contrast, and fluorescent techniques. But apart from brightfield illumination, all these methods involve varying degrees of light loss which, at high magnifications, can make film recording very difficult. A common problem with biological specimens is their inherent low contrast and, although counter-staining can produce artificial enhancement, not all specimens can be treated in this fashion, which means that special low-light options have to be employed.

The introduction of cooled high-resolution CCD cameras has improved matters considerably. First of all, their greater sensitivity allows low-light-level imagery to be recorded with ease, and secondly it is possible to enhance contrast either by software or, with cameras like those in the Hamamatsu C2400 series,[83] within the circuitry of the Argus-20 Image Processor.[84]

These CCD camera features provide considerable advantage over film, and make it possible to obtain high-quality images from specimens so low in contrast that they were previously unobservable. This is particularly the case with differential interference contrast microscopy, as shown in Fig. 10.16, and also with fluorescence microscopy.

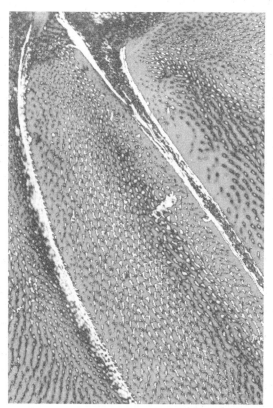

Fig. 10.16 Low-contrast microscopic subject (fly's wing), imaged by differential interference microscopy, and recorded with a scientific CCD camera. Image courtesy of AstroCam Ltd, Cambridge Science Park.

Transmission electron microscopy

Both Hamamatsu and AstroCam provide cooled CCD systems for transmission electron microscopy (TEM), both of which employ standard CCD cameras to capture a TEM image displayed on the instrument's scintillation (conversion) screen. The conversion screen is situated inside the vacuum chamber of the TEM so that image electrons can be converted to photons, which are then recorded by the CCD camera.

The conversion screen is a single thin sheet (0.5 mm thick) of yttrium aluminium garnet (YAG), and the CCD head is usually fitted with an $f/1.0$ lens focused to the front surface of the YAG screen.

10.10 Freelance Photography

Finally, among literally hundreds of applications one could mention, it seems appropriate to end this chapter with what must be one of the most well known, and perhaps exciting areas of imaging: that of the freelance photographer. It is particularly important given the alarming prediction made at the 1996 Photokina (Köln) exhibition that, by 1998, half of the freelance photographers would be out of work as a result of digital technology!

In an interesting article by Martin Evening in *Image* (the magazine of the Association of Photographers), the writer says that, in the future, it may become harder to define the difference between a photographer and an illustrator.[85] And that photographers will, out of necessity, have to invest in digital equipment: digital capture, modem/ISDN connections, etc.

As Martin Evening sums up so elegantly, when speaking on behalf of freelance workers: 'Digital technology has the potential to speed up the production process; time and money can be saved by taking full advantage of electronic communications. As with the cinema industry, it is not going to be the photographers who decide whether digital technology has a future or not – it will be the people buying our services.'

10.11 Conclusions

Chapter 10 illustrates a representative sample of digital imaging applications and, although most of the emphasis has been devoted to scientific and technical work, this was more to emphasise potential and diversity rather than anything else.

For professional photographers the image is the thing! And in their highly subjective business, artistry and originality are essential qualities, regardless of the medium employed. At a price, it seems that digital systems are now being accepted for quality work in product photography, portraiture, fashion and advertising. But success in this work goes beyond the technical and, provided that digital cameras can equal the photographic quality expected by their clients, the rest stands or falls on pure commercial grounds.

On the other hand, for the casual user, amateur, desk-top publisher, technologist or scientist, digital systems (and associated software) offer convenience, speed,

economy and technical expertise handed on a plate! With a little perseverance
anyone can master both computer and software, and produce images of a standard otherwise impossible to achieve outside an extensive course in photography.

There can be no doubt that CCD imagers are here to stay! And although
sensor technology may shift from CCD to complementary metal oxide semiconductor (CMOS) in the near future, we can expect further innovations and more
use of these cameras as they increase in quality and decrease in cost. Certainly we
can look forward to some drastic price cutting as market competition increases;
and as cameras, computers and software approach more attractive levels, so will
digital imagery become as normal as photography was yesterday!

Appendix A Binary and ASCII Codes

Binary code

Like decimal notation, the binary system of numbering is a positional notation, where the value of a binary number depends not only on the bits it contains, but also teir position in the number. The positional value increases from right to left by powers of 2, as the following list makes clear.

Decimal No.	Powers of 2	Binary No.
0	(0×2^0)	0000
1	(1×2^0)	0001
2	(1×2^1)	0010
3	$(1 \times 2^1) + (1 \times 2^0)$	0011
4	(1×2^2)	0100
5	$(1 \times 2^2) + (0 \times 2^1) + (1 \times 2^0)$	0101
6	$(1 \times 2^2) + (1 \times 2^1) + (0 \times 2^0)$	0110
7	$(1 \times 2^2) + (1 \times 2^1) + (1 \times 2^0)$	0111
8	(1×2^3)	1000
9	$(1 \times 2^3) + (0 \times 2^2) + (0 \times 2^1) + (1 \times 2^0)$	1001
10	$(1 \times 2^3) + (0 \times 2^2) + (1 \times 2^1) + (0 \times 2^0)$	1010
11	$(1 \times 2^3) + (0 \times 2^2) + (1 \times 2^1) + (1 \times 2^0)$	1011
12	$(1 \times 2^3) + (1 \times 2^2) + (0 \times 2^1) + (0 \times 2^0)$	1100
15	$(1 \times 2^3) + (1 \times 2^2) + (1 \times 2^1) + (1 \times 2^0)$	1111
16	(1×2^4)	10000
20	$(1 \times 2^4) + (0 \times 2^3) + (1 \times 2^2) + (0 \times 2^1) + (0 \times 2^0)$	10100
32	(1×2^5)	100000
100	$(1 \times 2^6) + (1 \times 2^5) + (0 \times 2^4) + (0 \times 2^3) + (1 \times 2^2) + (0 \times 2^1) + (0 \times 2^0)$	1100100

In order to convert from binary to decimal we multiply each bit in the binary number by the power of 2 with the least significant bit (on extreme right) having the positional value of 2^0, then add them all together. In the above examples (see under power of 2) we can see that the coefficient of each term is either a one or a zero and it is the coefficents that make up the binary number. Thus, for decimal 20, we add (from the right) as: $0 + 0 + (1 \times 2^2) + 0 + (1 \times 2^4)$ which sums to $4 + 16 = 20$.

184 ASCII Code

Binary digits (bits) can also be used to represent letters of the alphabet, numbers and punctuation marks. One such 7 bit code is the ASCII (American Standard Code for Information Interchange) which is used extensively in small computer systems to translate from the keyboard chracters to computer language. Since this code represents letters as well as numbers it is known as an *alphanumeric code*.

Character	ASCII	Character	ASCII
0	0110000	A	1000001
1	0110001	B	1000010
2	0110010	C	1000011
3	0110011	D	1000100
4	0110100	E	1000101
5	0110101	F	1000110
6	0110110	G	1000111
7	0110111	H	1001000
8	0111000	I	1001001
9	0111001	J	1001010
		K	1001011
		L	1001100
		M	1001101
		N	1001110
		O	1001111
		P	1010000
		Q	1010001
		R	1010010
		S	1010011
		T	1010100
		U	1010101
		V	1010110
		W	1010111
		X	1011000
		Y	1011001
		Z	1011010

Appendix B Fundamental Constants and Conversion of Units

Fundamental Constants

Constant	Symbol	Value
Velocity of light	c	$2.999\,925 \times 10^8$ m s^{-1}
Boltzmann constant	k	$1.380\,622 \times 10^{-23}$ JK^{-1}
Charge of electron	e	$1.602\,191\,7 \times 10^{-19}$ C
Rest mass of electron	m_e	$9.109\,5 \times 10^{-31}$ kg
Permittivity of free space	ε_0	$8.854\,185\,3 \times 10^{-12}$ Mm^{-1}
Planck constant	h	$6.626\,196 \times 10^{-34}$ Js
Mechanical equivalent of light	M	1.47 mW Lm^{-1}

Conversion Factors

Length	m	cm	mm	μm	nm	inch	feet
1 metre	1	100	100	10^6	10^9	39.3701	3.280 84

Length	km	mile	nautical mile
1 km	1	0.621 371	0.539 957
1 mile	1.609 34	1	0.868 976
1 naut. mile	1.852	1.150 78	1

Velocity	ms^{-1}	kmh^{-1}	mph
1 metre per second	1	3.6	2.236 94
1 km per hour	0.277 78	1	0.621 371
1 mph	0.44704	1.609 344	1

Appendix C Manufacturers and Agents, Institutions and Publications

Manufacturers and Agents

Adobe Systems (UK) Ltd, Hampshire House, Wade Road, Basingstoke, Hants RG24 8PL. Tel: (01256) 463344. Fax: (01256) 847163

Agfa-Gevaert Ltd, 27 Great West Road, Brentford, Middx TW8 9AX. Tel: (0181) 231420. Fax: (0181) 231457.

Apple Computer (UK) Ltd, 6 Roundwood Avenue, Stockley Park, Uxbridge UB11 1BB. FreePhone: (0800) 127753.

Arc/Info, GIS Consultants, ESRI (UK), 23 Woodford Road, Watford WD1 1PB. Tel: (01923) 210450.

AstroCam Ltd, Innovation Centre, Cambridge Science Park, Milton Road, Cambridge CB4 4GS. Tel: (01223) 420705. Fax: (01223) 423021.

Canon (UK) Ltd, Brent Trading Centre, North Circular Road, London NW10 0JF. Tel: (0181) 459 1266. Fax: (0181) 459 4202.

Comstock (Stock Photography), 28 Chelsea Wharf, 15 Lots Road, London SW10 0YY. Tel: (0171) 351 4448. Fax: (0171) 352 8414.

Digital Darkroom, West Park, Silsoe, Bedfordshire. Tel/Fax: (01525) 862456. E-mail: Digital Darkroom@.MSN.COM.

Fuji Photo Film (UK) Ltd, Fuji Film House, 125 Finchley Road, London NW3 6JH. Tel: (0181) 367 3560. Fax: (0181)367 6384.

Hamamatsu Photonics (UK) Ltd, Lough Point, 2 Gladbeck Way, Windmill Hill, Enfield EN2 7JA. Tel: (0181-367 3560. Fax: (0181) 367 6384.

Hewlett Packard, Cain Road, Bracknell, Berkshire RG12 1HN. Tel: (01344) 369222.

Kodak Ltd, Digital and Applied Imaging, PO Box 66, Station Road, Hemel Hempstead, Herts HP1 1JU. Tel: (01442) 845228. Fax: (01442) 845113.

Minolta (UK) Ltd, Rooksley Park, Precedent Drive, Rooksley, Milton Keynes MK13 8HF. Tel: (01908) 200400. Fax: (01908) 200391.

Nikon (UK) Ltd, Nikon House, 380 Richmond Road, Kingston-upon-Thames, Surrey KT2 5PR. Tel: (0181) 541 4440. Fax: (0181) 541 4584.

Photoair Software, Photoair House, 191a Main Street, Yaxley, Peterborough, PE7 3LD. Tel: (01733) 241850. Fax: (01733) 242964.

Pro Digital Imaging, South Point, South Accommodation Road, Leeds LS10 1PP. Tel: (0113) 245 4848. Fax: (0113) 4848.

Sony, Brian Reece Scientific Ltd, 12 West Mills, Newbury, Berkshire RG14 5HG. Tel: (01653) 32827. Fax: (01635) 34542.

Synoptics Ltd, 271 Cambridge Science Park, Milton Road, Cambridge CB4 4WE. Tel: (01223) 423223. Fax: (01223) 4200020.

188 Vision Corporation Ltd, Talmin House, Hogwood Business Park, Ivanhoe Road, Wokingham, Berks RG11 4QQ. Tel: (01734) 730911. Fax: (01734) 730910.

Institutions

Bath Spa University College (RSGIS Unit), Newton Park, Newton St Loe, Bath BA2 9BN. Tel: (01225) 873701. Fax: (01225) 874082.

British Institute of Professional Photography, Fox Talbot House, Amwell End, Ware, Herts SG12 9HN. Tel: (01920) 464011. Fax: (01920) 487056.

Mac/Windows Academy (UK), Gloucester House, Woodside Lane, London N12 8TP. (Photoshop training). Tel: (0181) 445 5225. Fax: (0181) 446 3314.

NESCOT, Nescot Epsom Centre, Longmead Road, Epsom, Surrey KT19 9BH. (Digital imaging courses). Tel: (0181) 394 3176. Fax: (0181) 394 3232.

Royal Photographic Society, The Octagon, Milsom Street, Bath BA1 1DN. (Digital Imaging Group). Tel: (01225) 462841. Fax: (01225) 448688.

University College London, Gower Street, London WC1E 6BT. Tel: (0171) 387 7050. Fax: (0171) 380 0453.

University of Newcastle-upon-Tyne, Department of Geomatics, Newcastle-upon-Tyne NE1 7RU. Tel: (0191) 222 6000.

University of Westminster, Imaging Technology Research Group, School of Communication, 18-22 Riding House Street, London W1P 7PD.

Publications

Advanced Imaging, 445 Broad Hollow Road, Melville, NY 11747, USA. Tel: (516) 845 2700. Fax: (516) 845 2797.

Computer Arts, Future Publishing Ltd, Somerton, Somerset TA11 6BR. Tel: (01225) 822 511.

Electronic Imaging, Market Link Publishing Ltd, The Mill, Bearwalden Business Park, Wendens Ambro, Saffron Walden, Essex CB11 4JX. Tel: (01799) 544200.

Image, The Association of Photographers, 9/10 Domingo Street, London EC1Y 0TA. Tel: (0171) 608 1441.

Scientific Computing World, Institute of Physics Circulation Centre, WDIS Publishing House, Victoria Road, Ruislip, Middx HA4 0SX. Tel: (0181) 845 8545.

Glossary

absolute temperature thermodynamic temperature expressed in units of Kelvin. Zero degrees on this scale (absolute zero) represents the lowest temperature theoretically possible, and is the temperature at which the kinetic energy of atoms and molecules is minimal. Absolute zero = 273 °C.

A/D converter a device that converts continuously varying analogue signals into discrete digital signals or numbers.

Adobe Photoshop well-known and very popular imaging software for Mac and PC computers. **Aldus Photostyler** now taken over by Adobe and no longer available, this remains an excellent image-processing program (replaced by Photoshop).

algorithm a rule for solving a mathematical problem in a finite number of steps.

aliasing an effect in computer graphics and bit-mapped images, where diagonal lines, curves or circles produce a stair-stepped appearance when resolution is too coarse.

alphanumeric consisting of letters, numbers, spaces and other characters (see ASCII).

analogue any device that represents changing values by a continuously variable physical property, such as voltage in a circuit. An analogue device can manage an infinite set of values within its range, whereas a digital device can only manage a fixed number of values.

analogue display a video display (such as VGA) is capable of a continuous range of grey levels or colours. By comparison, a digital display can only resolve a finite range of greys or colours (such as the old EGA system).

ASCII acronym for American Standard Code for Information Interchange. This standard code assigns numeric values to letters, numbers, punctuation marks and control characters, to provide compatibility between computers and peripherals.

bandwidth in communications and optics, bandwidth refers to the range between highest and lowest frequency (or wavelength) available for transmission.

binary a term reserved for any system that uses two different states, components, conditions or conclusions. In mathematics the binary system uses combinations of the digits 0 and 1 to represent all values.

binary numbers numbers stored in binary form (see Appendix A).

190 **bit** contraction of binary digit. A bit is the basic unit of information in a binary system of numbering, where 0 equals off and 1 equals on. Bits can be grouped to make up larger units, such as the byte, where 8 bits equal one byte.

bit-mapped graphics an image created by a series of dots (pixels), rather than a set of lines (vectors). Bit-mapped graphics consume large amounts of disk and memory space.

black-body radiation electromagnetic radiation (EMR) emitted by a hypothetical body that absorbs all the radiation falling on it. It thus has 100% absorptance and emissivity. The nearest practical approach to a black-body radiator is a small hole in the wall of an enclosure at uniform temperature.

brightness a subjective term that describes the sensation of light entering the eye. Roughly related to the objective term luminance, which is a physical unit.

buffer an area of memory used for temporary storage of data.

byte a contraction of the term binary digit eight. A byte is a group of eight bits that usually holds a single character. Bytes are further grouped into kilobytes (1024 bytes), megabytes (1 048 576 bytes), or gigabytes (1 073 741 824 bytes).

C a compiled programming language developed for professional programmers. Useful for writing programs that are fast, powerful and capable of being moved from one computer to another without difficulty.

C++ an object oriented version of C. Object oriented programming (OOP) views a program as a set of self-contained objects that interact with others by passing messages between them.

CAD computer-aided design.

calibration a term used in photogrammetry to define a metric camera (which has its focal length and image radial distortions calibrated to an exacting value). A calibrated camera is essential for topographic mapping.

CCD charge coupled device. A solid state imaging sensor that uses an array of metal oxide semiconductors (MOS) to produce an electrical output proportional to the amount of light (EMR) incident upon each picture element (pixel). Each signal charge is clocked-out to the output register by coupling all adjacent cells. Analogue signals then undergo A/D conversion to create a digital image.

CD-ROM acronym for compact disk - read only memory. A high-capacity (650 Mb) optical storage device used to store large image files, dictionaries, encyclopaedias, etc.

CFA interpolation colour filter array interpolation. Algorithm for improving a CCD colour image by using 'cross talk' between an array of coloured filters.

charge packets an optically induced signal charge stored in the potential well of each CCD storage element (pixel).

CIE system an internationally accepted system (Commission Internationale de l'Éclairage) for defining colour in terms of a modified triangle which contains all spectral colours. In the CIE system the three primary colours (red, green, blue) are designated X, Y, Z, thus a colour can be located within the locus of the triangle by quoting any two graph coordinates to find hue and saturation, while luminance (brightness) is provided by an additional value.

CMOS complementary metal oxide semiconductor.

CMYK cyan, magenta, yellow and black. The four colours used in printing, where CMY are the complementary colours.

conductor a substance or body that offers little resistance to the flow of an electric current.

D/A converter a device that will convert a digital signal into an analogue one.

dark current thermally generated electrical noise in a CCD imaging system.

decibel unit used to compare two power levels. Two power levels, P and P_0 differ by n decibels when $n = 10 \log_{10}(P/P_0)$.

dielectric a substance that is capable of sustaining electrical stress, that is, an insulator.

digital a term that describes any system that represents values in the form of binary digits (binary codes consisting of 0s and 1s)

DOS acronym for disk operating system.

DVD a high-density version compact disk. DVD increases optical disk capacity from the normal 650 Mb to 4.7 Gb (gigabytes) by using double tracks on both sides of the disk.

electronvolt a unit of energy (symbol eV) equal to the work done on an electron when it moves through a potential difference of one volt.

frame-grabber a device that converts a video image into digital form suitable for computer display. Sometimes called a video digitiser, most frame-grabbers can be attached to any video system producing an RGB signal.

full-frame transfer a CCD imager that employs its full array of pixels for imaging, in contrast to the frame transfer types, which employ half the total CCD elements for imaging and half for temporary storage.

grey scale a term used in computer graphics (grey levels) to describe a series of shades from white through any number of grey levels to black. The number of grey levels available depends on the number of bits dedicated to each pixel. Thus, a pixel with 8 bits (one byte) has $2^8 = 256$ grey levels.

ground state the state of a system (an atom for example) in its lowest energy level, in contrast to its excited state.

halftone when an original photograph is printed through a (halftone) screen, the image is broken up into a pattern of dots. Dark areas form dense dot patterns that can merge together, whereas highlight areas have few dots.

high pass filter an image processing operation which employs a mathematical 'filter' to provide image sharpening or edge enhancement when applied to the digital image array. A particular example is the Laplacian filter.

HSB acronym for hue, saturation and brightness, which are the three main attributes of any colour (HSB is also a colour model used in computer graphics).

Hue is the name of the colour, saturation is how pure the colour may be (freedom from other colours), and brightness refers to its visual luminance.

illuminance a photometric unit (symbol E). The light shining from a source onto a scene or subject.

image-processing the computer processing of a graphical image, made possible by the use of various software packages dedicated to image enhancement and overall control of the image.

insulator a substance that is a poor conductor of electricity due to a lack of mobile electrons.

ISO International Standards Organisation (based in Geneva), establishes world-wide standards in numerous fields, such as photography (film-speeds), and computer communications.

JPEG Joint Photographic Experts Group. A well-known image compression standard and file format. JPEG employs lossy compression methods, achieves compression ratios as high as 20 : 1 and stores 24 bit colour images.

LCD liquid crystal display. Usually found in portable computers (laptop and notebook) where display screen technology employs an electric current to to align crystals in a special liquid.

LED light emitting diode.

lightness lightness is the continuum running from a white to a black surface, and should not be confused with brightness. Whereas a grey cat in sunlight and the same cat in the shade will be of equal lightness (if constancy is perfect), in sunlight the cat will appear much brighter.

low-pass filter commonly known as a smoothing filter, a low-pass filter is generally used to remove image noise and speckle.

luminance the objective correlate of brightness (symbol L), luminance is a measure of how much light is coming from a surface. The unit of luminance is the candle/square metre ($Cd\ m^2$).

LUT look-up table. A collection of data values.

menu a list of commands, or options, available in the displayed software.

MOS metal oxide semiconductor. The individual light-sensitive elements that make up a CCD.

Munsell system a practical system for designating a colour, in terms of hue, saturation and value (brightness). The Munsell system can be purchased as a three-dimensional model (Munsell Tree) or in book form, with over 1200 colour samples.

Nyquist limit for a CCD sensor with pixel spatial frequency k_s, unambiguous resolution of image detail with a spatial frequency k_i, is not possible if $k_i > 0.5\ k_s$.

OCR optical character recognition. Computer recognition of printed matter.

PCMCIA PC Memory Card International Association. A standard for plug-in adaptors for portable computers and digital cameras.

photo-electron an electron emitted from a substance due to irradiation by EMR.

photometry the scientific study of visual radiation, where photometric quantities can be measured either by eye, or by photoelectric devices.

pixel contraction of picture element. The smallest element (resolution) of an image.

potential well signal information in a CCD element is carried in the form of a charge of electrons, localised under the electrode with the highest (positive) applied potential. This electric charge is said to be stored in a potential well.

RAM acronym for randon access memory. The principal memory system in a computer used for the operating system, application programs and data.

resistance symbol R.. The ratio of the potential difference (V) across an electrical component, to the current (I) passing through it. Related to voltage and current through Ohm's law as: $R = V/I$.

resolution a measure of the ability of an imaging system to separate individual components of an image. Classical theory suggests that a diffraction limited lens can resolve two points separated by a distance (r) as: $r = 1.22\lambda N$, where λ is the wavelength of light and N the relative aperture of the lens. With digital cameras, resolution is expressed in terms of the number of pixels within a CCD array, and in printing as the number of dots per inch (dpi).

RGB red, green, blue; the three additive primary colours.

ROM acronym for read only memory.

RS-232-C a standard interface between computer and a peripheral. RS-232 uses either a 9-pin or 25-pin connector, the C denotes a third revision of the Recomended Standard.

SCSI acronym for small computer system interface (pronounced scuzzy). SCSI is often used to connect hard disks, tape drives, scanners, printers, CD-ROM drives and digital cameras, in fact any peripheral that involves mass storage of data.

semiconductor a material that is in-between a conductor and an insulator, and whose electrical properties can be precisely controlled by the addition of dopants (impurities). The most common semiconductors are silicon and germanium.

SVGA super video graphics display (an enhancement to the standard VGA) which can display at least 800 pixels horizontally and 600 pixels vertically.

terabyte a terabyte is equal to 1000 gigabytes (2^{40}), or 1 099 511 627 776 bytes.

thumbnail a very low-resolution digital image, used for library file purposes.

TWAIN not an acronym. A somewhat humorous term for explaining an interface that is technology without an interesting name.

valency band the outermost electrons of an atom (those responsible for chemical bonding) occupy the valency band of a solid. If the valency band is filled and there is a wide forbidden band between it and the next highest empty band, then the material is an insulator. However, if the valency band is not completely filled, or if it overlaps with a higher empty energy band, then there are vacant levels that electrons can enter and the material will be a good conductor. Most metals have this property.

References

Part One

(1) Graham, R.W., The Optimum Photographic Representation of Brightnesses in Interior Scenes. pp. 105–117. Ph.D thesis, CNAA (1975).
(2) Stevens, J.C. and Stevens, S.S. *J. Opt. Soc. Amer.*, **53**(3), pp. 375–385 (1963).
(3) Hopkinson, R.G. *Architectural Physics: Lighting*, HMSO, London, pp. 324–351 (1963).
(4) Hunt, R.W.G. *J. Phot. Sci.*, **1**, pp. 149–158 (1953).
(5) Hurvich, L.M. and Jameson, D. *The Perception of Lightness and Darkness*, Allyn & Bacon Inc., Boston, pp. 62–64 (1966).
(6) Graham, R.W. The Optimum Photographic Representation of Brightnesses in Interior Scenes, *J. Phot. Sci*, **27**(3), May/June (1979).
(7) Klein, E. *Ber. Bunsenges. Phys. Chemie*, **80**, p. 1082 (1976).
(8) Metz, H.J., Ruchti, S. and Seidel, K. *J. Phot. Sci.*, **26**, pp. 229–233 (1978).
(9) *Kodak Data for Aerial Photography*. Eastman Kodak Co. 6th edn. (1992).
(10) Shannon, C.E. *Bell Systems Tech. J.*, **27**, p. 623 (1948).
(11) Brown, F.M., Hall, H.J. and Kosar, J. Photographic Systems for Engineers. *SPSE*, p. 99 (1966).
(12) Pearson, D.E. *Transmission and Display of Pictorial Information*, p. 115, Pentech Press, London (1975).
(13) Saxby, G. Practical Holography: Appendix 3 in *The Fourier Approach to Image Formation*. Prentice Hall, pp. 475–492 (1994).
(14) Graham, R.W. and Read, R.E. *Manual of Aerial Photography*, Focal Press, pp. 147–158 (1986). Also, *Manual of Aerial Photography*, 2nd edn. Whittles Publishing (in progress).
(15) Konecny, G., Schuhe, W. and Wu, J. Investigations on the Interpretability of Images by Different Sensors and Platforms for Small Scale Mapping, *Proceedings ISPRS*, Comm. 1, Symposium, Canberra, pp. 11–22 (1982).
(16) Makarovic, B. and Tempfli, K. Digitising Images and Automatic Processing in Photogrammetry. *ITC Journal*, **1**, pp. 107-126 (1979).
(17) Kosonocky, W.F. and Sauer, D.J. The ABCs of CCDs. RCA Booklet *Charge Coupled Devices and Applications*, April (1981).

Part Two

(18) Yang, E.S. *Microelectronic Devices*. McGraw Hill International Edition, p. 229 (1988).
(19) Yang, E.S. *Microelectronic Devices*. McGraw Hill International Division, p. 232 (1988).

196 (20) Crawley, G. The Solid State Still Camera and the Future. *B. J. Phot.* p. 1115, 30 October (1981).

(21) Mills, J.P. The Implementation of a Digital Photogrammetric System and its Applications in Civil Engineering. Ph.D thesis, University of Newcastle-upon-Tyne, p. 12 (1996).

(22) Shortis, M.R. and Beyer, H.A. Sensor Technology for Digital Photogrammetry and Machine Vision. *Close Range Photogrammetry and Machine Vision*, ed. K.B. Atkinson, Whittles Publishing, pp.120–121 (1996).

(23) Carnes, J.E. and Kosonocky, W.F. *Charge Coupled Devices and Applications*. RCA Publication, April (1981).

(24) Muller, R.S. and Kamins, T.I. *Device Electronics for Integrated Circuits*. 2nd edn. John Wiley & Sons, New York, pp. 411 (1986).

(25) Janesick, J.R., Elliott, T., Dingizian, A. et al. New Advancements in CCD Technology – Sub-Electron Noise and 4096 × 4096 Pixel CCDs. *Charge Coupled Devices and Solid State Optical Sensors, SPIE,* **1242**, pp. 223–227 (1990).

(26) Crawley, G. CCD in Solid State Video. *B. J. Phot.* 4th August (1972).

(27) Crawley, G. Sony Unveils Still Video Camera. *B. J. Phot.* 4th September (1981).

(28) Crawley, G. The Solid State Still Camera and the Future. *B. J. Phot.* 30th October (1981).

(29) Shortis, M.R. et al. Comparative Geometric Tests of Industrial & Scientific CCD Cameras Using Plumb Line and Test Range Calibrations. *International Archives of Photogrammetry and Remote Sensing*, 30(5W1), pp. 53–59 (1995).

(30) Mills, J.P. The Implementation of a Digital Photogrammetric System and its Applications in Civil Engineering. Ph.D thesis, University of Newcastle-upon-Tyne, pp. 18–19 (1996).

(31) Tinsley, J. *Electronic Imaging*, pp. 45–48, July (1996).

(32) Tinsley. J. *Electronic Imaging*, pp. 19–24, September (1995).

(33) Standage, T. Scan with a wave of the hand. p. 3 Connected. *The Daily Telegraph*, 28 January (1997).

(34) Warner, W.S., Graham, R.W. and Read, R.E. *Small Format Aerial Photography*, Whittles Publishing, p.12 (1996).

(35) Gulliver, B. *The Aerial Reconnaissance Co.* Obtainable from 6 Knowle Hill, Bodiam, Robertsbridge, E. Sussex, TN2 5UP, UK.

(36) Schowengerdt, R.A. *Techniques for Image Processing and Classification in Remote Sensing*. Orlando Florida, Academic Press (1983).

(37) Mather, P. *Computer Processing of Remotely Sensed Images*, John Wiley & Sons, (1987).

(38) Schalkoff, R.J. *Digital Image Processing and Computer Vision*. John Wiley & Sons, (1989).

(39) Pratt, W.K. *Digital Image Processing*. John Wiley & Sons, New York (1978).

(40) Ford, A.M., Jacobson, R.E. and Attridge, G.G. Effects of Image Compression on Image Quality. *J. Phot. Sci.*, **43**, pp. 52–57 (1995).

(41) Van Nes, F.L. Spatial Modulation Transfer in the Human Eye. *J. Opt. Soc. Am.*, **57** pp. 401–406 (1967).

(42) Campbell, F.W. and Maffei, L. *Sci. Am.* p. 106, November (1974).

(43) Graham, R.W. The Optimum Photographic Representation of Brightnesses in Interior Scenes.Ph.D thesis, CNAA (1975).

(44) Mullen, K.T. *The Contrast Sensitivity of Human Colour Vision to Red-Green and Blue-Yellow Chromatic Gratings.* J. Physiol., **359** pp. 381–400 (1985).

(45) Bartleson, C.J. and Witzel, R.F. *Phot. Sci. and Eng.*, **11**(4), pp. 263, July/August (1967).

(46) Tinsley, J. Jet Propelled. *Electronic Imaging*, p. 49, November (1995).

(47) Tinsley, J. Prime Example. *Electronic Imaging*. p. 44, August (1995).

(48) Pagoulatos, A. The Critical Mass Behind CD-ROM. *Advanced Imaging* pp. 10–12, June (1996).

(49) Warner, W.S., Graham, R.W. and Read, R.E. *Small Format Aerial Photography*. Whittles Publishing (1996).

(50) Stringham, A. GPS and Photo CD. *Earth Observation Magazine*, pp. 55–57, June (1994).

Part Three

(51) John Blishen Ltd. *Electronic Imaging* p. 12, July (1996).

(52) Lawson, J. *Electronic Imaging*, p. 33 May (1995).

(53) Anderson, P. A Networked, Industrial OCR Imaging System for Volume Inventory Control and Management, *Advanced Imaging*, pp. 54–56 September (1996).

(54) Hamit, F. Desktop NDT Vibration Tests. *Advanced Imaging*, p. 42 May (1996).

(55) Graham, R.W. Holography. *Printing Technology*, pp. 11–32, 16(1) April (1972).

(56) Graham, R.W. A Simple Power Density Meter for Holography. *J. Phot. Sci.*, **30**(3), May/June (1982).

(57) *The Sunday Times*, 4 August (1996).

(58) Linney, A.D. et al. Three Dimensional Visualization of Data on Human Anatomy: Diagnosis and Surgical Planning. *Journal of Audiovisual Media in Medicine*, **16** pp. 4–10 (1993).

(59) Personal communication from R. Thomson, National Technical Support Unit, Police Scientific Development Branch (PSDP), Woodcock Hill, Sandridge, St Albans, Herts AL4 9HQ, UK.

(60) Vanazis, P., Blowes, R.W., Linney, A.D. et al. Applications of 3-D Computer Graphics for Facial Reconstruction and Comparison with Sculpting Techniques. *Forensic Sci. Int.*, **42**, pp. 69–84 (1989).

(61) Griffiths, P. In The Army Now. *Brit. J. Digital Imaging*, pp. 15–16 (British Institute of Professional Photographers), 18 September (1996).

(62) Thomson, G.H. Aerospace Report No. 5. *J. Phot. Sci.*, **43**, pp. 36–37 (1995).

(63) Warner, W.S., Graham, R.W. and Read, R.E. *Small Format Aerial Photography*, Whittles Publishing (1996).

(64) Mills, J.P., Newton, I. and Graham, R.W. Aerial Photography for Surveying Purposes with a High Resolution Small Format Digital Camera. *Photogrammetric Record*, **15**(88), pp. 575–587 (1996).

(65) Fryer, J.G. Recent Developments in Camera Calibration for Close Range Applications. *International Archives of Photogrammetry and Remote Sensing*, **29**(B5), pp. 594–599 (1992).

(66) Thomson, G.H. A Practical Method for Determining the Ground Sampled Distance in Small Scale Aerial Photography. *J. Phot. Sci.*, **42**, pp. 129–132 (1994).

(67) Graham, R.W. The ITC Multispectral Camera System with Respect to Crop Prognosis in Winter Wheat. *ITC Journal* **2**, pp. 235–254 (1980).

(68) Graham, R.W. Multispectral Photography in Remote Sensing. *Brit. J. Phot.* pp. 23–25 (1992).

(69) Gavin, M. CCD Time Machines. *Astronomy Now*, pp. 15–16, September (1996).

(70) Jacobson, R.E., Ray, S. and Attridge, G.G. *The Manual of Photography*, 8th edn., Focal Press, pp. 187–189 (1988).

<u>198</u>   (71) Cox, R.J. *Photographic Sensitivity*, Academic Press, pp. 105–106 (1973).

(72) Todd, H.N. and Zakia, R.D. *Photographic Sensitometry*, Morgan & Morgan Inc., New York, pp. 95–105 (1969).

(73) AstroCam. *Astronomy Applications Guide to Cooled CCD Imaging Systems.* AstroCam Ltd., Cambridge Science Park, Cambridge CB4 4GS.

(74) AstroCam. *Camera Head Data Sheet and Selection Guide.* AstroCam Ltd., Cambridge Science Park, Cambridge CB4 4GS.

(75) AstroCam. *CCD Data Sheet and Selection Guide.* AstroCam Ltd., Cambridge Science Park, Cambridge CB4 4GS.

(76) Hamamatsu Photonics (UK) Ltd., 2 Gladbeck Way (see Appendix C).

(77) Santa Barbara Instrument Group (SBIG). PO Box 5047, 1482 East Valley Road, 33 Santa Barbara CA 93150, USA.

(78) Celestron International, 2835 Columbia Street, Torrance, CA 9053, USA.

(79) Jorden, P. New Detectors for New Astronomy. *Physics World*, pp. 40–45, May (1994).

(80) Mackay, C.D. Fast CCD Controllers Optimise Telescope Images. *Laser Focus World*, May (1996).

(81) AstroCam. *X-Ray Applications Guide to Cooled CCD Imaging Systems.* AstroCam Ltd., Cambridge Science Park, Cambridge CB4 4GS.

(82) Pitt, G.D. A Revolution in Raman Spectroscopy. *Physics in Business*, no. 13, pp. 6–7, Institute of Physics, February (1997).

(83) Hamamatsu. *C2400 Series Cameras for Video Microscopy.* Hamamatsu Ltd. (see Appendix C).

(84) Hamamatsu. *Image Processing and Analysis System for Optical Microscopes.* Hamamatsu Ltd., (see Appendix C).

(85) Evening, M. Digital Futures. *Image* (see Appendix C), pp. 5–7, January (1997).

Index

A

A/D conversion 66, 67, 82, 85, 87, 189, 190
Absolute temperature 57, 189
Absolute zero 19, 57, 189
Absorption 31, 32
Additive colour 32, Colour page III
Adobe Photoshop 85, 90, 92, 94, 98–9, 102, 105, 115–7, 119, 120, 126, 134, 142, 146, 147, 163, 169, 187, 189, Colour pages V, VI, VII, X, XII, XV, XVI
Aerial surveys 74, 96, 117, Colour page XI
Agfa ActionCam 99
Agfa StudioCam 101, 102
Aldus Photostyler 112, 113, 119, 162, 189, Colour page XI
Algorithms 81, 86–8, 96, 120, 189
Aliasing 47, 86, 89, 99, 120, 159
Allowed conduction bands 87–8
Aluminium gate 59, 64
Aluminium 56, 58, 59
Amateur photographer 151
Amplitude 9, 10, 49
Analytical processing 119
Antares 173, 178
Anti-aliasing 86, 120
Apparent stellar magnitudes 175, 177
Apple Photo-Flash 120
Arc Info 118, 125
Arc View 119, 125
Archaeology 159
Area Imaging arrays 68–72, 74, 79, 80, 81, 82, 85
Argon 55
Army 160
AstroCam 125, 173, 174, 175, 177, 179, 187
Astrochrome 175
Astronomical 39, 74, 125, 172, 174, 175
Atoms 55, 178, 189
Auto levels 121

200 B

Bandwidth 19, 23, 33, 189
Base 147, 148, 165
Bicubic 125
Bilinear 125
Binary digit 40, 42, 66, 90, 183, 184, 189
Bit 40, 41, 44, 88, 90, 107, 130, 173, 184, 190
Bit depth 108, 110
Bit-mapped images 89, 90, 107, 133, 190
Black body radiator 19, 73, 190
BMP 133
Boltzmann's constant 57, 73, 185
Boron 57
Brightfield illumination 178
Brightness 25–8, 33, 91, 120, 126, 127, 135, 190–1
Buffer memory 85, 190
Buried channel CCD 52, 63, 64, 65
Byte 40, 190

C

Cad 89, 190
Cadmium sulphide 56
Calibration 158, 162, 163
Camcorder 65, 66
Camera exposure 170, 171, 173
Cannabis 170
Candela 19, 21, 22
Capella 173, 174, 176, 178, Colour page XIV
Carrier, accumulation 59
CCD 14, 19, 25, 47, 51, 52, 58–61, 63, 67–8, 72, 75, 81, 87, 104, 114, 172–5, 177, 178, 190
CCD imagers 39, 47, 63, 67, 77, 84, 172, 180, 181
CCD linearity 30, 31, 76, 108, 118
CCD transfer efficiency 67, 72
CD-ROM 144, 145, 147, 148, 153, 190
CD-ROM writers 145
Celestron 174–5
Cessna 161, 165
CFA interpolation 85, 88, 90, 97, 170, 190, Colour page II
Channel palette 87, 92, 127
Channel stops 51, 60, 61, 65, 69, 70
Charge packets 62–3, 67, 68, 190
Chroma 33–4
CIE system 33–4, 190

Clocking voltage 62–3, 67
Clocks 62
CMOS 14, 104, 181, 191
CMY 32, 33, 91, 106, 138, 141–2
CMYK 36, 91, 106, 126, 138, 139, 141, 142, 191
COAST 176, Colour page XIV
Coherence 10, 11
Cold finger 174
Colour 30–3, 74, 159
Colour balance 120–1
Colour depth 36
Colour image 35–6, 85, 93
Colour monitor 90, 91
Colour wheel 127–8
Commercial photography 79, 153
Complementary colours 32
Computer 78–9, 88–9, 96, 103, 111, 121, 125, 135, 144–6, 151–2, 158, 172, 181
Comstock 144
Conductive bands 15, 55
Conductors 55, 194
Contrast 43–4, 47, 87, 93, 120–1, 162
Cooled CCD 174, 179
Copper 55
CorelDraw 123
Cropping 124
CRT 89, 91
Curves dialog box 128

D

D/A converter 66, 85, 87, 90, 191
Dark current 72–6, 173–4, 191
Darkfield illumination 178
Densitometer 44, 127
Density 27–8, 31, 38–9, 110
Density range 39, 110, 121
Depletion region 59–62, 65, 72
Despeckle 120
Dicomed Bigshot 100
Dielectric 58, 59
Diffraction 12, 104, 177
Diffraction limited resolution 12, 45, 46, 50, 51, 193
Diffuse reflection 22
Digital camera tone reproduction 28
Digital camera types 78, 92–3

Digital cameras 40, 67, 71, 74, 77, 89, 96–8, 145, 151, 160, 163, 177
Digital colour images 35, 81, 85–90, 120
Digital mapping 161
Digital Number (DN) 67, 86, 90, 125, 127–8, 130–1
Digital printers 137
Direct thermal printers 137
Discrete cosine transformation (DCT) 134–5
Distortion 89, 124
Distortions 163, 176
Dithering 86, 107
Donors 57
Dopants 57
DOS 98, 133, 135, 145, 191
Dot matrix printer 137
Download period 171
Dpi 106, 108–11, 114, 138, 143, 193
DSP compression 87–8
Dye sublimation printing 94–5, 97, 141–3, Colour page VII, IX
Dynamic range 74, 76, 78, 108, 110, 112, 143, 173–4, 178

E

Edge enhancement 130–2
EEV 176, 178
Electric current 55, 66
Electrode 60–2, 65, 70
Electron 14, 15, 55, 57, 61, 67, 72, 74, 75, 172, 174, 185, 194
Electron hole-pairs 57, 59, 70
Electron volt 15, 17, 191
Electrostatic printers 137
EMR 7–10, 14, 15, 19, 156, 169, 190
Energy bands 14
Energy levels 15, 55
EPROM 88, 93
EPS 133, 147
Epson printers 139
ERDAS 125

F

Facial scanning 157–8, 188
Fiducial marks 163
Field-frame transfer 68–9
File format 133
FILE menu 125, 135, 147
Fill factor 67, 74

Filter 13–14, 23, 30, 32, 34–6, 84–9, 163, 169
FILTER menu 121
Flat-bed scanners 67–8
Fluorescence microscopy 156, 179
Focal length 12, 163
Footprint 170
Forbidden bands 55, 193
Forbidden gap 57
Forensic science 157, 159
Forestry 170
Fourier analysis 48–50
Frame buffer 88, 90
Frame grabber 65–7, 89, 158, 191
Free electrons 57
Free space permittivity 60
Freelance photography 180
Fringes 153–5
Fujix DS-505/515 camera 96, 152
Fujix Pictrography 143
Full-frame transfer 71, 191

G

Gallium 57
Gate 59, 72
Gaussian blur 93, 120, 121
Geographic information systems (GIS) 145, 148
Geometric optics 11
Germanium semiconductor 57
GPS 148, 167, 171
Grains 38
Granularity 39
Grey levels 31, 41, 44, 107–8, 173
Grey scale image 30, 106, 191
Ground control 168
Ground sampled distance (GSD) 167
Ground state 15, 191
Guidescope 173

H

Halftone screens 106, 191
Hamamatsu 126, 174, 177, 179, 187
Harmonics 48–9
Heated capillary 138
Helium 55

204 Hewlett-Packard printers 93, 139, Colour page VI
High-pass filter 131, 191
Histogram 120, 121, 125
Holography 10, 11, 13, 153, 154
HSB 91, 126, 127, 191
Hubble space telescope 172
Hue 33, 90–1, 126, 191

I

Illuminance 21–5, 192
Image analysis 119
Image blur 120
Image compression 40, 87, 88, 96, 99, 103, 119
Image conjugate (v) 12
Image enhancement 119, 120
Image illuminance 24, 72
Image manipulation 121–3
IMAGE menu 123, 124, 128, Colour page V
Image processing 119, 192
Image transformation 119
Imaging sensors 59, 67
Incoherent emission of radiation 16, 17
Indicatrix of reflection 22
Industrial photography 153
Information capacity 39
Inkjet printers 30, 92, 93, 106, 109, 137, 139
Insulators 55–6, 59, 192, 193
Interference 12, 13, 153–4, 169
Interference microscopy 179
Interferometry 13, 153–4
Interline-transfer 68–9
Interpolation 85–6, 88–9, 124–5
Inverse square Law 21, 24
Inversion layer 59
ISO 84, 93, 96–7, 152, 156, 170, 172, 192

J

JPEG algorithm 134, 135
JPEG compression 82, 96, 133–5, 153, 156, 192
Junction diode 57

K

KDC 89, 94, 120

Kelvin 19, 35, 57, 189   **205**
Kernal 130
Kodak 30, 39, 177, 187
Kodak DC-20 92
Kodak DC-40 30–1, 81, 85, 88–90, 92–4, 134, Colour page VI
Kodak DCS-200 81–3, 85, 98, 120, 126–7, 162–5, 167
Kodak DCS-410 81, 88, 96, 152
Kodak DCS-42040, 81, 88, 94, 95, 98, 152–3, 156, 161, 169
Kodak DCS-420 CIR 95, 97, 169, 170, 188, Colour pageXIII and XIV
Kodak DCS-420 GPS 167
Kodak DCS-460 85, 97, 98, 172, 188, Colour page XV, XVI
Kodak DCS-465 103
Kodak DCS-597, colour page VIII
Kodak XLS 8600 141, 156
Kodak PCD Writer 145
Kodak Photo-CD 146
Kodak Pro Photo-CD 146, 147
Kodak Shoebox 147
Krypton 55

L

Laboratory 177
Landcare aviation 148
Landsat 169
Laplacian filter 131, 132, 133
Laplacian kernal 131, 132
Laser 7, 10, 11, 106, 140, 143, 154, 158, 159
Laser printers 106, 140
Leaf camera back 100
LED 111, 117, 140, 192
Lens flare 25
Lens transmission 24
Lightness 25, 33, 34, 35, 192
Lightness constancy 26, 27
Line art 106–7
Line overlap 165
Line-pairs 47, 50, 51, 86, 167
Linear arrays 67–8
Liquid crystal display (LCD) 84, 94, 156
Lossless compression 134, 135, 192
Lossy compression 134, 135, 192
Low-pass filter 130, 131, 192
Lpi 106, 108, 110, 114
Lumens 20, 21

206   Luminance 23–8, 88–9, 135, 172, 174, 190, 192
Luminous flux 20
Luminous intensity 21
LUT 87, 90, 103, 192
Lux 21, 22, 24, 27, 174

M

M-5 chip 82–4, 94
Macintosh 79, 92, 100, 102, 133, 135, 142
Macro 156
Magnification 12
Marquee 123
Matrix 33, 83, 85–6, 89, 107, 108, 130
Mavica 63, 77
Mechanical equivalent of light 20, 185
Medical imaging 152, 156
Metal oxide semiconductor (MOS) 14, 19, 25, 40, 57–8, 68, 190, 192
Metrication 127, 151
Microsoft 133
Military applications 160
Minolta RD-175 99
Modulation 47, 48, 49, 50
Modulation transfer function (MTF) 45, 50, 51, 52
Monitor 85, 87, 90, 133
Monochrome 24, 27, 28, 41, 74, 84, 92, 98, 105, 120, 140, 142, 147, 152, 159, 162, 169
MOS Capacitor 58–9, 61–2, 65
Mouse 121
Multispectral 68
Multispectral photography (MSP) 169
Munsell system 33–4, 192

N

N-type semiconductor 57
Nearest neighbour 125
Neutron radiography 177
Newsdesk 152
Nikon E-2 96, 152, 160
Noise 61, 75, 76, 173
Non-destructive testing (NDT) 154–5
Non-Image light 24–5
Nyquist limit 47, 52, 90, 159, 192

O

Object conjugate (u) 12
Object luminance 24
Object oriented graphic 89, 133
OCR 105, 112, 115, 192
OFOTO 109, 114
Ohm's law 56
Opacity 27
Optical transmission microscopy 178–9
Output gate 69, 70
Output register 67, 68, 69
Oxide capacitance 60

P

P-type semiconductor 57–8
Paintbrush 123
Parallel acquisition cameras 80
PC 82, 92, 98, 102, 133, 135, 144, 174
PC Image 126
PCMCIA 88, 94–7, 99, 103, 160, 169, 171, 192
Peltier cooling 174
Pencil 123
Perspective 1
Phase contrast 179
Phosphor dots 91
Phosphorus 57
Photo gate 67
Photo-CD 143–8
Photo-electric effect 56
Photo-electrons 61, 193
Photoair software 148
PhotoEnhancer 30, 88, 93–4, 119
Photogrammetry 117–8, 125, 163–4
Photo-journalism 152, 153
Photometric radiation equivalent 19
Photometry 19, 193
Photomultiplier tubes (PMT) 105, 118
Photon energy 17
Photons 14, 65, 70, 178
Photophase plus 102
Photopic sensitivity 19
Photoresistors 56
Photoshop (see Adobe)

208 PICT 133, 147
Pictrographic printers 143
Picture Publisher 120
Pipette 123
Pixel depth 88
Pixel filters 35, 80, 85, 86, 88–90, 93
Pixel picture 41–4
Pixel radius 74, 121
Pixel resolution 41–3, 45, 63,175–6
Pixels 35, 39, 41–3, 51, 61, 62, 67, 70, 73, 74, 86, 88, 90, 120, 130, 175, 193
Planimetry 161, 172
Point spread function (PSF) 37, 40, 45
Polarisation 12
Polarity 59
Police 79, 159, 160
Polysilicon gates 59, 63–5, 70
Positive hole 57, 58
Potential well 61–5,67, 193
Press photography 152
Preview 128
Print brightness 28
Print density 27, 28, 135
Print luminance 28–9
Printers 106–7, 137–9
Prism 30, Colour page II
Professional photography 77–80, 151–2, 180
Psychophysics 19
Push-broom 67, 101

Q

Quantisation 129, 130
Quantum efficiency 74
Quantum theory 14

R

R-Chips 125
RADC 87–8, 93, 134
Radiometry 7, 19, 119
Radon 55
Ram 94, 98, 145, 193
Raman spectroscopy 178
Random/Multilevel 38
Random/Stochastic 37
Rayleigh resolution 46

Reciprocity law 173
Reflectance 22, 27, 127
Reflection density 127
Refractive index 8
Regular/Multilevel 39, 41
Regular/Stochastic 37, 41
Relative aperture (f/No) 23
Remote sensing 125, 145, 167, 169, Colour page XII
Representative halftone 107
Resistivity 56, 193
Resolution 13, 45–7, 50, 86, 90, 104, 106–7, 109, 115, 139, 175, 193, Colour
    page V
Reverse bias 57
Rewritable-CD 144
RGB 36, 85–8, 90–1, 96, 99, 100, 102, 117, 126–9, 143, 193
RMS errors 163
Rotations 123
RULERS 126, 127

S

Saturation 33, 34, 74, 76, 89, 91, 126, 173, 191
SBIG 174, 175
Scale 128, 161–6, 168, 170
Scanmate 118
Scanner resolution 108–9, 111, 159
Scanners 89, 158
Scanners (drum) 105, 111, 118
Scanners (film) 105, 116, 117, Colour page IX
Scanners (flatbeds) 67, 105, 111, 113–6, Colour page IV
Scanners (hand-held) 105, 110–12
Scanning aperture 39
Scanning methods 102, 105, 158
Scanview 118
Scene luminance 26–8, 30
SCISSORS 124
Screen cell 107–8
Screen frequency 106–9
SCSI 82, 84, 87–8, 99, 100, 117, 142, 144–5, 193
Selwyn granularlity 39
Semiconductors 56, 57, 59, 63, 193
Sharpening 89, 121, 130, 162
Shift and difference filters 133
Shift register 61, 63, 68, 70, 72, 85
Signal-to-noise 74, 75
Silicon 57, 61

210

Silicon dioxide 56, 58–60, 65
Silicon semiconductor 57
Silicon substrate 60, 63, 70
Silver 55
Sine wave 48–50
Skew 124
Small format aerial photography (SFAP) 148, 161, 167
Smear 71, 72
Smoothing filter 130–1
Space-borne imagery 125, 169
Spatial coherence 11
Spatial filtering 129, 130, 154
Spatial frequencies 13, 45, 47, 50, 52, 135
Spatial resolution 13, 45, 47, 78, 86
Spectral power distribution 17
Spectrography 125, 178
Spectrum 7, 30, 32
Specular reflectance 22
SPOT 68, 101, 169
Square-wave target 46–9
Standard candle 19
Starlight Xpress 174, 177
Stochastic systems 37, 40–1, 44
Storage element 61–4, 70
Stored charge 60
Sublimation 141
Subtractive primaries 32, 35, Colour page III
Surface potential 59, 62
SVGA 90, 193

T

Telescope 72, 172–3, 176–7
TEM 180
Temporal coherence 11
Temporal multiplex cameras 80
Text 106
Thermal transfer printers 137
Thermal wax transfer printers 142
Thermo autochrome printers 142
Thinned CCDs 175
Three-phase 61, 62, 68
Thruster 166, 170
Thumbnails 85, 144, 147, 193
TIFF 89, 94, 96–7, 102, 119–20, 133, 147, 158
Tone levels 41, 43

Tone reproduction 27–9
Toner 140
Toolbox 121, 123, 127
Transformation 119, 124
Transistor 58
Transparencies 105, 110, 115
Transverse waves 7, 9
Travelling waves 10
TWAIN 85, 89, 98, 111, 114–5, 193
Two-phase 63, 64

U

Unsharp masking 93, 120–1, Colour page X

V

Valency band 15, 55, 193
Valency electrons 15, 55, 56, 57
Value (colour) 33–4
Velocity of light 7–8, 185
VGA 90, 99, 189
Video technology 65–6, 91
Visual optics 9, 19
Visual science 19
Voltage 56, 66, 71, 76, 193

W

Wave theory of light 9, 12
Wavelength 8, 9, 154
Wide-angle lens 161
WINDOW menu 123, 126–7
WINDOWS 126, 133, 135, 138, 142, 144, 145
Writable-CD 145

X

X-radiation 178
X-ray 156, 158, 177–8
Xenon 55

Y

YAG screen 180

212 Z

Zeiss PhotoScan 117
Zeiss VOS 80C 102
Zoom-in 123